SCOTLAND
(THE HIGHLANDS)
Scale of Miles

0 5 10 20 30

Dunnet Head
John o' Groats
Duncansby Head
Thurso

CAITHNESS
Wick
Ubster
Lybster
Dunbeath
Berriedale
Helmsdale
Brora

MORAY FIRTH

Findhorn
Culbin Bay Sands
Lossiemouth
Cullen Portsoy
Macduff Troup Head
Rosehearty
Kinnairds Head
Fraserburgh
Elgin
Fochabers
Banff
Rattray Head
Forres
Nairn
Fochabers
Aberchirder
Turriff
Keith
Deveron
Peterhead
MORAY
Rothes
Craigellachie
Dufftown
Huntly
Grantown on Spey
Rayne
Ellon
Old Meldrum
Insch
Bennachie
Inverurie
Newburgh
Lumsden
Spey
Tomintoul
Kintore
CAIRNGORMS
R. Don
ABERDEEN
Glen Avon
Aboyne
Balmoral
Ballater
R. Dee
Banchory
Inverey
Braemar
Lochnagar
THE MEARNS
Stonehaven
Glen Tilt
Ben y Gloe
Devil's Elbow
Milton of Clova
Laurencekirk
Inverbervie
Blair Atholl
Ben y Vrackie
Pitlochry
Glen Clova
Glen Shee
ANGUS
Brechin
Kirriemuir
Montrose

(CONTINUED ON BACK END-PAPER)

SUMMER
IN SCOTLAND

SUMMER IN
SCOTLAND

By

IVOR BROWN

COLLINS
ST JAMES'S PLACE, LONDON
1952

PRINTED IN GREAT BRITAIN
COLLINS CLEAR-TYPE PRESS : LONDON AND GLASGOW

In Memory of three Scottish friends
who died, before their time,
while this book was
being written

FREDERICK BAIN
JAMES BRIDIE
ARTHUR WALLACE

CONTENTS

Foreword

IT would be superfluous to write yet another topographical book about Scotland. The subject is rich and ample, but the covering of it has been rich and ample too. Guide-books and travel-books, national and local, abound and many of them are excellent. Edinburgh alone has produced a library worthy of its quality (what higher praise?) and some of the writers who have done so well for it have been no less excellent recorders of other cities and scenes. James Bone, Moray McLaren, and George Scott-Moncrieff, to mention but three, are most in my mind when I walk about the capital, but the first two have also been lively recorders of Glasgow life and the last of the landscape and architecture of the Lowlands. With so much writing born of learning and affection already on the shelf, I could not decently enter this field unless I felt that I had some slightly different approach.

Places, as I see and feel them, are the nursery of personality and the workshop of things. It is of people and events as the product and abiding presence of the countryside that I wish to write. The national history of Scotland has often been composed of savagery and gallantry mixed, forming a macabre pattern of intrigues and treacheries, slaughters and revenges. So the landscape, as well as the urban scene, flickers with ghosts. Much of the majesty of Scotland, from the northern wilderness to the ballad-echoing Border, has a haunted quality: inevitably the mind and art of the people have been backward-looking, fighting interminably the old battles, recapturing the old glories, or escaping into worlds of fancy from the ugly world of fact. My kind of travel blends past and present, the cities with the things of grace (or otherwise) which they have created, and the hills with the ardours and endurances of the hillmen. Places are the background and the forcing-ground of passions and loyalties: they echo the laments which are the staple of Highland minstrelsy and music. They echo, fortunately, the triumphs and rejoicings too. I do not hear only pibrochs in the air, but the great gusts of Scottish laughter, the clash of minds above the social glass, the high debate of forum or of tavern, and the ever-lasting argle-bargle of the race. The Scots are as quenchless in contention as the winds and tides of the Pentland Firth. Their intellectuals generalise with unfailing energy about their fellow Scots, their strength, their failings, their grievances, their character, and their destiny. When, escaped from sluggish southern air, I feel the keen wind in an Edinburgh street, on East Lothian links, or on a Highland moor, I feel, inlaced with it, the old and new conflicts about all things sacred and profane. When the Scots mitigated their wars of theology, they did not cease from mental strife; in work they ' drive at practice ': in leisure they enjoy theory.

Places on the map fascinate not only as scenery but as the parade-ground of the industrial march and as frames of the sporting print. Some people detest scenery. Somerset Maugham has frankly affirmed his sympathy with the scenophobia of the eighteenth century and with its distrust, even its loathing, of the horrid hills. Defoe would have been written down as a potamophobe by our jargonists of the new psychology: he was terrified of rivers and regarded them as enemies likely to rise and slay, which they occasionally do. But Scotland's rivers are its glittering necklets as well as its serviceable arteries. As for its Highlands, many people are oppressed by mountains in mass, and it is certainly difficult to be elated by a day of thick cloud in such a menacing, peak-prisoned chasm as that of Glencoe. I myself am on the side of the mountain-addicts, most of all where the sea invades them. But I admit that a surfeit of summits can become tyrannical: even the addict can be sated and demand more of a country than its loneliness.

The natural prospect, however magnificent for the moment or for the holiday month, demands some acquaintance and sympathy with the aspirations, sufferings, rejoicings, and achievements of its people, if the view is to have its full value. Land is living-room and the Scotland of this book is not simply a piece of scenery, a ribbon of grandeur, unwound for the tourist's gaze; it is the place of the Scots. The tenacity of those who have tried to scrape a living from the rain-swept, wind-stripped void, who have fought the heather and the weather, the bog and the rock, to win a lean harvest or to feed what flocks can endure the climate and the pasturage, are of as much appeal as the terrain itself. The story of this land is as much the chronicle of those who were driven out as of those who held on. The greeds and cruelties of men as well as the severity of soil and climate emptied the glens; the crimes and follies have been as notorious as the beauty of the glens themselves is notable. That spectral quality of Scotland, to which I alluded, hangs not only over the ruined shieling and the tumbled harbours of the West: it is the companion of all imaginative map-reading and a chart is only coloured canvas unless the mind can play upon its names and contours. This drama of place and person everywhere quickens the imagination with its conflicts, while it makes the senses tingle with the strange beauty of its scene.

History and geography, economics and topography, create a design that is not to be dissected without loss. As a traveller I naturally have my case of maps, since reading and pondering over the charts is the proper end of a wanderer's day and his best preparation for the next. But I want other books in the bag, the novels and the plays, the chronicles and the fiction, that have flowered in each sector of the countryside. To this our contemporaries contribute no less than do the classics. It would be ridiculous, for example, to assail the far North East without something of Neil Gunn's to be the map's companion: he illumines the Caithness shore just as Scott or Hogg light up a Border journey. One cannot carry much; so a shrewd selection must be made. It is in this spirit of one with many interests that I have tried to approach the fabric of Scotland: even the barest landscape contains the secrets of its nakedness and it is the spice of travel to unravel the history, as well as to enjoy the beauties, of a wilderness. Out of the earth, or lack of earth and presence of rock and water only, came the character of the people and the ideas and myths for which they passionately stood or fell. The map is a chequer-board of agonies and exultations as well as of shaded contours and blue inlets of the sea. The toils of the breadwinner and the pleasures of the sportsman, the campaigns of the rebel and the austerities of the zealot, are always interwoven with the filigree of cartography.

The right of an absentee Scot to enter the Caledonian Forest as even the humblest kind of woodman and botanist may well be challenged, especially as there are now so many Scots writing with experience and brilliance about their own land. My excuse for adding a book on ' Summer in Scotland ' to a previous one on ' Winter in London ' is simply that this has been the division of my life. When away from Scotland—and admittedly London has provided the larger part of my residence, though not of my affection —I have followed as well as I could its current affairs, the arts and the politics, the plays that are written, and the stories that are told. One periodical alone, *The Scots Review*, starveling though it was to the shame of its unheeding countrymen, provided those across the border and the seas with a lively survey of the needs and cravings of a nation that is trying to remake itself as well as with a selection of the new Scots writing in poetry and in polemic. It is a scandal that it should have been allowed to dwindle away. Scotland has been my winter reading as well as my summer refreshment. It is a thing in my blood and in this book I am liberating the sentiments and expressing the surmises, I hope not altogether ignorant or absurd, of an Aberdonian born in Malaya and educated and mostly employed in England.

I had chosen the title 'Summer in Scotland,' to follow my 'Winter in London,' since the two are coupled in spirit, before I read J. R. Allan's book of the same name as my own, published by Methuen in 1938. Since there is no copyright in titles (and could not be since it is now almost impossible to find names not used on any occasion in past decades and centuries), I have no legal need to apologise: but in fact I do and would like to pay tribute to this spirited survey, mainly of the East and South, and to express my hope that I do not overlap Mr. Allan's work in detail as I have done in title.

With that self-justification, I set out, proposing to abandon the usual order of books about Scotland. I shall not begin at Gretna Green where 'tourism' is seen scarcely at its best. The relics of matrimonial romance are there on view for those who would bang the first sixpence or two

13

in their conquest of Caledonia by motor-coach, but they are no more typical of Scotland than is a tartan hand-bag in a gew-gaw shop. Nor shall I start at Carter Bar where a worthier Scotland, the surge and tumble of the Cheviot sheep-lands, is so handsomely presented. Instead, I shall go straight to the far top of the mainland, since of Orkney and Shetland, another world, I have a miserable ignorance. In any case, they are, I am assured, themselves and different. They need their own book-shelf. So I drive straight into the heart of desolation, in the emptiest counties of all, a Scotland unclothed by nature and now scarcely peopled by man, a miracle of beauty and yet, in some ways, the patriot's despair. The climate has denuded the farthest mountains of soil and tree and man has continued that violence of scouring by sweeping from the small fertility of the inlets and crevices many of such indigenous stalwarts as once managed to live tolerably in these limited oases. And so to Sutherland and Ross, superb yet melancholy, a paradise to the eye, yet increasingly deserted by the sons of McAdam.

CHAPTER I

Far Corner

IT was a private passion for wholeness that sent me to the Pentland Firth whose turbulent waters race under the gales between the mainland and Orkney. When I see a hill I want to be on top of it and that has caused me some considerable slogging in my time. Neither wind nor muscles being what they were, I must reluctantly abandon this kind of conquest now and abjure my greed for total occupations. Just as I always longed to master the whole of a mountain and felt the peak to be a challenge and a prize, so I could not look at the Scottish map without a curiosity about corners. People collect many odd things: for a traveller to crave corners seems scarcely whimsical and, indeed, natural enough.

Some corners are easy to reach. In my youth Cornwall was the pet nook of the English novelists and was almost the back-garden of the publishing trade. Charles Marriott as well as ' Q,' Compton Mackenzie (before he returned to his Highlands and Islands) and Hugh Walpole were constantly finding their matter to good purpose in this old colony of the ancient mariners, tin-questing up the west of Europe, and in this last English refuge of the hunted Celt. The Great Western Railway made it extremely easy to walk among the sea-sprayed barrows and the Standing Stones and to tramp the cliffs where ' Carnival ' came to its sad, gull-clamorous end. It is pleasant recreation to follow books, like rivers, to the source, to track down Tess in Dorset, or trail the spoor of the numerous and excellent Dartmoor novels of Eden Phillpotts over Devon's central waste. I have followed Arnold Bennett's Old Wives and their grandchildren into the Duck Banks and Trafalgar Squares of the Five Towns, as I have chased the Dickensians round London. Re-reading one or two of William Black's romances of the farther Highlands, saccharine stuff at times and now I think entirely neglected by an age which prefers bitters, I felt a renewed impulse for corner-collection in the farthest north of my country.

Both the western tips of Scotland have been undervisited. Galloway, in the south, is superb country, but it needs a left turn which the southern traveller will not make. By road or by rail, he rushes past Lockerbie, urgent for the north. A slight deviation would give him Glen Trool, which has Highland quality to the full, and the great spine of the Rhinns. But few will pause and turn. So the wine-red moors and the curlew-plaintive graves of the martyrs remain familiar in Stevenson's oft-quoted verses, but unfamiliar to the eye. This is absurd, but it is a gain to the solitudinarians, to the readers of S. R. Crockett and of some of the best of Sir Walter, and to those who prefer their country towns to be few, douce, and uncrowded like Castle Douglas, Newton Stewart, St. John's Town of Dalry, and Kirkcudbright of the estuary and the artists, one of Scotland's happiest echoes of the past and of the French influence.

Galloway is easy, if you turn. Sutherland is not easy at all. To go seven hundred miles is a trifle to an American or an Australian, but to a Londoner it seems an intolerable distance and the ever-mounting costs of travel by steam or petrol still further discourage the penetration of the ultimate Scotland. To see Ben Hope and Ben Loyal (as we have Englished Laoghal), those last, superb and many-peaked monsters of the northern rocks, is high experience: but few enjoy it. They may at least argue that they can slake their senses with similar grandeur without the expense of time, funds, and trouble incurred by a journey into Sutherland.

The eastern tip can be tackled by the railway which runs from Inverness away up to Wick and the great cliffs of Thurso. It is a long, meandering, day's-work run, if run is not altogether too flattering a term. But the eye is grandly rewarded on a fine day, with sea and strath and heathery hinterland in glorious reiteration. Do not look for violent motion. Here Time is not taken by the forelock: he is overlooked and snubbed into humility, as if he had no business with the affairs of travelling folk. Things may have improved now, but it is not long since my last journey north from Inverness was of a sweetly farcical type. Here was I in Inverness, the capital of the Highlands, waiting for the train of the day, the Link with the North, to carry me to the remote province. The train stood ready, a fine train: it even had a dining-car: but it lacked an engine. Inquiry as to the provenance of this necessary adjunct was not encouraging. The appropriate authorities were not asleep. Eyes right, eyes left, they were looking for an engine. They might, it seemed, have to look as far as Aviemore, some forty miles away to the south. To get that engine along and refuelled and all aboil for the great North enterprise might take some hours. Could I go away and be given a time for my return? Oh no, something might turn up. Micawberism prevailed. Something did turn up. The missing article had been suitably routed out from its repose or cannily replaced by a sudden newcomer. So off we went, only forty minutes late at the start.

It was a curving, halting, hour-consuming, sight-enchanting journey. The sun gleamed generously on the Firths of Moray and of Dornoch to our right. These smiled in something subtler than Technicolour Blue. They had ' the countless laughter of the waves ' which Aeschylus saw in the Aegean around Athens. To the left, instead of Hymettus, was Ben Wyvis. On past Nigg Bay to Tain, whither once came royal pilgrims to the shrine of St. Duthas and where the usual atrocities that seem to be inseparable from the fervours of the medieval faiths were duly and bloodily committed. Dornoch lay across the water, Dornoch acclaimed in 1630 for having the ' fairest linkes and green fields of any in Scotland, surpassing for golf, archery, and riding even the fields of Montrose or St. Andrews.'

The train turns inland by the Oykell River to make for Lairg, the base of all far-westerly excursion, before it turns back to the Caithness coast. Then comes Skibo Castle to the south, whither for twenty years, to his neo-baronial, many-turreted splendour came Andrew Carnegie, the lad from Dunfermline in Fife and, more rewardingly, the steel-master of Pittsburgh, U.S.A. There is a spice of paradox about this coast; just north is the ducal castle of Dunrobin, the seat of the Sutherlands, long so wealthy and so powerful. Nearly a century and a half ago it was the Sutherland factors (agents) who conducted the most remorseless of the Clearances, banishing the old crofter-tenants to make room for new and profitable sheep. Those bitter wrongs are still keenly remembered in the townships and clachans of the very far north. I remember Eric Linklater telling me before I went there that I would find the Clearances to be still current politics. He did not exaggerate.

18

Hard by the source of the unforgotten evictions sat, later
on, the self-made man of Fife, millionaire and benefactor,
busily filling Britain with libraries and church-organs,
lavishing books and hymns by the millions on the millions,
endowing University careers for the young of promise,
founding his four charitable Trusts, of which the United
Kingdom Trust is the largest, a monster of cautious
benignity which continually assists, after due care, the
Movements that are held to be on a promising and ethical
move. Sutherland may be reckoned the poorest of the
Scottish counties since its population is the thinnest. But
it has long housed a sumptuous dukedom, famous for its
hospitalities, and it once contained the fountain of charity
that Skibo's Andy turned on with pious zeal. It is not his
fault that so many of the libraries that he scattered like
leaves were built when British architecture was at its worst.
He meant to elevate, and no doubt did. But he signally
failed to decorate.

Keeping to the east the traveller comes to the best of
Caithness, which is the southern end of the county. The
little towns of the coast have taken all the tossings of
fortune that befall the fishers of the sea. The herring-
harvest that is gold to-day is dross on many a morrow: the
lairds by the rivers running seaward have taken (or their
vassals have poached) the finest of Scottish salmon from
their chill, unsullied waters. Behind them are hills, at
first of moderate height and then of increasing loneliness.
It is sixty odd miles as the eagle flies (if there are any eagles
still where once they almost swarmed) from Helmsdale to
Loch Inver, its opposite mark upon the western coast.
There are certainly not six hundred people living on or near
that sixty-mile line. Higher up, from Wick to Kinloch
Bervie on the Atlantic side, the distance is over seventy
miles. Your flight-line, should you emulate the eagle,

would prudently skirt Ben Loyal and Ben Hope; once off the Caithness levels it would cover or take in view little more of human habitation than a fishing bothy, a game-keeper's cottage, and the shelter of a shepherd.

Should you wilt at the thought of so much wilderness, you can keep east and press north through Wick to John o' Groats and the two heads of Duncansby and Dunnet which are a proper target for corner-questors since here is the northernmost top of the mainland. The motor-coaches, which have proved a salvation to many hard-pressed Scottish Hotels, including some of the best, grind on to John o' Groats where the sea-view is better than the land-look and the beaches are famous for their shells, including the rare cowries or Groatie Buckies. This part of the world used to have a considerable export of stone, especially for paving purposes. Many London streets have been paved by Scotland's North East corners: but cement has been a strong rival. This most northern phase of Caithness is not remarkable for its scenery, and, should some of the travelling party insist on reaching John o' Groats, it would be a wise enough plan for those less corner-minded to await their return and dig in somewhere between Dornoch and Dunbeath. For company, if your inn-mates incline you to misanthropy, take the stories of Neil Gunn. This is his land, his sea, his mystery. The wise man sees not the same mountain or the same river that the fool sees and Gunn's wisdom is visionary, searching, making the earth seem as limpid as water, with all its secrets manifest. He finds the universe in a salmon-pool or even a sheep-fank. But he is not only a prose-poet and a seer: he can tell a good human tale of the drifters or the crofter, of the milord and his sport. For the last get hold of ' Second Sight,' which contains a more striking picture of deer-stalking than even John Buchan ever made. To know what shepherding in Caithness under snow can be, read ' The Drinking Well.' You may well prefer a leisured stroll with these authentic fictions for company than pressing on to John o' Groats.

But suppose we have no time for both corners and vote for the far wilder west. Then we leave the railway at its leftward bend, get out at Lairg, take one bus from that station to the village, and wait for another. There will be time to look round and Time, as I said, goes jog-trot here. Two buses will then be available, one striking west by the long water-snake that is narrow Loch Shin, the other driving due north across the moors to Altnaharra, then down to the Pentland Firth at Tongue and eastward to Bettyhill. That little place lies above a cove of Cornish aspect at the end of Strath Naver. It is apt to be beset by those who can afford the costly salmon ' beats ' on the Naver or take a more economical chance with the trout-lochs in the moors behind. So it is well to see about accommodation in advance.

I took the latter, the Bettyhill coach, and had, on a glorious September afternoon, a journey of magic. The deer-forest of Ben Armine rolled away in lovely rhythms of desolation to the right, gentle-seeming on such a day, but fierce to the shepherd or the sportsman when the storms are massing. An occasional sheep-farm dotted, at first, this noble void. The bus-driver, who is the general carrier as well as the local Director of Passenger Services, threw out letters and parcels and papers on the road-side for the farm-folk to collect at their leisure. Doubtless Sutherland has no pickers and stealers. In any case, where there are no people, there can be no thieves. And here there are no people.

At Altnaharra the great skeleton of Reay Forest loomed away to the left, while to the north towered Ben Hope and

Ben Loyal. After dropping down to Tongue and stopping for refreshment we swung right on switch-back roads, rough, narrow and alarming, to end at Bettyhill. It was now about 7.30 and I thought that the driver had done plenty. But, rid of us, he was off to take the locals to a dance in some other township (here ten crofts make a township) and to cover, in the dark, many more miles of those dizzy, scenic-railway tracks. The dance, I gathered, lasted from eight till two! Pleasures and gatherings are taken seriously in a desert. When they dance here, they do dance and their time-table is that of a London night-club. Back at Bettyhill about three in the morning, this indefatigable dancer and coaxer of a bus up and down ways more proper to a goat, would be on the job again in a few hours to get his vehicle back on the early morning run to Lairg, fifty miles away. When they dance, they dance: and when they drive, they drive.

At Bettyhill I struck one exquisite day of shimmering sunlight and then a Pentland gale: it did not rain, but it blew beyond belief. The rain, if it had rained, would have been whisked into spray. The hay-stacks of the little crofts perched round the cove were hurled about like single straws: it must have taken their owners weeks of drudgery to recover something of their scattered possessions. We were not allowed to use the front door of the hotel, because, if the wind got in under the porch, it would certainly throw it skyward like the hay-stacks. The storm raged like a frenzied bull, tossing everything on invisible horns. So I crept out into the yard at the back and took a walk, innocently going westward with the hurricane to help me. I stupidly did not realise what would happen when I turned for home. I had weight on my side and even so could only just force my way into the wind: a light-weight or a woman hampered by skirts could never have got back on foot at all and

would have had to sit and wait for a passing car or lorry.
I did at last ' make it,' buffeting slowly on, head down: it
was a mere mile or so, but it was equal to a dozen in normal
weather. They say, justly, that there is good air in these
parts: true, and there is also plenty of it. The victuals at
the hotel were excellent and plentiful. They were needed.
Barons of beef and saddles of mutton would seem like mere
snacks in such a climate. So try, if you want ' a breath of
fresh air,' an equinoctial gale upon the Pentland Firth.
Here is ozone. The cobwebs that could stand up to it
would have to be made of steel.

There can be no trees in such country, except in a few
hollows. The very moorland is shorn like sheep after
clipping. The landscape is reduced to the roughest elements
of its anatomy: here are the bare bones of geography,
unfleshed of fertility, except beside a river or for an acre
or two in a nook of the sheltering cliff. They have long
spells of hot weather, I was assured, at Bettyhill, weeks of
anti-cyclone, fantastic in blue and gold with the sun dipping
only for an hour or two. (The English sounding name of
the place is attributed to an Elizabeth who was Duchess of
Sutherland and made this, during the anti-cyclones, her
darling coign of vantage and her belvedere.) I was told
also of the glories of sea-bathing in the bay, where the
combers were now crashing and crumbling in white ruin,
house-high before the hurricane, immensely menacing and
shiversome. I believed in the long spells of radiance, but
was sceptical about the joys of immersion in these waters
in any weather. The visitors who find a Lido on the
Pentland Firth must be of sterner stuff than I am.

This sense of Nature in the absolute nude was even more
powerful later on as I drove, with the gale exhausted, to the
westward, past Tongue, over a huge bare plateau called
A'Mhoine and so to gaunt Loch Eriboll, an inlet that has

23

been of some naval service in the past. In modern warfare, if you have a fleet, you must also have somewhere to hide it and the north-west of Scotland is not lacking in cloud-girdled fastnesses which are conveniently similar and baffling to the searching eye of the aeroplane's pilot. Eriboll is a superb name for a marine abyss and looks the part. And so to thinly inhabited Durness where life almost ends.

Beside the estuary of the salmon-rich river Dionard stands the Cape Wrath Hotel, a good ten miles from the Cape itself. This has to be reached by ferrying across the Dionard and then by getting some portage over a rough road to the ultimate tip; the road wanders across a tumble of loneliness called the Parph. By this time a fine morning had turned to unhelpful mist: it was obvious that if I did achieve Cape Wrath, I would scarcely profit by the effort. Mist looks much the same in Ultima as in Proxima Thule. So the corner of the corner, which I had come to ' bag,' remained inviolate.

Then, after lunch in the surroundings which fishermen create and relish (they are not for nesh creatures who want a padded and a steamy lounge) I went south to Rhiconich and Scourie with the surge of Foinaven on my landward flank. Here is a kind of majesty of nothingness; it is surprising that deer can subsist on such a surface of wind-scraped rock. I am told that the stags run lighter and smaller in this forest than in the Central Highlands, which is scarcely strange.

Scudding mist broke to reveal infinities of emptiness. I have never on British soil felt so completely sundered from mankind. I wondered what would happen if the car broke down. Then we suddenly came to a car which had surrendered; it contained a District Nurse who had been driving herself alone through this rain-dark limbo to a case. We lifted her to Rhiconich where there is a garage; thence she could be driven to her task. Rescue of her own little car would follow sometime. To be a District Nurse round about Cape Wrath demands, I should have thought, a bit of feminine machinery with an all-weather body made of rust-proof metal, with nothing so human as nerves, and as handy at a breakdown as at a lying-in. Our companion was a little heroine who, from the look of her, might have been going to the pictures in Glasgow.

Scourie is 'quite a place.' It has a number of crofts scattered on the hills around the bay, a famous fishing-hotel, at least two shops, three kinds of religion, rivalling each other in fiery Protestant fervour, and a Corpach or grave-yard on the sands. Since the land is all bone, so bony that rabbits cannot dig their shelter and have given up the region as useless, man's digging has to take place beside the beaches, where alone a spade can penetrate. Here lie the McKays, home from the hills, home from the seas. Here happen the funerals which are usually the prelude of a feast, sometimes of an orgy. When folk so isolated do get together, either to marry or to bury, they miss no social chances. The men of the wilderness are not awed by last rites any more than District Nurses are awed by fifty miles of mountain road. Having assembled, from far-flung crofts or tiny townships many miles away, they do not part without a dram.

At Scourie I settled in, with time to look and read and think and ask questions. The admirable Mr. and Mrs. Knowles, who had made the drastic alteration of habitat from the Sudan to Sutherland, then managed the hotel. Mr. Knowles was eager to prove that the climate of the north corner is reasonably mild, which may well be true. (It was by no means mild when I was there—but the village shop stored hot-water bottles.) The Meteorological Office has recently pointed out in an official publication that

' Cambridge is a distinctly colder place in winter than Lerwick in the Shetlands.' Mr. Knowles, by importing soil, created two gardens in which to prove that the sea-coast of this region, with a bit of wind-shelter and some extraneous earth, can grow all manner of flowers and vegetables locally declared to be impossible.

Really the local industry is the pursuit of salmon, sea-trout, and trout. The natives themselves, by their highly paid service as ghillies and boatmen, flourish on the sport. Through the summer they can get a full agricultural wage plus tips by attending on a sporting visitor from 9.30 to 5.30 or thereabouts. The ghillie is driven to and from a loch where he takes out the boat and advises and assists his client; this may be chilly or boring, but it is much easier work than slogging away for longer hours on a farm. He has his cheaply-rented croft which he can tend in the long evenings: he has sheep on the hills, with subsidies attached. His daughters can get summer work in the local, or other Highland, hotels, at Catering Wages Act rates with good tips to follow. It was obvious that plenty could be put by for the winter, which admittedly is long and dark. Small wonder that the Sutherlanders will travel huge distances in their wild Decembers to a dance or ' a social.' In a place like Scourie the crofter who will take his chances is not now a distressed person, because the summer opportunities are so rich and the agricultural subsidies so bountiful. But he must be ready to be a servant to win the easiest rewards. Highland pride does not seem to be offended.

The visiting fishermen of Highland hotels, doctors, lawyers, and professional men from the South or from England, are men and women with a single thought. They talk fish, they dream fish, and occasionally they catch fish. Their passions leads to such masochistic routines as wading about in the Tay and the Dee in February and March or facing any weather that summer may bring to the far north. The hotels often have a weighing-scale in the hall and the day's catch is deposited there in the evening. This machine was never in danger of collapse through over-loading while I was at Scourie. Fishermen always have their good reasons for a barren day: it is too hot; it is too cold: it is too windy: or there is a thundery calm. They explain, but they do not grouse. They are ecstatic in their hour of triumph. They are content in their days or weeks of failure. They do not mope or grizzle.

I, though not a fisherman, was kindly tolerated at Scourie, but, because of my arriving rodless, I was plainly regarded as deficient in a proper sense of values, if not a trifle insane. My retaliation was to solve the fairly easy cross-word puzzles over which my betters boggled at night. Skill at fishing and lexicographical ingenuity appear to be strangers. All the visitors disappeared for the whole day in all weathers. Mrs. Knowles was toiling at 'packed lunches' long before breakfast. Organisation was thorough. A notice was chalked up in the hall at nights scheduling each party's loch or section of loch for the next day, so that all had a turn at the best. There were two non-angling ladies from Lancashire, devotees of wilderness, who went off all day with sandwiches and mackintoshes, indefatigably walking. They came back at the time of general reunion, sunburned or sodden, but inevitably rejoicing. We had days varying from the perfect to the atrocious, but climate did not seem to count. I have rarely been in, or on the fringe of, a society which seemed so resolutely, so un-quenchably happy.

My own solitary wanderings provoked some reflections on the beauty and tragedy of wilderness. These were con-firmed when I was driven south, on a day of September's most serene and shimmering performance, across the

27

Kylestrome Ferry, past the peak of Quinag to Loch Assynt and Inchnadamph. Later we dipped between Canisp and the gaunt, sheer pyramid of Suilven on the west and the vast Ben More Assynt on the east and so down to Ullapool on Loch Broom. The road was often bad, but the view was never less than superb throughout the whole fifty miles. The mountains, when you get to Ullapool, are not quite so bald as those to the north of Scourie, surging starkly above the Laxford River and beyond Loch Stack. (It is odd to meet such a Surrey-sounding name as Laxford Bridge in these parts, but Lax is the Scandinavian laks, meaning salmon; and ford is fiord. The Duke of Westminster knows all about the rich content of his salmon-fiord and has a house thereby.) But everywhere, in Wester Ross as in Sutherland, there is this incessant expanse of the utterly empty and the wholly exquisite. Probably not two hundred people live along the road (there are no others) or even within ten miles of this fifty-mile route that I traversed. The entire county of Sutherland contains close on three million acres; it had just over 16,100 inhabitants in 1931. Now, according to the Census of 1951, there are 13,664, which is about the population of a single English country town. And down the numbers go, while elsewhere increase is general.

First of all I realised that even a lover of scenery, which I am, can become surfeited and even sickened with scenery. There it all was, stretched out in purple and blue and in greys as lovely as either, an ocean of wilderness in which the myriad lochs twinkled like jewelled islands. This land-ocean surged around peaks of rhythmic splendour or of sudden, staggering, conical sharpness. Beyond lay a blue and dancing sea. I had been taken across to Handa Island and had looked from its colossal western cliffs, a sea-birds' metropolis and nursery in May but bird-empty in the

28

autumn, over the Minch to Lewis. Most of the north-west was to be seen, glimmering in its September pride, beauty after beauty for multitudinous miles. The bare-bone summits shone like regalia. But, after a while, the senses began to ache. I was not only numbed by the keenness of the air, I was actually oppressed by the enormity of my visual banquet. I was reminded of the Scot who said of a friend's poem, ' I dinna like it. It's far ower sublime.'

Over-sublime. It can work out so. But there was something more than excess of geographical nobility. My queasiness was partly caused, I am sure, by the implications of all this void. Waste country can be more than a fascinating wilderness; it can indeed be just waste. Must this largesse of Nature's giving, a benison on such scale as well as of such quality, be frittered away on a few deer-stalkers and fishermen, coming only for their brief seasons, on an occasional landscape painter, or on a vagrant writer like myself? The touring motor-coaches do not, as a rule, reach so far over such rough going: there are not the hotels in the far North West to accommodate a largely expanded tourist traffic. One does not feel so much enraptured, it is true, after a week of driving rain and all-obscuring mist. But beauty in the ends breaks in, beauty so limitless as to be almost a bore, at least when you have been there for some time. You feel ashamed to be the monopolist of such entrancement. So a melancholy seeps into one's felicity. After all, there had been, in the coves and niches, more cultivation in the past. Why not now?

Just south of Scourie there is an easy walk to Badcall Bay, a tangle of rocks and islets and lapping waters, with the kind of sea that travel-films pursue and cannot catch. It is all as pretty, weather permitting, as a Victorian painter's dream. Then, strolling by the shore, you suddenly encounter the usual evidence of Highland ruin, in short the ruins

29

themselves, the testament of old surrender. Badcall has a sad wharf and warehouses tumbling in decay. A trim little haven was there once, and now nothing but a broken habitation. The deserted stones of the quay were sepulchral. They chilled the heart as well as the feet. They smudged the celestial afternoon.

I used the hard word surrender. Perhaps that was wrong. Betrayal by circumstance might be fairer. Man had come here with cargoes and had taken cargoes away. Coal and victuals in, beasts and fleeces out? Whatever that commerce had been, it no longer was. The sailors of the ships and the loaders of the ships gave up or were given up and their descendants are doubtless enjoying ' full employment ' in some murky city-port. Badcall Bay, at once bleak and benign, beneath a temperate sun, was typical of Caledonia stern and mild. It occurred to me that in this alteration of Scott's famous phrase lay the secret of the lovely wilderness through which I had been travelling. The Highlander is, like his land and his climate, a baffling mixture. He is the grand fighter on fields of battle, but not so tenacious on fields of grass. He has handed his home to the alien rich: he once allowed the lairds of his own blood and birthplace to drive him into the sea. He has been happily a ghillie, tying flies to foreign rods, not deeming them to be rods of affliction. He has been charming and polite and deferential and, in exile, he has gone to the ends of the earth for the enrichment of those ends as well as of himself. He has a fierce religion, perhaps, and an aspect of grandeur. But he has touched his cap to the conquerors; he has been a man both stern and mild.

CHAPTER II

In the Dead Vast

BADCALL reminded me of moorland days in North Yorkshire. Those who walk in the Northern Pennines will see, as I have often seen, scratchings on the sides of the fells and a few grey ruins beside them. Sometimes they are farms which could not be held against the heather. Man had desperately fought the hills to yield him pasture and tilth and fought the climate to yield him a crop; at last he was beaten. More often they are the relics of the lead-mining industry which was as old as the Romans who flung their great road across the bleak heights between Scotch Corner and Brough, carrying the legions and auxiliaries to Carlisle and the west of their Wall. They even built a bath for the warm relief of troops and travellers; its uncovered remnants are still to be seen at windy, desolate Bowes, where Dickens was later to discover Mr. Squeers and the unwashed urchins of his Dotheboys. Foreign competition beat the lead-workers and we cannot altogether regret the fact. For it was a hard, poor, lung-damaging life that the miners had to endure in dark Swaledale or in the ghylls around the high-flung wilderness of Teeshead, so majestic to a tourist in summer, but not easily habitable in wild Decembers. But at least the lead-men were not savaged by their fellows: the trade was broken by alien pressure and the changing economy of the world; it was not massacred by a section of its own people. And that is the horror whose ghosts still linger in the North and West of Scotland. The staples of far north and far west, sea-fishing and farming by self-reliant individuals grouped in small communities, were deliberately assailed and slaughtered and the assassins in this case were the old Highland chieftains themselves. Later the English and American ' sportsmen ' were to complete the destruction begun by the native lairds.

The Clearances drove the crofters, as the Scottish small-holders are still called, into or over the sea or into the menial status of ghillies, stalkers, and boot-cleaners to the rich renters of a castle with a forest and a river, while their women scrubbed and cooked in the vast grim cellarage that supplies the usual domestic offices of a baronial ' place ' in the Highlands. These mass-evictions from the land are familiar history to the Scots—or should be if Scots, even now, are taught their own history. (For a long time it was not so much a neglected as a forbidden subject, so strong was the domination of England and of the Anglicised Scots who accepted and profited by that domination.) But the English tourist, as a rule, knows nothing of all this. He surveys the desolation, rejoices in the scenery, and asks no questions while his car or motor-coach sweeps past a cluster of roofless walls in the glen that is so fair to see and would appear to be a better dwelling-place than is a Glasgow slum. So, if I am to interpret the mystery of this dead vast of wilderness, this Caledonia Deserta, a mystery typified in the tumbled warehouses of Badcall and its similar empty havens or in the crumbled steadings of a seemingly fertile river-bank, I must, at the risk of boring Scottish readers, recount a little history.

After Culloden and the final breaking of the gallant, feckless Jacobitism of the Catholic and Stuart-loyal clans by the Anglo-German army of Cumberland with the support of those Scots chieftains who had despaired of the Stuarts (and not without reason), the clan system which had been feudal and even paternal in its way, was broken, the tartan forbidden, the Highlanders hunted and slaughtered, and a new rule of legal contract, agreeable to the lawyers of the South, was imposed on the old rule of family custom. The Heritable Jurisdictions Act and its companion laws which abolished ward-holdings sound little and dry enough on paper. But they made an economic and social revolution.

Some Highlanders found their escape in emigration; others, by a brilliant stroke of English and Hanoverian policy, were recruited to serve in the very army that had been their ruin. They were disarmed as Scottish rebels: they were promptly rearmed as British patriots, when the Highland regiments were formed to do England's work.

Only twenty-one years after Culloden the Earl of Chatham could boldly claim that he had looked for merit wherever it could be found and that was in the mountains of the north. The men who 'had gone nigh to have overturned the State in the '45 were in the last war brought to combat on your (the English) side: they fought with fidelity, as they fought with valour, and conquered for you in every quarter of the world.' Wolfe, of Quebec fame, was riding, as a young Major, over the field of Culloden with the Duke of Cumberland. A wounded and helpless Highlander was thought to look defiantly at them. The Butcher ordered Wolfe to shoot the dog for his impudence. Wolfe and some other officers decently refused this filthy command, but the man was shot by a private. The victim was Charles Fraser of Inverallochy who had led the Frasers on that day. Only thirteen years later the First Fraser

Regiment was to scale the Heights of Abraham for England under Wolfe's command! The Highlanders, in this case, were no elephants: they easily forgot. The English have been very good at this contrivance and later persuaded the Indians to be as valiant on their behalf as the Frasers and the Camerons, whose clans were so neatly transformed into crusaders for the very power that had overwhelmed them.

The rebellious Chieftains, some of them wandering as Displaced Persons in more hospitable France, saw their lands sequestered for nearly forty years; but England knows when to forgive and the laws of property were not overlooked. When they came back it was in a new form. The clan-system had gone. They were no longer fathers of a family; they were landlords renting land under contract to what was left of their men. Old customs and traditions had vanished; the Industrial Revolution and the reign of the ' Cash Nexus ' were about to begin. Edinburgh was no longer a medieval fortress; with its superb New Town in the making it had risen to be a city of great elegance and attraction, as well as a nest of lawyers who controlled the new régime. It was a tempting magnet to the old chieftains who had become new lairds. London was no longer hostile to them. It, too, was gay and alluring. But the key to both was money and money in abundance. And money, which could never have been screwed out of mere crofters, could now, by a surprising turn of fortune, be wrung from the hills of their recovered homeland.

The new prop of the lairds was the sheep. The sheep has often been a cruel master of men as well as an excellent servant. It was the flourishing English wool-trade of the sixteenth and seventeenth centuries that enriched the weavers and flockmasters, especially in Suffolk and the Cotswolds and, since English architecture was then at its highest level of performance, the new rich of that epoch left their mark handsomely in towns, manor-houses, Churches, and markets of consummate beauty. But to get the wool they had to have wide pastures and to get these they destroyed the simple farming of the time and got rid of the old agriculture that was cumbering their potential ranches. They enclosed common lands and the English Enclosures, imposed by that symbol of innocence, the sheep, were the prototype of the Scottish Clearances. One shepherd took the place of six peasants. How cheap and how rewarding, except for the displaced peasantry! Sir Thomas More said curtly, ' Sheep eat men,' and what he said of England was true, later on, of Scotland. ' The sheep's in the meadow, the cow's in the corn,' is an old rhyme. It is also an epitome of economic history. The sheep got into what poor meadows the crofters possessed —and ate both the Englishman and Highlander out of them.

The mills of the northern English and Southern Scottish towns began to demand wool on an unprecedented scale. Here, in the early nineteenth century, was the new laird's chance. What is well-nigh incredible to us now is the inhuman savagery with which he took it. Sheep on the land were to relieve his poverty and to pay his way to the genteel (or profligate) amenities of the South. But the crofters were in the way, scraping their living contentedly enough with the hand-plough and by the service of simple farming with strong right arms. The lairds, with their legal documents of tenure replacing old customary rights and duties, could raise rents as they chose or order the crofters out and, if the order was stubbornly neglected, the law could be enforced and the men thrown out. And not only were they thrown out: their homes were burned over their heads. In some places of this Far North, now toured by us in all its lonely calm, there were appalling scenes of violence and misery; it is true that some of those who were shipped to Canada survived the hardships of the voyage and of the penniless arrival in a strange and empty world, with the result that those of their descendants who stayed there to prosper could become Prime Ministers and millionaires. But that accidental good fortune of the children does not excuse the infamy practised on the fathers.

It was in the county of Sutherland that the evictions were most heartless and severe. The heiress to the Sutherland estates had married a nobleman with an English title, Leveson-Gower, Marquess of Stafford; he could hardly be expected to understand the old ways of the clans and he was ' progressive ' in spending on roads and bridges, but his factors were ' progressive ' also in the drastic shifting of the men who got in the way of the sheep. In Kildonan Strath a population of 2,000, which had previously divided 133,000 acres, was squeezed into 3,000 acres of the worst land, while the remaining 130,000 acres went to six sheep-farmers. If the men would not go, they were put out by force and kept out by the firing of their houses. Should a visitor at Scourie inquire why there is a township there at all, he will be told that the Sutherland Clearances drove many of the Mackays out of Strath Naver, which reaches to the sea at Bettyhill and has a small stretch of covetable soil. The refugees were allowed to stop at Scourie because its land was deemed worthless. But somehow they managed to cling on, doubtless using that harbour at Badcall, where my excursions into history began.

Then the wheel of lairdly fortune took another and less happy turn. There was a kind of rough justice in that. The rich lands of Australia and New Zealand, farmed sometimes by the very Scots who had been driven out of

Scotland by the Clearances and the ensuing poverty, began to produce wool in great quantity and cheapness. The problem of the sheep-farmer is that of winter keep. The tourist, as he is whisked up the glens and over the grassy uplands of the gentler hills, sees a few hundred sheep grazing there in summer, and naturally wonders why there are not thousands instead of hundreds: there seems to be room for countless flocks, with grass and to spare. But the grass has withered by October and then the sheep must be mainly fed on crop-products; and where are these to come from in sufficient amount in a land so bare as this? But in warmer climates it may be possible to find grass all the year round: the cropping problem then vanishes. So, with the flocks self-maintenant, wool becomes plentiful and profitable. This kind of competition began to press on the Highlander from the Antipodes in the eighteen-sixties. The lairds were to find to their dismay that they had shifted their troublesome crofters and smashed up their clans in vain; some of the lowlier clansmen, who had been forced to quit Sutherland, were hitting back, from over the seas and far away, and were not so lowly now.

But the deer came to the rescue. The Highlands had been discovered by Royalty. Queen Victoria had fallen in love with them at first sight when she stayed at Taymouth Castle on her first visit to the North. She insisted on a Highland home for herself and built Balmoral in Deeside, which showed her sagacity in choosing a perfect site. The architectural taste was that of the period; her patronage of the baronial confirmed that mode. We are rash to be rude about aesthetic fashions. They may always come again.

She fell delightfully in love with the Highlanders, so 'cheerful and happy and merry,' as she wrote, 'and ready to walk and run and do anything.' The perfect ghillie was already being formed from the old cateran. Prince Albert, more gravely, remarked of these aboriginals that ' he highly appreciated the good-breeding, simplicity, and intelligence which makes it so pleasant and even instructive to talk to them.' The Prince was ready, even eager, to be a sportsman as well as a conversationalist. So, with this abundance of tame Highlanders and wild deer, the joys of the country were complete. And, naturally, a fashion was set. The soaring wealth of Victorian English capitalism was seeking new holiday outlets for the end-of-the-summer vacations. Caledonia Deserta was discovered, and its bare hills were suddenly changed from the now unprofitable sheep-runs to the more saleable deer-forests. What the sporting tenants shot, Landseer publicised by his painting. The monarch of the glen had magnificently arrived in high society. The Lairds found a new salvation, in the blood, not of the sheep, but of the stag. Were there not natives ' ready to walk and run and do anything '? Yes, but the stalking and the carting of corpses and the cleaning of rifles and boots did not occupy all that was left of the clans. There were still a few crofters about, disturbing the romantic loneliness, getting in the way of the deer, keeping their own dogs, and possibly even helping themselves to a trout or a rabbit from the land of their inheritance, the land which they had to inhabit through the dark and soaking winters while the September sportsmen were sitting by their London fires.

So the Clearance policy was carried to the uttermost. There was indignation, but there was no rebellion. The discontent was sufficient to cause a Commission of Inquiry, whose report, issued in 1884, was a dreadful record of eviction and persecution. Donald McKinnon of Skye, for example, reported that in Elgoll forty-four families were removed from the little township of Keppoch and fourteen of them went away to Australia. The absentee landlord who arranged this form of Empire-building by compulsion was a Mr. Macallister who had not been seen in the place for forty years.

The Clearances for deer had the old technique, but new dictators. The Scots had already been exiled by the Scots; now they were to be the prey of the English. A. G. Macdonell, who recounted this rape of Highland life with his characteristic trenchancy in ' My Scotland,' ended his chapter on the subject with the reminder that, as early as 1884, of the thirty-seven deer-forests which were recorded in the county of Inverness thirty-one were owned or rented by men with Anglo-Saxon names: Ross and Cromarty, to the north, had forty-four forests and thirty-seven of these were owned or rented by people who were not Scots. Moreover the Americans, who had, one would have thought, deer enough in their own Continent, were coming over to join the fray; it was a fray which was then carrying social distinction. The stag was the target of the titled. Innocent of the economic background into which they stepped, they concluded, from the examples on the spot, that the way to get more stags for their rifles was to drive more men into destitution and exile.

A Mr. Winans, who can hardly have known what he was really doing to an ancient, if humble and narrow, civilisation, took over nearly a quarter of a million acres for his own style of sport. This was described by one of the Commission's native witnesses as ' gathering the poor animals together and driving them before the muzzles of the guns.' The Winans way was similar to that practised by the ancients, who, lacking rifles, coralled the driven deer and massacred them with any weapons at their disposal. That was the manner in which Queen Elizabeth had got her bucks when she made a ' progress ' through the great country-houses and their parks. There was then no alternative. But Mr. Winans and his friends had rifles of range and accuracy.

In Winans's trail, up Glen Cannich, there was left, as witnesses deposed and any eye could see, the usual wrack of ' crumbled walls, empty but substantial homes, some slated and some thatched, still standing at intervals in the Glen, their windows bolted and their doors locked up.' But we must not put all the blame on the stranger who had become a dollar-king in Caledonia. When it was asked who cleared the land and made it forest for Mr. Winans, the answer was, ' First and foremost Mackenzie of Kintail.' The English and Americans were only accessories to the social crime.

The Lairds' fortunes flourished on the rents for forests thus obtainable, with ups and downs, until 1930. The world-wide economic depression of that year and the following years reacted severely on the Highlands and by our time the rich have been largely taxed out of this form of pleasure. Certainly, unless they were to take the Winans way, it was a strenuous form of self-indulgence, demanding great physical fitness, long exposure, and hard climbing and crawling on the rain-swept hills.

New forces have intervened. Glen Cannich, when I was last there, had a huge camp of workers creating roads, dams, and power-station for the North of Scotland Hydro-Electric Scheme, of which more will be said later. ' Hydro-Electrics ' do not directly repopulate a countryside after the initial work has been done; the turbines themselves depend on water-power and can be manipulated by a very small staff of specialists. But they are intended to distribute heat, light, and power which will bring amenity and new industry and so draw back again at least a few of the Highlanders whose ancestors found the Highlands barred against them.

The stag is no longer monarch of the empty Glen nor is the salmon the king of the rivers now pressed for larger service.

Everybody knows the haunting lines of the ' Canadian Boat Song,' written for the exiles of the glens, perhaps by John Galt:

> *From the lone shieling of the misty island*
> *Mountains divide us, and the waste of seas,*
> *But still the blood is strong, the heart is Highland,*
> *And we in dreams behold the Hebrides.*

But less many remember what follows:

> *When the bold kindred, in the time long vanished,*
> *Conquered the soil and fortified the keep,*
> *No seer foretold the children would be banished,*
> *That a degenerate lord might boast his sheep.*

The poem can hardly be popular even in these humaner times with certain ducal and baronial families. Did Mackenzie of Kintail and his like ever hear its sonorous rebuke? The last quatrain of this poem has proved nobly untrue:

> *Come foreign rage—let Discord burst in slaughter,*
> *O then for clansmen true and stern claymore!*
> *The hearts that would have given their blood like water,*
> *Beat heavily beyond the Atlantic shore.*

Back from Canada and Australia came the men of Highland name to the challenge of two great wars and their Niagaras of blood. The Frasers and the others, who a little more than a decade after Culloden were sailing with Wolfe to

41

Quebec, sailed again and in reverse. Perhaps they had forgotten: if they remembered, they forgave, both Cumberland's butchery by the sword and the long century of persecution by legal process which followed after.

Of course there were two sides to all that. It is not suggested that every laird was a greedy tyrant or every factor a fiend. The crofters themselves had often a very hard life and a low standard of living by modern standards. Some of the Clearances have actually been described as 'assisted emigration' for the people's good. (Hitler, in this sense, may also be said to have 'assisted emigration'.) Some who survived the exposure and hardship of oceanic voyages in ill-found vessels 'made good' and saw their children prosper beyond the dreams of a Sutherland crofter. But the essential factor is that they went under duress. They wanted to stay where their ancestors had enjoyed such freedom as clan-feudalism allowed. Their new legal liberty, as rent-payers liable to eviction, was no freedom in fact. They might as well have been slaves. Sometimes good news of a better world might come from overseas to make the parting less bitter. A band of emigrants leaving for North Carolina in 1752 gave as their reasons 'poverty, oppression of landlords, and encouraging letters from friends already settled in America.' But it can hardly be denied that the present emptiness of Caledonia Deserta is based on a misuse of law which made the crofters as helpless as slaves. It is an astonishing fact that Harriet Beecher Stowe, the champion of Liberation, whose 'Uncle Tom's Cabin' raised fires of indignation across the world, actually defended the Clearances.

Given, as I said, some bounty of weather, this Dead Vast of Scotland's farthest verge is lapped in a beauty that is serene as well as savage. You may bask by a sky-blue inlet, as I basked by Badcall Bay, and fancy yourself in a

42

Cornish cove, with the grim wilderness behind you and the gaiety of blue sea, green isles, and the rippling Firth or Minch spread out in miles of salutation. Stern and mild! This extraordinary mixture of extremes has been typical of the people who lived there. The Highlander has been both the most ferocious of warriors and the most courteous man of peace. Clans have butchered clans for centuries, raiding and slaying in a dreary succession of reprisals. Yet their descendents were those whom Queen Victoria and the incoming milords of the new deer-forest economy found so cheerful, so polite, so ready ' to walk, run, and do anything.' Highland pride was linked with Highland poverty by Robert Burns, but that pride could melt to make the perfect man-servant, the ghillie of irreproachable manners.

It is sometimes said that the men of the far North are not ordinary Highlanders. When you get to Lairg you do feel a change from the romantic Gaelicism that flourishes in Central and Western Scotland. (That romanticism you may dismiss as partly commercial, but there is more to it than the tartan trade.) Scandinavian influence is there. You are out of the Balmoral Belt. There is very little Catholicism. When the crofters of the Pentland Firth go a-dancing, their music is ' the boxy ' (accordion), not the pipes. The kilt is not much seen; as a matter of fact, the poor rarely wear it anywhere in Scotland to-day. But, for all this, Caithness is not Norse. It was a Gaelic-speaking area well on into the nineteenth century. The top-corner county must come into any discussion of Highlanders.

The central truth of it all, as I see it, is that the Highlander was not a stubborn fighter of defensive actions. Macdonell made this point strongly. (This has no bearing on the quality of contemporary Highland Regiments which must, since the Highlands have been so stripped of population, be largely recruited from the central industrial

43

regions. Despite the kilt, the Highland soldier is now, as a rule, a Lowlander.) The Highlander of history was magnificent, almost irresistible, in assault. But he could not organise a victory; he got bored with the business; rearguard actions did not appeal to his martial romanticism. The most striking example is the Battle of Killiecrankie in July 1689, fought in a romantic gorge which every visitor to Central Perthshire stops to see.

'Bonnie Dundee' led an overwhelming charge of his shoeless, claymore-brandishing madmen against a mixed and well-trained army of Scots as well as of English and European troops, led by an experienced General, Hugh Mackay, actually a Scourie man. Mackay had far the bigger force. Yet the Highlanders' victory was, for a day, absolute. But Dundee himself was killed and there was no capable successor. The triumph was utterly wasted. As one historian, W. C. Mackenzie, author of ' The Highlands and Isles of Scotland,' put it, ' So this, the first of the Jacobite risings, fizzled out after an initial success of spectacular completeness.' Within three years of this tremendous yet barren victory, Dutch William had the Highland chieftains in total submission and could counter the least sign of native intransigence by such an abominable stroke as the Massacre of Glencoe.

The lesson of the '45 was no less striking. The men who routed Cope at Prestonpans and marched to Derby without defeat were not the same when the order, justified or not, came for retreat. In the ardours of war they were superb; but in its patient endurances, deficient. Long-drawn retreats and bitter rearguard actions were not their idea of war. If the ardours win battles, it is the endurances that win campaigns. It was not true, except in a few cases, that the Highlanders were too much concerned with loot. It was impatience of spirit that sapped them.

44

That perhaps gives some explanation of a mystery which has baffled many readers of Scottish history, namely the surrender of the crofters to the Lairds. The amount of organised force with which the evictions could be carried out against a tough resistance was small, but it sufficed. There was no chance here for Highland charges: what was needed was house-to-house fighting, hill-side resistance, the use of ambush and of arson, the organisation of an ' underground.' Those methods were used by small bands of Irish peasantry to defeat the armed might of Great Britain in our own time. But the Highlander could not organise that kind of savage, bestial, long-drawn, stick-at-nothing civil war. He could not improvise weapons and a guerrilla army that would lurk behind dikes through long, dark nights. It was not his way of warfare. Ireland has seen numbers of its Big Houses burned out by the rebels; the only smouldering ruin of that kind that ever I saw in Scotland was a mansion fire-gutted by the Suffragettes. The arson was all on the side of the Lairds; it was the thatch of the crofts that blazed.

Ireland has had centuries of Peasant Revolts; London, too, has seen landless men march on it more than once. But the Highlands, though obviously suitable ground for guerrillas, have seen no such fury of the poor. Fury there was, and to spare, when clan raided clan or when Highlanders could make their devastating charge. But the crofters did not go back into the hills, to survive somehow and to fight again. They were driven to the beaches and went into their exile.

They were bewildered men. The old chieftain had become, out of all belief, a new kind of merciless master. Their ministers of religion, with a few courageous exceptions, were no help to them. The thing done to them was so vile as to be unsuspected, almost incredible. Moreover there was a fundamental gentleness in the Scottish Gael that the Irish Republican Army never possessed. The Scottish army that reached Derby in 1745 was led by a tender Prince who genuinely loathed bloodshed and was merciful to prisoners, while their Anglo-German enemies were under one who genuinely earned the name of Butcher. The Highlanders behaved far better to the civil population, all the way to Derby, than the people on the road expected. The man who is irresistible in a charge is not the man to organise cold-blooded cruelties.

If the Highlanders were to defeat the sheep-farmers and the Clearance Lairds who created Caledonia Deserta they needed qualities not their own. There was in them that 'complaisance,' to use the fine, old word which has degenerated into our complacence, the quality which Queen Victoria discovered to her pleasure. In many ways it is to the poor men's credit that the Lairds won this civil war without fighting it. Crime would have had to fight crime and there was no stomach in the glens for waiting a week behind a wall in order to shoot an oppressor in the back. Donald Macleod, whose wife and family were hurled out of their homes on a stormy night during his absence, has left the record of atrocities in ' The Gloomy Memories ' and the Rev. Donald Sage, one of the Ministers who refused to be complacent in the modern sense, has confirmed them. To combat such enormities there had to be the willingness to be atrocious in return. The Highlanders of Caithness behaved more Christianly. What greater humility than to be ghillie for the families who once kicked your forefathers into houseless misery and banishment? The Englishman may well be astonished at the meekness of the Scottish Gael in the face of persecution and tyranny. There may be a relic of the old acceptance of the clan-chieftains' feudal power in the readiness to knuckle under when a landlord decrees. In the isle of Rona a Mr. Rainy, who had cleared fourteen townships and their arable land to make a sheep-farm, enacted that no one should marry in the island, except, of course, the rams. Could Hitlerian absolutism go further? In Tobermory, a proprietor blocked up the water-supply to discourage the natives from remaining. It seemed to be taken for granted that no one would unblock it. (One would have thought that enough water descended from the skies on to Mull to guarantee water for myriads.) Only two years ago, in the Isle of Jura, I asked why so lovely an island, with its fine beaches in the south, as well as the many-tinted beauty of its three soaring Paps and its twisting, isleted sea-lochs, did not support more summer visiting to improve its economy. The answer was so simple. ' The Lairds would not like it.'

That the will of the Lairds, who want solitude for their stags, could be questioned or even challenged, was apparently not conceivable. The power of the landlord has been strong enough in England, but now it dwindles. It was more potent still in Scotland, where the stranger in the glen was odious to the sportsmen-rulers. Inns were allowed to decay; new hotel-building was forbidden. Because of that the urgent need for developing tourist facilities now has been sorely hampered in many places which might attract a steady flow of money-spending, even dollar-spending, travellers. The tourist, if he is able to notice anything except the mountains and the rivers, must be struck by the enormous mileage of fine stone walls built round the ' policies ' (grounds) of the Big Houses. Hundreds of Highlanders must have toiled without demur and with small reward to erect these fortifications that were to keep the Scots out of their own land. The heroes of the brief, irresistible charge in the battles long ago hardly considered resistance to the chieftains and the succeeding lairds. It was not the custom of the country to snarl at authority or refuse its levies and behests. Behind the ferocious battle-cry was the moral disarmament of pacific courtesy. The hand that waved the claymore touched the cap.

There are sour memories still. I spoke of Linklater's observation that the Clearances are still contemporary history in the region of Cape Wrath. I was told that the name of Elliot was an ill passport in some remote parts, because the Elliots were the men from the Border, long skilled in sheep-ranching, who were brought in to make the new economy work profitably and to see that sheep prospered in the empty glens. But that does not mean any active spirit of revolt. Caithness and Sutherland have been represented by a Conservative in the recent Parliaments. Cape Wrath is in name more true to the weather than to any wide, abiding anger of the heart.

It is customary to generalise about the Highlander. (I have just been doing that myself.) He is said to be lazy, apathetic, unreceptive of new and helpful ideas; he does not welcome those who would come to his rescue. It is absurd to be thus sweeping to his discredit. In a discouraging climate on discouraging land, living often in great isolation, the remaining crofters of the Dead Vast have developed their own protective qualities and may view the would-be benefactor askance. Their history has been a dark one; they are children of the mist, of the long winter and of the long night. The summer tourist is in no position to pass easy and dismissive judgments.

The land is still being cleared, though not in the old way of violent eviction. Caithness had a population of 25,656 in 1931; in 1951 it was 22,705. Sutherland, as I have said, had an even greater percentage of loss. During the same time the town of Inverness put on nearly 5,000 and it goes on growing quite rapidly. The seeping of men from the bleak corners continues. One new disintegrating force is the Standard of Living. We live in a centripetal age. Everywhere the countrymen are lured by the town, the suburbans by the Town Centre, Neon-dazzling and cinema-strident. These glitterings are the welcoming beacons of the twentieth century. Though our electricity shortages and cuts are apt to diminish and even extinguish them, they still act as beckoning signals. If wireless be in many ways an alleviation of loneliness and a cordial contributor to the 'Cottar's Saturday Night,' it is also an advertisement for the towns because it constantly describes all the supposedly great, gay doings of the cities and builds up the personalities of the urban world of entertainment. The crofter had a struggling time, and the modern agricultural market and the subsidies, as well as new medical and social services, have eased it in some ways. But the Welfare State and Full Employment are powerful lures to the streets where the pubs and the films and the dance-hall are the magnet.

What can be done with the empty glen is a subject so large and so frequently debated and officially reported on that I do not propose to discuss it in a book of this kind. On the Highlands and Islands the rain of Blue Books descends and a Scotch mist of minutes and memoranda drifts up from London and Edinburgh. But much more is said than done. The renewal of the old Highland trade in cattle is practised by Lord Lovat of Beaulieu and Mr. Hobbs, who has ventured upon stock-rearing of this kind in the unlikely region of Fort William. The Duke of Westminster is briskly afforesting some of Sutherland. Men of spirit try new methods of coping with harsh climate and sparse soil. Cheap electrical power from the rivers, the organised exploitation of the huge deposits of peat, and scientific treatment of sea-weed are other factors which should stop depopulation and even start the reverse process.

Tourists will be the more encouraged as the value of desolate deer-forests shrivels away. Those who once drove out the invader with proclamations of privacy and campaigns against trespassers may, in their new poverty, be glad to sell their castles as hotels or to take in paying guests. But all these things move slowly. And the towns keep up their lustre for the young.

The Dead Vast can hardly be said to be quickening yet. It is natural to feel ecstatic about its beauties on a bright day of high summer or of that golden autumn with which the wilderness is often blessed. ' The memory of a trip north from Scourie,' Neil Gunn has written in a composite volume called ' Scottish Country,' ' is curiously jewelled. The greenness of mountains where one had expected to find heather, the land between mountain and sea assuming every shape, fantastic, ancient, grey, brooding in peat black, glistening in loch blue, unexpected in goblin green, dreaming in brown, the wind touching it, passing over it, carrying away its loneliness to some place still more deeply withdrawn.' (So moved was he that he forgot to end his sentence.) Again, ' Watch Ben Laoghal play with its four granite peaks on the legendary stuff of history, or is it of the mind? Sometimes they are the battlemented towns of a distant Medieval Age: in the smoke-blue drift of the half-light they are ramparts to the high hills of faery; a turn in the road, or in the mood, and they have become perfectly normal again, unobtrusive and strong as the native character.' I know; I have been there. The great bens of the Far North are Nature's Cathedrals. But for weeks on end they may be invisible, with dense cloud on top and the on-ding of the pelting rain below. We privileged creatures of the summer day leave the winters to the natives, the few who grow still fewer.

The place on which to find ' the stuff of history ' is in the

50

grey corpach, the cemetery on the beach. The burial stones are not as striking to the careless eye as are the ruined brochs, the circular ancient forts that are unique to North Scotland in their construction. The old walls of the brochs were very thick and high. They are tremendous things even in decay and Caithness has them in plenty. But they say nothing to the casual traveller while they remain the fascinating themes for conjecture by the specialists in archaeology. It is the tombstones, on the sandy sea-shore patch, where burial is possible, that tell the Highland story if you stop to read. Very often the father's 'lair,' which is Scottish for grave, records the dispersal of the sons; here lies a Mackay or a Macdonald whose scattered children are under Canadian, African and Antipodean soil. Many who died at home did not live the proper span. Disease ran through them, helped, no doubt, by hunger or a thin, monotonous diet. Among the lairs at Bettyhill or Scourie I have seen in the mind's eye the remnants of the clans in the great wanderings of far-flung, adventuring men.

Wars have consumed them and the seas have claimed them. So beautiful it all seems at Badcall on a gleaming afternoon. Must there have been these ruins, this void, the trek to the Fraser River, the burial in the veldt and the back-blocks? Will ye no come back again? Will it ever be discovered that such a place can once more keep its own and be a nurse of men, not in great plenty, that can hardly be—but in some number, as of old? Perhaps the busy Civil Servants in Edinburgh will find an answer with their plans and projects. Perhaps not. Deserts are more easily made than restored. Meanwhile I rise and walk back to the hotel; the visitors are back from the fishing and the ghillies, in the bar behind, are taking their dram before they go back to the crofts on the hill-side. It is time for dinner and the crossword puzzles. 'A word of nine letters. It must begin with C.' But for me the biggest puzzle of all is Caledonia Deserta, bright with its beauty, dark with its history, unfathomably, fascinatingly cryptic, dreamily brooding on what is still to come.

CHAPTER III

Charles's Country

CHARLES EDWARD STUART wandered, during the spring and summer of 1746, from Culloden to the Isles and back to the mainland. No traveller in the mid-western Highlands, on one day rain-sombre beyond endurance, on another exquisite in sudden sunshine, can escape the feeling that something wanders there still. Whether we travel south from the Dead Vast by way of Inverness and the east or whether we keep along the sea-lochs and promontories of the intricate western shore, we run into Stuart memories with equal certainty. Charles achieved nothing but an honoured name; by his reckless adventure he brought many good and brave men to ruin or a bloody end on field or scaffold. Yet, with his battle lost and his cause vanished, he has survived in dreams and is an immortal presence in the air. Such a piece of Highland magic must prick the curiosity of every stranger who is sensitive to atmosphere.

My westerly journey went by way of Kylestrome Ferry to Ullapool on Loch Broom; this shining little town is well north of the Stuart-haunted country; it is exciting because it makes a break in the great void of the top corner. One realises, almost with a shock, that here there are Scotsmen as well as Scotland. Yet the Scots who give it periodical bustle and vitality are not Highlanders of the west, often not Highlanders at all. It is a holiday centre whence you can take ' bus ' to Inverness or meander north-westward to Achiltibuie and the cluster of the Summer Isles. There is a circuitous way south-westward to Poolewe and the Gairloch and so eventually to Ardnamurchan and Loch Nan Uamh, where the Prince touched the Scottish mainland for the first time, with an astonishing confidence, and left it for the last time, with a spirit unbroken.

Ullapool is worth some dalliance, not merely because its white terraces can gleam so fairly in the sun but because it is so strangely symptomatic of Scotland in the petrol age. It has a good harbour for the herring-fleet, but the boats are chiefly worked by men of the Moray Firth, imported Easterners who come over in motor-buses at the beginning of the week, fish the Minch, see their catch packed into lorries, and then are themselves driven home for the week-end to the grey fisher-towns lying between Nairn and Banff.

It is a hard life: the five days and nights in the western waters may yield a chance of good money and a certainty of little sleep. The local men, I was told, do not care for it and, in any case, there are very few of them. So the mid-week immigrants come to and fro, a hundred miles or so each way, annihilating distance in the manner of our time. By Nairn, by Inverness, by Glascarnoch they arrive to fish the tangle of the Isles, packed in great vehicles that grind across the deer-forest of Ben Derg. They do well for themselves, and take the money home: the inn-keepers of Ullapool say that the town is only ' lit up ' when the lads from Stornoway have a good week. The Moray men are not for drams galore. Theirs is a stern, religious coast —at least so Ullapool decides.

Petrol has thus tilted the balance of Highland life: east

is east and west is west in habit and feeling, but easily the twain can meet. It is now quite difficult to imagine what the Dead Vast was like when only horses carried men and news. There were more men, but what of news? Even when the railway came and carved its ingenious way to Kyle of Loch Alsh, it was still, as the gull flies, a hundred miles from the Pentland Firth—and far more by the devious road. The easterly railway, seeping inland as far as Lairg, is still some fifty miles from Durness and sixty from Cape Wrath. I fancy that in some of these parts they never heard, at least for weeks or months, that the Jacobite standard had been raised at Glenfinnan and that a Prince was calling them to a last bid for his cause. The Far North gave him little support, partly, perhaps, because it was not interested, but more, I surmise, because it heard no more of his southward swoop than a few, belated rumours. The Scotland in which he landed was not one, but many; its remoter clans were severed and suspicious, with a policy of minding their own business when they were not raiding the adjacent herds.

Suppose we come south by the eastward route. Inverness, bridging the broad waters at the top of the Great Glen, is the inevitable link. Traffic is now plentiful and extremely crowded do its narrow streets become. It has outgrown its original purpose which did not include 'tourism' on the grand scale. So its town-centre is a clutter of cars and coaches nosing into one-way streets. But, by Scottish standards, it is gay with its shop-windows a blaze of tartan, hotels and cinemas abundant, and the pretty chain of the wooded Ness Islands illumined in summer for the spectacle of Highland dancing and the skirl of pipes in plenty. When I was last there some favourite comedians and minstrels of the South were performing in a Summer Show of consider-able quality. During the day I could watch the locals

55

wading in the rapid (and public) waters of the Ness and casting for salmon which, at current prices, would make any success at the sport pay handsomely; this it frequently does. I myself have been privileged to fish the Ness between Inverness and the Loch of the Monster. Salmon leaped gaily into the air round about us, but none of the three rods engaged, two of which (not mine) were handled by experts, had any success. It seems that salmon in the leaping mood are not interested in flies, however lush and garish. My suggestion was that we should wait quietly until one jumped slap into the boat in its careless rapture; then we could knock it on the head. That really might have happened, so many fish were taking the air. But my plan was not accepted. Fishermen are solemn folk and have their rituals. I am a humane man and think it kinder to knap salmon over the head, as the Fool in 'King Lear' said of the eels, than to 'play' them on a barb.

Another Inverness sport is shinty, which may be called hockey with knobs on or hockey with a smack of lacrosse in it. The teams are small, the field large, the pace fierce. It is a favourite diversion of the Gael. On a mellow September afternoon I watched a tournament of local teams ultimately won by the men of the Lovat country who triumphed over representatives of townships drawn from as far as Kingussie to the south and Fort Augustus to the west. I have mingled memories of a tea-van busily patronised by the team-supporters and almost buried under swarming wasps; also of a fair-ground adjacent whose swings and roundabouts were noisy and popular, and wholly un-Gaelic. The shinty supporters did not become possessed like football-crowds, but swatted wasps amid much gulping of tea and amicable conversations. Inverness and its environs breed sedateness of mien and manner. The shinty game is suited to the élan of the Highlander whose supremacy in the speedy martial charge I have discussed: but its galloping hurly-burly evokes a considered approval, not hysterics, in the ' fans.'

Prince Charles went straight south by way of Perth after landing in the summer of 1745: but he was at Inverness and in the surrounding country after the retreat from Falkirk which lost him Scotland, as the retreat from Derby had lost him England. It was not Charles who wanted to retreat: desertion and divided counsel among the Chiefs were the disintegrating factors. Back at Inverness, which he took on February, 1746, he was gay and a popular host at Highland balls. But accidents were happening. A ship with money and supplies from France, both direly needed, had been driven ashore by English warships away up at Tongue, beyond the Dead Vast, and the Reays and Mackays helped the English cause to hold the treasure: they were realists, as that word is unkindly used in these days, not romantics, in the very far north.

Inverness holds the Prince in memory still. Jacobite relics are curiously abundant considering the brevity of Charles's return to and sojourn in Scotland. He must have acquired a considerable wardrobe of the finery now deemed indispensable to ' the best-dressed Highlander ' of the haberdashery competitions in the Games. For he left a fair amount behind him to enjoy immortality under glass. Museums at Inverness and Fort William and privately organised exhibitions are not short of matter for display. But I am not greatly moved by waistcoats, napkins, and shoe-buckles however genuine their provenance. The moors hold more of Charles Stuart for me than do the Museums.

The town of Inverness is now too busy, too prosperous, with its coming and goings of tourists and its new-found industries, to be historically atmospheric. It has no ghost of Banquo in the air, no echo of Macbeth's crime-haunted agonies, no smell of witchcraft. ('How far is't called to Forres?' The answer is 26 miles to the east and Forres is now a douce, well-seeming town with a fine hotel on the hill, good golf, brisk air, and nothing hag-ridden about it.) The modern castle of Inverness, a red-sandstone pile that certainly does not look half as old as time, is a County administration centre, whose clerks conduct the un-romantic paper-chase imposed by modern legislation. Where lay the murdered Duncan, 'his silver skin laced with his golden blood,' we build the Welfare State with buff forms and the abominable prose of bureaucratic formulæ. True

> *This castle hath a pleasant seat; the air*
> *Nimbly and sweetly recommends itself*
> *Unto our gentle senses*

(Shakespeare was more complimentary to the Inverness climate than those who find it as relaxing as Perth, which it somewhat resembles with its wide river and narrow streets; but it is nearer to the sea than Perth and the alleged nimbleness and sweetness of atmosphere is not mere flattery.) The 'pleasant seat' looks over the mid-town salmon-fishers to the green, sepulchral pyramid of Tom-na-hurich. There are a harbour to the east, the famous distilleries of Glen Mohr and Glen Albyn and a burned-out theatre that must once have been a handsome house of secular pleasure in a town whose kirks abundantly remind one of the sterner call. There is a serene river-front whose terraces and cottages look as homely as a high tea.

If witches are wanted, turn west to Loch Ness, whose immensely long, narrow, dark, scarcely fathomable waters 'deeper than did ever plummet sound,' fill, in dark weather, a chasm of infinite menace. Here Monster-

58

watchers gather and their prey, fairly frequently seen—or deemed to be seen—is often dismissed as a phantasm. Here, not in green-wooded Perthshire, should Macbeth have fought his last battle: here, not near to blithe Forres which is ' a veritable sun-trap,' as the house-agents say, should he have met the weird sisters. Loch Ness, it is true, did not frighten Dr. Johnson: few things, save death, did that. But it frightens me.

Compared with its western scenery and the sad Culloden Moor to the east, Inverness is gentle, affable, and smiling. If a bell still rings on the Castle knoll, it is probably a summons to down pens and silence typewriters. There may be shard-borne beetles humming drowsily about (I have not heard them), but you are unlikely to see a mousing owl strike at a falcon over Miss Melven's all-supplying book shop or hear the raven croak fatally above the numerous stores retailing Highland gew-gaws and the daedal trinkets which later commerce has so lavishly invented for the earlier clans. You will not eat your meal—probably a very sound one—in shivering fear nor will you

> *. . . sleep*
> *In the affliction of those terrible dreams*
> *That shake us nightly.*

There is not the beginning of a nightmare in this swarming-ground of motor-coaches and of the patrons of substantial teas. Edinburgh's wynds and ' lands,' with the medieval houses soaring in gaunt severity, once private fortresses, next salons, and then slums, might well cry ' sleep no more ' in the sensitive traveller's ear: but the capital of the North is benign and defies a nervous insomnia.

Yet the shade hovers round about: the Abiding Prince abides. Culloden is close by and nearly all tourists have time for the Moor, where forty minutes of disaster finished for ever the declining fortunes of Charles Stuart and his hungry, out-worn Highlanders.

The battlefield is a melancholy spot; even though the sky be blue, a sort of darkness hangs about it. Undignified building has been allowed on that ground which should have been left with the simple dignity of nakedness. The Memorial Cairn is unpretentious but impressive and the pitiful little gravestones of the clans create poignancy by their insignificance; judged by size they might be the lairs of a few pet dogs. Beside them is an appeal to the public to pay to the dead the slight honour of tidiness and to spare this little space of turf and heather their revolting offering of cigarette-cartons and sandwich-papers: even that modest demand on decency is not always observed. I do not think it is only the alien tourist who plays the litter-lout here.

There is the bleak aroma of defeat, as well as of petrol, in the air. Culloden was a small battle, as numbers go, but big in destiny and calamitous for the conquered, who were to be so savagely harried and murdered in cold blood. It settled an epoch: it gave yet another imprimatur to the Act of Union, for, though Charles fought for the English throne in his father's name, he, who dreamed and brooded much on the Highlands during his long, unhappy exile, would not have allowed his own country and the source of his support to be later submerged with the status of an English province. But now the once-ensanguined soil offers no striking prospect: it is as though the descendants of the brave had lost the spirit to make a decent job even of salutation.

Burial had hereabouts been practised with more size and memorials made with more dignity very many hundreds of years earlier. The Clava Stone Circles and huge stone-graves of the neolithic men who settled by the Nairn River, just under the table-land of Culloden, have their own grandeur and should be visited by travellers to the Moor. These old monoliths and tombs are more carefully tended than are the lairs of the clans on the hill above and are well opened to the view in their little belt of trees beside the water. They stir one's curiosity about the archaic seafarers who wandered up the Scottish coasts from the Mediterranean, leaving their spoor of standing stones and sepulchres. One thing is obvious. They had an eye for a site. Their barrows have lordly positions on the hills: their Circles are set in delectable places. They wisely avoided windy Culloden for this nook by the running water.

The Hanoverian victory of Culloden was in large part a victory of victuals. The young Duke of Cumberland, whom one pictures in the mind's eye as a gross monster of middle years but who was, in fact, only twenty-five, the same age as Prince Charles, had managed to give to his once sullen and home-sick army of Germans, English, and a few Scots, long campaigning in unknown desolation, the spirit that comes of good supply. When he celebrated his birthday at Nairn there was a liberal issue of brandy all round. The Highlanders had lost sleep and rations; with little inside them and dissension around and above them, they were 5,000 against nearly 9,000. The day was dark and rainy; Cumberland's men had good artillery support, the wind at their backs, and meat and brandy in their bellies. Even the traditional Highland charge was powerless against them and the onslaught was lessened by a deplorable example of Highland pride. The Macdonalds had been piqued by what they deemed to be an inferior posting in the line of battle and delayed their attack; the Mackintoshes were impetuous and made their dash too soon—against desperate odds. The end was immediately plain and the reckoning dreadful. To those with a little of this history in mind the

61

now undistinguished country of Culloden Moor, with its modern building where the doomed Prince stood as a target undismayed, may still be a stimulant of reflection and compassion: to the ordinary ' bus-load ' it is, I fancy, a disappointment and a bore. Battlefields often are. What can they be, at least to the unimaginative, the unfancying mind, when the battle is long past and only a field or a built-up area remains? However, like any other sight, Culloden is ' done.' The engines are started up, the company reseated. What's next? Loch Ness, this afternoon, with a hoped-for glimpse of the Monster thrashing its way past Castle Urquhart and Drumnadrochit.

The modern tourist who is westward bound will take the well-made road on the north bank of Loch Ness rather than the hilly road by Foyers (See Falls, two stars, as Baedeker might put it) and so to Fort Augustus, where Catholicism monastically abides. The inn there was so wretched in Dr. Johnson's time that the Governor was obliged to do all the entertaining, for which the Doctor suggested the tribute of an additional salary. But hotels now serve all needs and provide needed shelter between showers or downpours. It has not been my luck to visit this one-time Hanoverian stronghold in weather of any benevolence. And so to the West, where Charles landed and whence, fourteen months later, he sailed.

At Glenfinnan, where the Standard was raised in August 1745, there is a memorial column with a lonely figure on top: it is a work of piety rather than of art and piety can transcend aesthetics. A simple statement in stone is what is seemly and it is there. Two hundred years later, to the day, there arrived a great concourse to celebrate the Jacobites' deed of daring. The weather had an unaccustomed blaze: the road from Fort William had shown the West Highlands in clear outline and exquisitely tinted forms.

It was a true march of the Highlanders as well as a congregation of the curious motorists. There was no disloyalty to the reigning house of Windsor; this was obeisance to courage and a tribute to those dead yesterdays whose death had the majesty of endurance as well as the pathos of disaster.

It was not on the surface a display of Scottish Nationalism, but subconsciously there was more than a salute to the bravery of an immortal escapade. There was the inherent conviction of the Scots that, with the Act of Union, they were ' beguiled into the very heart of loss.' Of course some economic advantages accrued from the absorption in a larger unit of commerce and very many Scots were to profit thereby. But Economic Man is washed away beside the waters of Loch Shiel, where the Prince arrived to find a nation in arms and, finding nobody, waited, well assured that Highlanders are unpunctual folk, until 150 Clanranalds and 700 Camerons marched in with no less an aim than the conquest of all Britain. In country of such whispering memories city folk do not chiefly remember bank-balances. They are caught by fancy and become men of feeling. It had happened before. The London Scot Boswell, tough of fabric, could not refrain from tears in this glen.

' There is a certain association of ideas in my mind upon that subject, by which I am strongly affected. The very Highland names, or the sound of a bagpipe, will stir my blood, and fill me with a mixture of melancholy and respect for courage; with pity for an unfortunate and superstitious regard for antiquity, and thoughtless inclination for war; in short, with a crowd of sensations with which sober rationality has nothing to do.'

The meeting of the clans in 1945 was not an act of ' sober rationality ': but ' a crowd of sensations ' fell upon that crowd of the kilted and the trousered, the few locals and the many car-borne strangers.

Anywhere in Arisaig and the adjacent isles it is natural to reflect on the strange figure of Charles Edward Stuart. I have no Jacobite sympathy in general; I can believe that Charles, had he prevailed over Lord George Murray and the chiefs on that black December Thursday in Derby, had a fair chance to succeed in his march on London, where there was panic in the City, grave shortage of defence, and hasty bribing of drunken recruits unlikely to stand up to a Highland charge. True, there had been apathy among the English Jacobites, but the solvent of apathy is victory and another Prestonpans in the Midlands would have been powerful persuasion. Compton Mackenzie states boldly the future that was lost by the policy intended to be cautious but which in fact, as Culloden was to show, turned out to be calamitous. In his brief and passionate volume on ' Prince Charlie ' he claimed:

> ' The history of the world was changed by the fatal decision of that December day. There is no doubt that James III intended to abdicate in favour of his son, who would have made an ideal King. The American colonies would never have been lost. The French Revolution might never have happened, for it is not outside possibility that Charles would have become in fact, as he still was in theory, King of France too. The long martyrdom of Ireland would have been avoided. Religious toleration would have been achieved long before it was. There might have been no exploitation of the poor by cynical industrialism. But let speculation cease.'

That Charles would have reigned wisely as well as triumphantly over Britain and France, inaugurating a golden age and taming, if not defeating, the onward drive of the

French and the Industrial Revolutions is a considerable guess. The gallant leader of a desperate venture is not necessarily a statesman after victory and my estimate of the Stuarts as a reigning family is very different from Mackenzie's. Were they notable for religious toleration? There is, incidentally, an interesting point of debate for Discussion Circles and Debating Societies in the likely date of American Independence if King Charles III, reigning in London, had not been as foolish as King George III. The break was bound to come some time. The small does not contain the greater and the Pilgrim Fathers and their followers had preferred to quit an England that was Stuart-ruled. I wonder what affection Charles could have felt for rebellious colonists. Yet Flora Macdonald's husband fought for King George across the Atlantic. It is a queer muddle. As Mackenzie says, ' let speculation cease.'

That Charles ever did get so far as Derby is the astonishing thing: he landed on the island of Eriskay, where the flower whose seeds he brought from France is still to be seen, at least by the faithful, and moved on to Loch Nan Uamh an unwanted man. He touched Scottish ground with confidence, but really that soil was no ground for hope. His personal backing was mainly French and Irish and the French were casual and slippery in supporting him, if not completely false. His entourage, the Seven Men of Moidart, was made up of five Irishmen, one Englishman and one Scot. He himself had only a trickle of Scottish blood, for the Stuarts, Norman in origin, had long married into foreign dynasties. His father James, ' Old Melancholy,' a devout, strict, unglamorous man, had begotten this son of glamour—I use glamour in its proper sense of magic and not in its vulgarised meaning of sex-appeal—by an arranged marriage with the Polish princess, Clementina Sobieska: behind James on the female side of the pedigree were the royal or noble families of Italy, France, and Denmark. The royal blood was mixed blood.

In his early childhood the boy baptised and christened as Charles Edward Louis John Casimir Silvester Stuart was not Charles to his parents. He was Carluccio or Carlo Mio. If his subsequent supporters turned him into the Scottish national hero, he was, in fact, much more the International Man and his primary aim was the recapture of the English throne for his House, not the destruction of the Act of Union between England and Scotland. The wonder is that he 'Scotticised' himself so quickly (one can hardly say 'nationalised' in these days) after landing in a landscape so strange and in a climate so trying to one accustomed to the Italian sun. It was a characteristic as well as an apt retort to Macdonald of Sleat, who had told the Prince to go back home, to reply 'I am come home.' But he may have sneezed as he said it. For he suffered, quite naturally, from a continual catarrh during his year's experience of the Scottish climate. His rapid acquisition of some Gaelic speech and a sufficient mastery of the bagpipes were a victory of versatility over up-bringing. Nationality, after all, is more what a man feels than what he is: heredity is less than affection, blood thinner than resolve. Charles felt himself a Scot, despite his mixed ancestry, his Italian boyhood and his early lack of Scottish support. And he backed that sensation with adaptability and resolution.

Romance has built the image of the Beau Chevalier and the adjective Bonnie has stuck to his name. The portraits do not confirm it. Painting in the eighteenth century was picturesque, not photographic, and the 'likenesses' of the period vary considerably. The Antonio David portrait, full face, makes the Prince lively, but not handsome. The portrait (artist unknown, c. 1750) owned by Donald Nicholas and used by him in his very interesting book

'The Young Adventurer,' a closely detailed examination
of the 1745 campaign and the escape, is far from attractive.
It shows a pop-eyed, puffy, weak face. But Mr. Nicholas
is obviously not using it for policy. He is an enthusiast
for his subject, but he quotes Andrew Henderson (1749)
concerning 'a savageness discernable in his (the Prince's)
eyes, which, while rolling in his head, while turning about
without speaking to one who was inquiring of him, appear
rather terrible than mild: his emitting his saliva which he
forms in his mouth is really nauseous.' Again Mr. Nicholas
alludes to Charles's unfortunate weakness of nose-bleeding
which came upon him in moments of emotion. But, since
he adds that Charles II had the same affliction, it does not
appear that this malady need diminish attraction for the
ladies, at least when the blood is royal.

The Bonnie Prince did not always impress people as
such: he was not a universal charmer. (Film-stars have
usurped his name and person, but never with much success,
since so much of his life was a Failure Story and the cinema
public prefer success. Had he fallen at Culloden, which
he well might have done, for he was never one to lead his
army from behind, great tragedy would have been written
about him: the forty years of anti-climax that Charles had
to suffer do not make things easy for the dealer in heroics.)
It is on record that the women of Glasgow were disappointed
by the invader's looks. 'Our very ladies,' wrote Provost
Cochrane in an often quoted passage, 'had not the curiosity
to go near him and declined going to a Ball held by his
Chiefs. Very few were at the windows when he made his
appearance and such as were declared him not handsome.
This, no doubt, fretted.' There is probably some spite in
this, for Charles had been refitting his army at the expense
of the city of Glasgow, a process which 'no doubt fretted.'
Another Glasgow citizen described his dejection and down-

cast eye. If Charles had just heard of the fall of Carlisle, he had no reason to parade in Glasgow as a Smiling Prince.

I find it impossible to visualise the man: both reports and portraits are contradictory. But, whether 'Bonnie' is a later fiction or not, he obviously had a soldierly charm, which nose-bleeding and excessive salivation did not destroy. No doubt he felt himself, against the evidence of his features, to be handsome, as he certainly felt himself, against the evidence of his blood, to be essentially a Scot. Such faith works its wonders, as many a plain countenance has proved upon the stage, where confidence in good looks so often makes up for the lack of them.

What is indisputable is his failure in the role of Ladies' Man. He never had a successful and enduring relation with any woman. Refusing to relax the royal claims of his House, he desperately needed a male heir to sustain the succession. He raged against his brother Henry for entering the Roman Church and so denying himself a son. But Henry could tartly reply (and perhaps did): ' What have you done about that?' In view of his dynastic opinions it is astounding that Charles did not marry until he was fifty-one. He then failed to be a father. His union with the Princess Louise Maximilienne Caroline Emmanuele de Stolberg was a failure. She was only nineteen: and he, not unnaturally, considering his life, was older than his years, moreover, so his critics said, he was not only a tippler but a bore with a Scottish nostalgia and with all too fluent and repetitive a conversation about his battles long ago. However that may be—and Charles was always the target of malice among the supporters of the Hanoverians—he signally failed to retain his young wife's affections. She was soon preferring the attentions of Vittorio Alfieri, a fiery-headed poet of small quality. The claims of the

Sobieski Stuarts to have been descended from a son of this marriage were pure fiction. There was no child.

Charles had been greatly served by Flora Macdonald while hunted by the English soldiery in Skye: that she allowed him to masquerade as her maid and so secured an escape is true. That there was any 'affair' or lasting affection between them is mere legend: their acquaintance was brief, friendly, and utilitarian. He seems to have forgotten her easily. He parted from her on July 1st, 1746, after repaying her half a crown of borrowed money and with the formally courteous remark, 'For all that has happened, I hope, madam, we shall meet in St. James's yet.' She never heard from him again. Mr. Nicholas adds: 'Indeed, though Charles did not die till 1788, he never communicated with any of these faithful friends to whom he owed so much. The Stuarts are not celebrated for long memory or gratitude.' It might also be said, on Charles's behalf, that those who are born into a family that had long asserted the Divine Right of Kings are likely to take much for granted from their subjects.

Sentimentalists have ridiculously revelled in a Stuart-Macdonald romance. There was none. But Flora was not downhearted. She was later on arrested and taken to London by sea. There she surprisingly enjoyed the rare experience of Hanoverian clemency. She was well treated and became more the idol than the victim of the Londoners, who, released from their first panic, were recovering that spirit of toleration which has so long been one of the finest of English qualities. On returning to Scotland Flora did not sit dreaming of her Prince, but married Macdonald of Kingsburgh. They entertained Dr. Johnson and Boswell in 1773. The travellers did not discover a stalwart Amazon. The Doctor spoke of her moderate size, 'soft features and gentle manners' while Boswell described her as 'a little woman of a genteel appearance and uncommonly mild.'

In the following year she emigrated with her husband to North Carolina, a name apt to her deed of rescue. But they were evidently not in love with the enemies of England. In the War of Independence both her husband and her sons joined the Royal Highland Emigrant Regiment in order to support the Loyalists (and King George) against the Patriots. That was a queer sequel to the defiance of the red-coats in the islands. In 1779 Kingsburgh and his wife came back ' over the sea to Skye ' and she died ' a respected old lady ' eleven years after that.

Charles did have a daughter, by his Scottish mistress Clementina Walkinshaw. He quarrelled with Clementina; but with their daughter, Charlotte, he was reconciled in his decline and Pouponne, as he called her, was the comfort of his dismal years of dwindling into death. Made legitimate as the Duchess of Albany, she was a loving nurse of a difficult invalid, but she only survived him by a year and left no heir. On her tombstone in Bologna she was described as ' Virgo Clarissima.' Burns, who never made up his mind whether he was Jacobin or Jacobite, had given her his own kind of immortality, with his ' Bonnie Lass of Albany.'

> *Alas the day and woe the day*
> *A false usurper won the gree,*
> *Who now commands the towers and lands,*
> *The royal right of Albany.*
>
> *We'll daily pray, we'll nightly pray*
> *On bended knees most fervently*
> *The time may come, with pipe and drum*
> *We'll welcome hame fair Albany.*

Her mother, Clementina, reasonably suspect among the Jacobites because she had a sister in the household of Frederick, Prince of Wales, lived to be eighty. Her relations with Charles were comparatively brief, and soon unhappy. We need not try to apportion the blame.

Compton Mackenzie, in ' Prince Charlie and his Ladies,' has frankly discussed the failure of Charles as a lover and husband. Lord Elcho, the Prince's enemy, said that the Prince was embarrassed and cool in the company of women. He was also sneered at for his chastity in the anti-Jacobite papers. Mackenzie adds ' Mary (Queen of Scots) and Charles were both essentially cold sexually. . . . It is probable that Charles in 1745 was still to some extent sexually immature or at any rate virgin. The Marquis d'Eguilles, the representative of France who was with him, stated positively that Charles was neither *coquet* nor *galant*.'

It is one of history's greatest ironies that Charles should have been given by legend the status of Prince Charmed as well as of Prince Charming. Fascinate he could, especially men, but fascinated he was not: in his melancholy maturity he had in him, I fancy, all the makings of a club-frequenting bachelor, fond of his bottle and of his talk about bygones. That amazing year of the campaign had, after all, given him much to remember and recount. He can hardly be blamed for harping back: men without a future—and he surely knew from 1746 till his death in 1788 that he had no future—may be permitted the weakness of a continued regret for thoughts of old times and a certain discursiveness about the might-have-been. He had to endure forty-two years of frustration and during them did some foolish things, especially at the expense of the French. But France had played with his hopes, instead of either denying them outright or supporting them with energy and conviction:

71

to insure peace with England the embarrassing exile was even imprisoned and flung out of the country.

A wanderer, uncertain of income and inclined to the bottle, without a function and without a future, he none the less became legendary as the Bonnie Prince. Nobody can travel Scotland from Culloden to Skye without being aware of it still. The shelves of the libraries are packed with histories of the man and of his campaign as well as with novels based on the last, brave throw of the Stuarts in the game of dynastic power. Those who travel in these regions will not lack abundance of required reading. Charlie was the darling of the later ballad-makers; a wave of sentiment broke over his name. He was beautified and idealised, and garlands were hung upon his memory. It was lucky for the English that they never captured him after Culloden: they were often very close upon his heels and I sometimes wonder whether their officers were not actuated by shrewd policy in letting him slip them yet again. A Highlander who betrayed him stood to win £30,000, then an enormous sum to a mostly penniless and persecuted people. But, to the eternal credit of the race, no Highlander played false. Would the red-coats have had the prize-money if they had earned it in pursuit of military duties?

If so, they were certainly incompetent hounds on the trail of a wearied fox. Charles in chains would have been a far graver problem for England than Charles hiding in the heather and finally an exile in France, there to become a nuisance to the French King and a persuasive advertisement for the stability of the Hanoverians. Had they caught their man what could they have done but send him to execution, with his followers, on Tower Hill? In that case the headsman's steel would have at once been turned into a fiery torch kindling the heather as never before. Even the apathetic Scots would have shed their lethargy or their

Laodiceanism. A man so well remembered without being martyred would have been an unquenchable source of revolt if there had been occasion for another Marvell to write, as the first Marvell did of the earlier King Charles

> *He nothing common did or mean*
> *Upon that memorable scene,*
> *But with his keener eye*
> *The axe's edge did try;*
>
> *Nor called the gods, with vulgar spite*
> *To vindicate his helpless right,*
> *But bowed his comely head*
> *Down, as upon a bed.*

It is now generally accepted as fact that within ten years of Culloden's disaster Charles visited London under the name of Mr. Brown and walked into the card-party at Lady Primrose's house in Essex Street, Strand. He also called upon Dr. King, the Principal of St. Mary Hall, at Oxford. King said he spoke fluent French, Italian, and English, the last with a foreign accent. He could have added Gaelic. It is incredible that the Government can have been so deaf to rumour or so lacking in information as not to know that the old enemy was in town, for he went about quite a lot, inspected the Tower, and was received into the Protestant Church, since he judged his Catholicism to have served his cause poorly, at St. Mary's in the Strand. Charles returned to the Church of Rome later; his religious principles were not rigid. The Government had the sense to leave ' Mr. Brown ' to his friends. He could do no explosive harm at card-parties. In gaol or on the block he might have been dynamite. Charles was obliged to Flora Macdonald for his escape; the English owed her another and perhaps a greater debt.

But in Scotland the legend grew. Long after Culloden the songsters were taking boat and sail to live and die with Charlie, over whose defeat the national Muse began to utter a continual pibroch. It is as easy as it is common to call the Scots incurable sentimentalists, but there was more in the building of a Bonnie Charlie myth than an emotional debauch. The shade of the Prince continued to haunt a nation which, with the dynastic issue finally settled, went on to achieve a new urban prosperity and a tremendous intellectual flowering in the second half of the eighteenth century. But this glory of the new Edinburgh and this wealth of the newly and rapidly growing Glasgow belonged not to essential Scotland but to the northern province of Great Britain, a considerable difference.

So the legend of the Prince, brave and bonnie, grew steadily instead of withering with time. He had stood, it is true, to restore a House whose record of kingship was not encouraging, but he began to stand, in his absence and after his death, for something that Scotland subconsciously knew that it had lost, the National Being. (That is a phrase which George Russell, the poet 'A.E.,' liked to use of Ireland; it applies no less to the sense of Scottishness that has lately sprung up again.) Now that Scottish Nationalism is having a vigorous renewal, the subconscious awareness of abandoned values and a vanished legacy comes to the surface. Of course there is no Jacobitism now, but the Prince, who raised a standard, against all warning, in Glenfinnan is, in his own spectral way, having his resurgence. There is an echo of his courageous voice in the demands of those who, while in no way disloyal to the successors of the Hanoverians, are raising the issue of self-government on countless platforms and have put their names to the new Covenant of freedom under the Crown. Perhaps the tripper-trodden turf of Culloden, like that of the isle of

74

Eriskay, has seeds in it yet, seeds not of an angry thistle only, but of plants more nourishing to the Scotland of to-morrow.

While national sentiment sang its lays of Charlie the darling, history was busy with the Prince's faults. That he greatly dared, that he was indomitable in defeat and in the hardships of a hunted man, that he was no lover of bloody revenge, that he preached and practised mercy to prisoners while inhuman savagery was employed against his followers, has been too easily forgotten. Much has been made of his later decline into a state of drunken self-pity. The article on Charles in 'The Encyclopædia Britannica' says nothing of his virtues and reminds its readers only of his ' debauchery.' One would think, from the Whig commentary of his own times and the sneers of many subsequent historians, that none of his conquerors in Georgian England ever wined from five till midnight and had to be removed as a matter of routine by the footmen. But the legend of Charles the hero grew amid all the scorn of Charles the sot. So it happens that people still peer affectionately at the mementoes in a Highland Museum and cannot pass Glenfinnan without the tribute of something more than a sigh. The traveller feels a presence. The ghost has not gone West; it stays there.

I do not consider myself a Romantic; I have never felt myself a partisan of the Stuarts. The common-sense of the eighteenth century and the age of reason, with its Whiggery, so cool in its philosophies (while so coarse in many of its pleasures), has more appeal for me than the panache of cavaliers. The Edinburgh of Hume had an intellectual climate more bracing than the Paris of the Stuart-faithful exiles, still havering about Divine Right. Yet there is something in the Western Highlands that has enduring power to undermine logic and the wind on Culloden Moor echoes with intimations which even the motor coaches cannot brusquely silence. But many, it seems, are less affected by the sentiments and leave their sandwich-papers instead of flowers upon the little graves of those who were lucky enough to die in battle instead of being hunted to a slower and more horrible end.

CHAPTER IV

Banff and Barley

THE road east from Inverness, with the bodeful ridge of Drummossie Moor (Culloden) above you to the right, leads to the levels of the Moray Firth, and to country which is comparatively populous; it is a chequer-board of green and gold, the light green of the parks—which is Scottish for meadows—the dark green of forestry, and the gold of the barley. Here are good fishing, of sea and river: here the white-washed walls and queer pagoda-roofs of the distilleries which the barley feeds. All this benign prosperity is not far from the Dead Vast; a gull's flight across the big marine triangle whose extreme points are Lossiemouth in Moray, Inverness, and Dunbeath in Caithness would be less than fifty miles. But the difference in scene and way of living is incalculable.

One has left the rocks and the melancholy ' Clearance' glens for land and people in good heart. The tattered, rain-swept oat-patch is replaced by broad acres of sun-golden barley-crop. Once east of Inverness the rain does really stop: many a time have I passed from the storm-bearded clouds of the west into the radiance of Nairn and Elgin, thence to look back on the darkness that one has dodged. There is an open, flat, straight road with ample visibility, where the speeding motorist can ' step on it '

77

with a safety unusual in Scotland. Nairn, sedate and tranquil, has become a bourgeois settlement because of its climate rather than its scenery: it has renowned golf and secluded villadom. The castled Cawdor of Macbeth is, like Culloden, close by: but their old, macabre world of fortress and of massacre is right out of Nairn's map. And modern Forres, too, as you move eastward is spick-and-span, with a notable hotel to cap its hill: instead of witches' brew it offers a Martini now. A deviation to the coast will bring you to the Culbin sands, where the sea did its best to overwhelm the land and piled up a monstrous desert, a Sahara of the Moray Firth whose dusty, village-obliterating invasion has now been checked by careful planting of conifers and marram-grass. From the defensive verge one looks over a wilderness with a vanished town and harbour underneath it.

For the catastrophic history of Elgin's once superb, still nobly naked cathedral see any guide-book. Marie Lloyd sang her own Alcoholic Interpretation of History.

> *The gay old days,*
> *There must have been some doin's*
> *With all them Abbeys*
> *Battered into ruins.*

The local water of life, usque-baugh (whisky), may have assisted the Wolf of Badenoch, the Scots Privy Council who stripped the roof to sell the lead in 1568, and the Covenanters and the Cromwellians resentful of beauty in a fane, in their various blastings, burnings, and batterings of Elgin's sanctuary. But those were hardly gay old days and the ' doin's ' were of a gloomier kind than the water-of-life should stimulate. For a more cheerful view of Elgin consider its domestic architecture.

Away past Fochabers, ducal and well-sited by the lordly

Spey, most fruitful of Scottish rivers in its yields of salmon and whisky, we enter Banffshire, which I always regard as Scotland's forgotten county. The guide-books, so loquacious about Aberdeenshire, because of royal Deeside, and about the Highlands, because they are just that, are mum about the slice which lies between: yet it is dear in my memory and has been dear again in new acquaintance.

I spent nearly a year of my boyhood in the county of Banff; that was at Glassaugh on the northern coast between Portsoy and Cullen. There had been an earlier six months at Cobairdy, near Huntly, which is in Aberdeenshire but close to the Banffshire border. Naturally I have been back there since. Glassaugh seemed to me, in childhood, a wonderful kingdom, yielding cover to roe-deer which, to a nine-year-old, were as monstrous as elks. The stubbles of autumn, where the partridge fed, were prairie-wide in my eyes. In the dense woods of the Seafield estate round the Bin of Cullen were dappled fallow-deer in plenty. At that age all things of earth and air have a romantic enormity about them. Revisited, they dwindle. Those who return to the empires of their childish explorations, the deserts and jungles of their young excitements, smile sadly at diminished splendours, at poetry turned to prose. The rivers are burns, the burns mere trickles, the forests thickets. But one does not go back altogether in vain. There is a spell about it still.

The Scots, being a dispersed nation, widely emigrant, do, in their later and more prosperous years, take a look at the old home. It is often disappointing, since they have passed from the small scene to the large, from the croft in the hills and the wynd in the market-town, to Continents and Dominions with their monstrous mileage and considerable capitals. Was this indeed the burn of our delighted paddling, were these the forests of mystery? Was this wee school the great academy we deemed it, this huddle of grey biggins the town whose visitation was an adventure in a larger world? Yet it was worth the journey, they probably feel. Even the little and the mean have served, like the Ithaca of Ulysses, to be a rugged nurse of goodly men. (To visit Greece, incidentally, is to see another Scotland in a brighter air, sea-indented, mountain-soaring, bare, barren, yet once a great breeder of the human brain.) The return of the Scottish native has its pangs and also its rewards.

The little hills of the Banffshire coast, from the conspicuous Bin of Cullen to the gentle Hill of Durn and the once fir-covered ridge above Fordyce, were mountains to me. Durn had then a single pair of barren grouse, but they were duly pelleted into the larder on one August 12th. By our small standards of sport it was as though a major battue had been achieved. On the Fordyce Hill the woods quivered with blackening darkness and its menace. I imagined monsters there. Now it is a waste of stumps, a treeless void as empty of strangeness as an urban playing-field. England has lost trees enough in the wars, but Scotland's forest casualties were far larger and the scars on the hillsides are horrible to see. Yet all that country, its glamour shorn away by years, comes sweetly to the eye. It is essential Scotland, with its mingling of moor and tilth, of hills and the sea. About it hangs the sharp, clean smell of neeps after rain while the smoky tang of well-cured fish is in the air of its harbour-towns. Countries are to be known by their impact on the nostrils as well as on the eyes and Scotland has a smart fume as its mark. Smoked haddocks, good whisky, a field of neeps—they strike the senses with a similar keenness. John Keats, when visiting Scotland and tasting whisky for the first time, said ' This is smart stuff.' Smart, taken as brisk, keen, challenging,

80

is exactly the right word. In that sense Banffshire is a smart county.

Why has it had so little praise? Where are its singers? What have the banks and braes of bonnie Doon that Deveron lacks? Were I a bard, I would sing Banffshire to the uttermost. Aberdeenshire has had the nostalgic Muse of Charles Murray, crying in ' Hamewith ' for the rain-green Howe of Alford from his exile in the sun-drenched veldt. Forfar and the Mearns have had Violet Jacob, Marion Angus, and Sir Alexander Gray to sing of the neep-fields by the sea, of Tam i' the Kirk, and of the crofts in the lithe of the hills. Banffshire has been overlooked by the choir who have chanted, in prose as well as in verse, that rich tumble of parks and woods with a Grampian back-cloth through which the trains whirl their usually imper-cipient and snoring travellers up the glorious eastward track to Aberdeen. Where are the odes to the river Spey, where the ballad of Fiddich, or the lay of tribute to Glen Avon? Has Tomintoul no salutation in a rhyme?

Banffshire revisited is, inevitably, Banffshire diminished in size, but not, most certainly not, demeaned in quality. If the burn, which was a decent young flood to a boy, now seems, on a summer day, no more than a trickle, if the trout that looked worth the pursuit are now discovered to be tiddlers and minnows, if the heron and the squirrel have left the hollow that once beckoned with all the glory of a major glen, then we must discard, as mature realists, the dreams of a younger romance. But the county abides, so various, so sensibly, so unfussily Scottish, a fair rival to Angus and the Mearns to the south-east, and yet so strangely lacking the regard and relish that have been lavished without stint upon the general Scottish scene.

Putting counties in order of scenic merit is a foolish, but tempting, pastime. Nature and the things man does to it for good or ill are not to be assessed in terms of arithmetic; nor, incidentally, are works of art and entertainment. You can measure, especially with photography's decisive aid, the inch or two by which one horse has outpaced the rest over so many furlongs, but how can we match a tragedy with a comedy, fell-country against weald, Yorkshire against Devon?

In Scotland the possibility of listing counties in a reasonable order of superiority is even more remote than in England. I have heard it claimed that Wester Ross is supreme among the Highland areas, but wander farther north, into still wilder Sutherland, whose surge of peaks is skeleton-bare, or south amid the sea-lochs of Inverness and Argyll and the folly of comparing the incomparable becomes the more conspicuous.

But one thing did strike me during a wet-day conversation on these matters; and that is the way in which some exquisite counties are neglected or even forgotten altogether. In England is there enough salutation of Herefordshire? In Scotland, as I have asked, who proclaims the shore that looks across to Caithness with Banffshire's gently rhythmic hinterland of unassuming hills? Looking through a number of topographical books on Caledonian splendours— and these written by informed and well-approved Scottish wayfarers—I was astonished by their silence about this curiously inclusive county. Yet it stretches from the towering summit of the Cairngorms to the famous distillery glens and thence to the barley-fields that serve them on the rich lands running to the links and havens of the Moray Firth.

Banffshire is long and slender. It is, on the whole, very thin, as Counties go, and the east-west traveller by car is soon across it; in the neighbourhood of Keith a walker could be out of Aberdeenshire, across Banffshire, and into

Moray in a single afternoon. At this point it is a mere sliver of the Scottish scene, not a solid helping. In that nice old Scots phrase for a delicate slice it is ' a sensation of cake,' not a slab of it. But it broadens notably at the coast and mysteriously grabs a piece out of what is really Buchan as it does its cliff-walk along to Troup Head and nearly into the charmingly entitled township of Rosehearty. As a matter of fact, this name has no more to do with flowers than has the Roseland of South Cornwall. Both come from the Celtic Rhos, a headland, or jutting height. The mystery of County boundaries, with their wayward deviations and plunges and lunges, their snatchings and withdrawals, is nowhere more apparent than here.

If people were asked to name the Highland Counties how many would mention Banff? Yet at the southern tip it does more than Ross, Sutherland, and Argyll ever do: it climbs over the 4,000 feet level on the summits of the Cairn Gorm and Ben Macdhui: it includes Loch Avon, the watery gem below this gaunt carcanet of stone, and then takes in the huge moorland surge that runs to Tomintoul. This desolate high-pitched town one would expect to be all ruggedness; but it turns out to be trim, couthy, and fairly planned. All this region, it is true, is massive in its outlines, rather than serrated. The Summits assault the sky classically, like a solid phalanx: they do not stab it savagely with spears, like the Coolins or the queer pinnacles of Sutherland and Wester Ross. But Banffshire's share of major majesty is undeniable. The county is not sensational: it is content to be superb. It has not Nature's Gothic, the flying buttress or the gargoyle crags. But it has grace and proportion; its summits are Palladian.

It is rarely realised that Banffshire, in its lofty south-western corner, only fails by 108 feet to include the loftiest point in Scotland. The shire climbs to the second highest of the Caledonian tops, Ben Macdhui (4296 ft.). This monster it shares with Aberdeenshire: the two counties march, or rather scramble, together on the summit. Banffshire is a partner, not a possessor, of the grandeur hereabouts. Cairn Gorm itself (4084 ft.) it divides with Inverness-shire. As on Macdhui, the peak-bagger can stand at his journey's end with his two feet in two different counties. That feat of poise admittedly adds nothing to the view. But the view is one to which nothing need be added. Those who talk of the Highlands often refer only to the sovereign splendours of the West. But, if the word height means anything in the computation of Highland quality, Banffshire soars higher than any other county except those of Inverness and Aberdeen. Perched among the lingering snows on Ben Macdhui, a man may well cry, like the Edinburgh playgoer who questioned the grading of Shakespeare, ' Whaur's your Perth and your Argyll noo? ' Ben Nevis is the absolute monarch of Caledonian altitudes, but it has no near neighbours of 4000 feet.

Of the other 4000 ft. giants in the Cairn Gorm group, Cairn Toul (4241 ft.) is all Aberdeen's, while Braeriach is divided between Aberdeen and Inverness. Nowhere in the British Isles do three counties meet in such colossal and desolate splendour; they actually collide on the south shoulder of Cairn Lochan at a height of 3931 ft. This intrusion of Banffshire into the highest mass of the Highlands gives to our forgotten county the whole of Loch Avon in the majestic chasm between Cairn Gorm and Beinn Mheadhoin. Then the boundary drives east into the peaks above Braemar, scaling the North Top of Bheinn A' Bhuird and so on to Ben Avon. The Ordnance Survey hesitates between its Bens and Bheinns. Presumably the better known are de-gaelicised for benefit of the alien. But the spelling makes no difference to the scene.

84

The glory of this mountain-mass is enhanced by the difficulties and distance of the approaches. There are three principal ways of fighting a passage into the soaring desert of South-west Banffshire. The best known is the defile of the Larig Ghru which brings the foot-sloggers from Aviemore through the forest of Rothiemurchus right between Braeriach and Cairn Toul on the west of the track and Ben Macdhui on the east of it. The pass reaches within a half a mile of Banffshire under Cairn Lochan just before the rocky track works round Ben Macdhui to meet Glen Dee: it cuts across to Glen Lui and Derry Lodge, and so descends to Inverey, Braemar, and Deeside. But I would not call that half-mile into Banffshire a ten-minute walk. The contours ask for study. The Larig Ghru thus gives two entrances to the kingdom, from Speyside and Deeside. The third is from the north, by Tomintoul and Glen Avon, a yet more tremendous walk, even for those who can get a lift up to Inchrory where the track swings west into the grand canyon which ends with Loch Avon and the corrie under Cairn Gorm.

I said that the glory is enhanced by remoteness and surely that is more than ever true to-day. One of the major crimes of progress has been the abolition of distance. Nobility of scene is infinitely more exciting when you have to work to find it, instead of being whisked there in a motor-car or over it in an aeroplane. The wear of winning makes victory slow and severe, but satisfying to the core. Nobody can drive mechanically into this niche of Banffshire; the infantry alone are its sweating combatants and its enraptured connoisseurs. Long may the Larig Ghru continue to defy the surveyors and engineers; it should be spared for eternity the presence of petrol-pump and road-house, as the Sty Head Pass between the Scawfells and Great Gable still receives the mercy of mankind and is a track instead of becoming a well-roaded beauty-spot, with the litter, the Kosy Kafes, and the invitations to partake of ' Snax ' which are so often the familiar marks of our most favoured scenery.

It was in Banffshire recently that I was most strongly reminded of what we have done in the last forty years to make nonsense of distance. In our old horse-carriage days at Glassaugh we had one of those open vehicles so romantic-ally—and at the same time classically—called a phaeton. To its modest speed Cullen, less than four miles away, was decently remote. My father presented a Silver cup to be run for at the Games in Fordyce; the organisers of the Games, pleasantly astounded by this generosity, determined to provide value for money and, with Scottish thoroughness, made the race a cruelly long one; round and round the Glebe in the hollow by the village went the frantic com-petitors on a hot summer afternoon until the local hero, probably carrying some local money, as well as his own considerable weight, fainted. The trophy was carried off by a man from Cullen, which caused, I remember, some strong resentment. Cullen was almost four miles away: therefore he was an invader, a foreigner. That the coveted cup might as well have departed to Aberdeen was the opinion of Fordyce.

Now all that niceness of separation has been torn from us. The Cullen lads, with motor-car, motor-bike, and motor-bus, can tear about the county and see the pictures in Buckie and be citizens of the world. That may have its immediate gains in amenity; the doctor can come quicker to patch up the driver who has already been too quick. But in knowing and loving a countryside the slaughter of distance is death to appreciation. Properly to get the feel and to savour the essence of a place, whether it be in Bedfordshire or Banffshire, you have got to work your passage. This means that nobody has ever had a superficial acquaintance with the Cairn Gorms; he may have staggered along the Larig Ghru in dense mist and seen very little. But, while his eyes were cheated, his legs told him quite a lot. There have been many invasions repelled by the weather. But any invasion that does win its positions wins them with an ecstasy denied to all but the takers of the hard way. So this can be said of Banffshire, that it contains a notable share of that wilderness most coveted and enjoyed by the sturdy devotees of solitude. Ben Nevis is the king of Scottish mountains; but he has Fort William at his feet: rail, road, and steamer bring up his courtiers by the thousand. He has, I believe, suffered the insult of a successful assault by machinery. Nobody can play such larks with Ben Macdhui. Banffshire's skyline is inviolate.

Among the County's rivers are the Spey, the Fiddich, and the Deveron. What more could one ask? Spey, indeed, it only shares, but to have any part in that majestic flood is sufficient for high pride. Of the gentler Deveron it has a plentiful portion; at its mouth the towns of Banff and Macduff confront each other with the old rivalries and suspicions that often linger in adjacent spots. The man from one does not like to be told that he comes from the other. No sensible person would object to being a citizen of either.

The rolling country that lies between the Cairn Gorms and the coastal plain is a typical mixture of Scottish virtues. The distilleries of Glen Fiddich and Speyside are its wealth, but distilleries, looking inside like spotless laboratories with their gleaming vats and stills, employ comparatively few workers. So the towns, like Dufftown and Craigellachie, are small. Industrialism does not smirch this shire, whose fortune is in the flavour of its waters when the magic of the malted barley is mixed with them. Because the rivers are not fouled they provide some of the finest of Scottish fishing as well as helping to cream the barley into bottles.

Behind and above the rivers are the sheep and the grouse and the deer. Those who want to see the middle aspect of the county in all its smoothness of rhythm and richness of colour should take the road from tidy, demure Huntly in Aberdeenshire, a pretty piece of old, easy, unaffected town-planning. The road wanders first above the Deveron and then above the Fiddich and on by way of Dufftown to the meeting of the waters at Speyside's Craigellachie. No view will take you by the throat, as in the Highlands proper: but every view, especially when the heather is out, has an enchanting serenity. Here are hills rather than mountains, but hills of exquisite moulding, hills made for man to work in, not merely to play in, hills of the shepherd, hills dropping with caressing folds to the little towns of stone where he goes to the austerity of school, to the profit, the chatter, and the bottle of market-day, to the sonority of the kirk, and to the long silence of the grave-yard.

Being essential Scotland, this is highly educational country. The towns may be little, but their academies are large of fame and even tiny Fordyce has a notable record of scholastic achievement. Keith is another mother of distinguished sons and the present Principal of Aberdeen University was one of the many talented lads who climbed the ladder there. For those with less exalted interests, I may add that you may chance upon a good beef-steak more easily in this region than in most. Banffshire feeding is luckily not vaunted in the guide-books, but many will vouch for it.

Tomintoul, a trim gateway between North Banffshire and the huge mountain area of Glenavon and Deeside, is high-flung and well-planned, a very civil spot where one would expect uncouthness. Scotland, being a land of high bens and deep glens rather than of lofty plateaux, has few mountain-towns. The Scot usually, and of necessity, builds for shelter and follows the strath. The county lacks a Buxton. Tomintoul, at 1124 feet, is not so loftily set as English Dartmoor's sinister and prison-dark Princetown, but it is a happier looking place and even offers arts as well as altitude. To my surprise, during a visit some years ago, I found that a touring company was established and playing a series of those antique melodramas which delighted the ' flea-pit ' audiences of the Victorian age. I suppose that the holiday public was big enough to support these adventurers, who even threw in a little variety of song and dance as well. But I could not help thinking that to go barn-storming in Banffshire must be as risky to the purse as climbing the Cairn Gorms can be to life and limb, at least for those who start without some local knowledge and precautionary measures.

So to the sea. The coast of Banff, cliff-bound with inter-mittent harbours for the herring-fleets and sweet, sandy bays for the paddlers and for the hardy bathers, is full of beauty both in name and scene. I have never forgotten the titles of the stations that charmed my young ears as we went by rail from Glassaugh to do our shopping in Elgin. Cullen, Portknockie, Findochty, Portessie—like Kipling's flowers, ' almost singing themselves they run.' Grey places, of course, they are, and now some of them are less prosperous than of old, for successful Buckie has drawn the local wealth and population towards it. Its harbour has grown to imposing size and its great, broad main street has risen to cinemas and stores of magnitude.

But nothing in Banffshire seems to turn squalid. Buckie, facing out on the Moray Firth whose white fish are said to be the best around our isle, is a clean, well-mannered looking town and appears to have ample money in its lap. One way to judge the prosperity of a town is to look at the toyshop windows. If there are fine, expensive pedal-cars and the like, then the parents are well-to-do. The children of Buckie struck me as being in clover from what I saw. But fishermen have always their ups and downs. Behind the harbour there is ever a fear of the morrow when the market fails.

The maritime view from the Banffshire coast includes, to the west, the coastline running up to Caithness, with many a shadowy peak, Ben Wyvis conspicuous, merging gently in the blue. Landward there is the noble line of the moors which rise with pleasant gradations to merge in the final Cairn Gorm mass. Nobody would recommend Banff-shire for the wonderments of Nature (outside the Cairn Gorm tip) or for especial beauty of man's contrivance. It has no city of size; it has nothing so rich in sacred and profane architecture as near-by Elgin. Indeed, there are not many places in the whole shire where the visitor without private hospitality would be inclined to stay, unless he were an eager fisherman or found Banff or Cullen to be a sea-side resort of a likeable, unassuming kind. The famous golf-links of Spey Bay and Lossiemouth are away to the west; the Spey should logically be the county-boundary and so give Banffshire the Spey Bay golf-course, but the curious, jinking spirit of county-makers has been at work again and their line leaves the river. Dr. Johnson came hither on his way from Aberdeenshire where he strode beside the Bullers of Buchan in a way to frighten Boswell. He had there hired a boat and been rowed by men 'wonderfully stout and alert' into the circular basin or boiling pot of waters. (Buller is the French Bouloir). Banffshire would be a little tame after these excitements of neighbouring Buchan.

' We breakfasted at Cullen,' wrote Boswell. ' They set down dried haddocks broiled brown with our tea. I ate one. But Dr. Johnson was disgusted by the sight of them, so they were removed. Cullen has a comfortable appearance, though but a very small town and the houses mostly poor buildings.' The Doctor was a fool to be averse to a Banff-shire dried haddock: even in Aberdeenshire, the heaven of ' haddie ' fanciers, he would hardly have found better. They got to Elgin for dinner.

So much for their survey of Banffshire. Had they plunged inland and made for Tomintoul, the adjective employed for the scenery would have been the favourite eighteenth century epithet for mountainous country, ' horrid.' But our notions of horror have been broadened by progress. There are worse things for us than a corrie, a loch, and a framework of peaks.

As a rule those making up the centre of Scotland for Perth and Inverness have no easterly inclinations. Why swerve? Romance lies to the north or to the west. But serenity—and also sunshine—should beckon those at least who are not too frantically pursuing the accepted ' sights ' and cause them to wander aside from the gracious domesticity of Grantown, so handsomely designed by Sir James Grant in 1766, into Moray and Banff. The myriads who sweep up Royal Deeside are ignorant of Donside to the north, with its lonelier fascinations, and have no notions of what country they will reach if they press still farther up the map and explore the landscape that sinks in gradual beauty from the great hills to the Moray Firth.

The staples of Banffshire are the good farming in the north of the shire and the good distilling in the heart of it. It is, pre-eminently, the County of Whisky. Mr. Marshall Robb, in his Guide to ' Scotch Whisky ' lists 63 Highland Malt Distilleries, of which 17 are in this narrow strip of

Scotland. These include some of the most famous, the various Glenlivets. In years of grain-rationing (and sometimes lately of total denial of supply) the distilleries cannot be working regularly: the job is a seasonal one in any case. Now they may be idle for long stretches, as they were during the war. A bad, rain-spoilt harvest can impede or delay distilling. But it can fairly be said that, when the malting is on, Banffshire will enjoy 'full employment.' Dufftown, Craigellachie, and Aberlour are names of power and Glenlivet has as much claim to glory as a notable vineyard of France.

The Englishman does not often taste Scotch malt; he is more familiar with its Irish cousin or with a blended Scotch. The 'single' whisky, the pure malt, is too heavy for the sedentary life and, since whisky has been made, by villainous taxation, too costly for the manual and out-door workers who most need it, it is increasingly a comfort of the 'tired business man' and is allotted, if available at all, to the hotels and bars, as well as reaching (in a meagre trickle) the more prosperous homes. This means that a lighter whisky is the more popular and this lightening is achieved by blending the traditional malt of the individual 'pot still' with the grain whiskies mass-produced in the 'patent' stills of Scotland's industrial South. Mr. Robb lists fourteen West Highland distilleries of 'single' whisky in Islay and Campbeltown and ten more Lowland makes: the grain whisky is distilled at eleven centres in mid-Scotland and the blending is done in many places. To mix 40 per cent of malt with 60 of grain is to please the present taste. Cold countries naturally prefer the heavier, hot countries the lighter blends.

Many learned and aromatic books have been written on whisky: Aeneas Macdonald and Neil Gunn, as well as Marshall Robb, have been my literary advisers. It is, I think, generally agreed that the Highland Malts are the proper drink of the Highland life: for those who have been farming, fishing, or shooting all day the dram is not too sturdy and, if its strength is to be mitigated and thirst quenched with a long drink, the peaty water of a burn is the perfect companion of the malt. The townsman takes his less formidable draught of blended whisky with soda-water: many Scots despise this practice and take water. This seems to me absurd. Most urban water supplies are now chlorinated for necessary purposes of safety. The highly chlorinated water originally drawn from sluggish rivers, such as Londoners obtain whether they like it or not, is so remote from the natural water of the mountain spring that to substitute good soda-water (and some soda-waters are paltry) is not only to obtain a liveliness in the glass but to escape a flavour of chemical that destroys the natural tang of the whisky.

The history of whisky, which is also the history of Banffshire, is a sad one for the Scot. He did not invent the usquebaugh, the water-of-life. The Irish Gaels may have preceded and taught him. But he perfected it. Nobody else can make the true thing. Scotch whisky is a mystery, a magic of locality. The foreigner may import not only Scottish barley but Scottish water, Scottish distilling apparatus, and set a Scot to work on them, but the glory evaporates: it will not travel. All the triumphant ' know-how ' of American technology cannot counterfeit Scotch whisky. ' Stand fast, Craigellachie.' Craigellachie obediently stands fast.

The ancient Greeks imagined spirits of the tree and the brook, the Dryads and the Naiads, elements made persons, forces with a fairy status. In Scotland there are, in the same way, animations of the burn and the river: furthermore each separate distillery has its own daemon and creates a unique effluence. Mr. Maurice Walsh, introducing Marshall Robb's book, stresses this amazing diversity. (He entered the Excise Service in 1901 and has memories of the almost untaxed years and of the greatest Speyside distillations.)

'I knew one small town with seven distilleries and I knew an expert who could distinguish the seven by bouquet alone. These seven distilleries were in one mile of Highland river; they used the same water, peat, and malt and the methods of distillation. One, the best, mellowed perfectly in seven years: another, the least good, not a hundred yards away, was still liquid fire at the end of ten years.'

So there really is a double wonderment about this noble invention of the 'barley-bree.' The genius of it is so volatile that it cannot be captured out of Scotland: and inside Scotland, inside one glen, it is again so capricious that neighbouring distilleries evoke distinct qualities of their own. In the town of Inverness Glen Albyn and Glen Mohr distilleries are adjoining and have the same management, the same water. But their product is not identical.

All sorts of reasons have been advanced, such as the exact shape of the still and its influence in holding or dismissing essential oils. But, whatever the explanation may be, all this subtlety of the craft working upon the curious diversities of nature now matters little enough. The 'single' whiskies are swept away to be blended into the multiples. The blends can still have character, but to the champions of the malt it is a kind of massacre and sacrilege.

And even the blends are not for Scotland. The whole world thirsts for them. The Americans insist on them and Banffshire lives in service of the dollar. The British Treasury first taxes 'Scotch' as though it were a vice and then battens on it as liquid gold. In the year ending March 31, 1950, three million gallons were allotted to the Home Market, of which Scotland, the producer, is a very small part, while about eight and a half million gallons went abroad. In that year whisky and gin paid nearly a hundred million pounds in Excise Duty, while wines paid less than twenty millions. The levy on a bottle of whisky was five-pence in 1840 and climbed slowly to one and eightpence in 1901. In 1918 it was three shillings and sixpence. It is now one pound, four shillings, and seven pence. The entire cost of raw material, of distilling, of transport, and of retailing Scotch whisky is about only a third of the levy made by the British Treasury.

In recent years I have found it hard enough to obtain whisky in bottle in London, but it is certainly no easier for my Scottish friends in Scotland: usually it is more difficult. The Gael began this usage of his grain and the Scot 'sublimed' it. But the English sweep it nearly all away and make it so costly that what might be fourpence a tot sells at two shillings—that is, if there is any to sell. It is a monstrous injustice that a Banffshire farmer who has toiled at the harvest in his barley-field, the Banffshire ghillie who has served the shooting tenant beside the salmon-river or on the moors above the barley, and the Banffshire distillery-worker who kindles the peat, dries the grain, and tends the mash-tub and the still beside the river whose water he bewitches with his craft are all denied the cheap and general enjoyment of the homely miracle they have made.

The natural impulse of the Scot to keep his own treasure once produced plenty of secret stills: in days of elementary transport and communications the free lance was hard to catch. Then the discipline of the Excise was steadily strengthened and the bonds of the law closed upon the liberty of the glen. But the old freedom has left its mark upon the map. Glenlivet not only did wonders of distilling: it was profitably remote. Those who go north from Tomintoul to Dufftown will pass it. In ancient times it was the proper nook for a man who wanted to use the grain and the water in his own way and to his own advantage.

We know that whisky of a sort had reached London by the beginning of the seventeenth century. In the bitter winter of 1606-7, when the Thames was frozen over, it was one of the cordials sold to the skaters by the river-side in Southwark. Shakespeare may have had his nip, an improvement surely on the sweet wines of the time. (Whisky renders far better all the services that Falstaff claimed for his sherris-sack.) But Dr. Johnson did not know of it until he travelled north. ' Let me know what it is that makes a Scotchman happy ' he said, and then drank a gill of whisky: that is the equivalent of about four English ' doubles,' to name the contemptibly vague measure with which English caterers and publicans fob off their customers. The Scots, mild as ever, have recently allowed this nonsense of ' small ' and ' large ' whiskies, with quantity undefined, to sully their own bars.

The true Scottish measure is a half-gill or a quarter-gill and such should be demanded. A good innkeeper will serve them. The half-gill is almost double one of the debased English ' doubles.' The English have not only wellnigh emptied Scotland of its native nectar: they have been unconscionable robbers in the retailing of it. As Robb puts it, ' The small whisky measure of one-sixth of a gill (a ' six out ' as the publicans call it) can be filled very nearly thirty-two times from a standard bottle and thirty-seven times in some districts of London where the measure is as small as one-seventh of a gill.' At two shillings a nip this gives the publican seventy-four shillings a bottle! And sometimes he charges half-a-crown. Robb says 'the one-seventh measure was sold early in 1949 at 1s. 9d.' It was sold, in many places, at 2s. or even 2s. 6d. (And sometimes, I fancy, watered at that.) In some luxury hotels of London a so-called 'double' was six or seven shillings, the excuse being that they had to buy in the uncontrolled market. (The Distillers Company does control price and quality, but cannot be responsible for the 'free' market and for what goes on in bars.)

> *Here's a bottle and an honest friend,*
> *What wad ye wish for mair, man?*

An honest inn-keeper as well, is my reply.

The 'bree' of the eighteenth century was a powerful matter. Burt, the English officer of engineers who worked for road-builder Wade in the 1730's, has some startling tales of the native absorption of what he spelled 'usky.' Children of six or seven were given nips containing as much as a wine-glass. Some of his fellow-English rashly took on the Highlanders in an usky-drinking match. The locals won with ease and suffered no losses, whereas of the Englisher challengers, 'One was thrown into a fit of gout without hope: another had a most dangerous fever: a third lost his skin and hair by the surfeit.' (Whisky as a depilatory is a curious idea.) Burt took against the usky and said that it contained the seeds of anger, revenge, and murder, and made men behave like barbarians 'beyond the effect of any other liquor.'

This is nonsense. Any alcohol can inflame and spirits are likely to inflame more rapidly than wine. But whisky properly savoured and not grossly gulped is essentially a pensive and a philosophic liquor: it is the natural companion of reasonable conversation: while it warms on a cold day, it can assuage the fatigues of a hot one. Whether

or not we agree with Smollett that it is an admirable salve
for infants assailed by the confluent small-pox, we can take
it in our maturity as a purge of lassitude and as food for
thought. The Scots of the industrial areas have misused it,
when in funds, to get a quick escape from the squalor of
the abominable cities into which they were born; they have
tossed it down rapidly and 'chased' it with beer to get
release as effectively and as economically as possible. I
do not myself care for all the songful clamour of the 'Whisky
Johnnie' type or for the advocated recourse to whisky as
Dutch Courage, a favourite theme of Burns:

> *Inspiring bold John Barleycorn*
> *What dangers canst thou make us scorn!*
> *Wi' tipenny we fear nae evil,*
> *Wi' usquebae we'll face the devil.*

(Tipenny was ale at twopence a pint.)

The Scots, it is true, are shy, suppressed, and often silent
folk. The dram of whisky does more than 'refocillate'
(John Aubrey's word for warming up the inner hearth).
It unties a slow tongue. It reassures the apprehensive.
But, for more than that, it adds ease to discourse, quickens
wit, and gives substance to meditation. It used to be said
that fish makes brain: if that be true, which I doubt,
Banffshire, with its pride of fish in sea and river and its
leadership in distilling, both builds and animates the mind.
It has served the body with its beef and the head with its
barley. Wrote a Scottish Gentleman, visiting the Highlands
in 1737:

> *Where Corn and Grass, Enclosures all around.*
> *Where fitt supplys, for men and horse, are found;*
> *There various Meats and Liquors too are got,*
> *And Usqueba must never be forgot.*

Nothing inspired this labouring rhymster, but his facts and sentiments are sound. For ' Fitt Supplys ' Banffshire from Cairn Gorm to Cullen has truly served and its Usqueba, by me at least, will ' never be forgot.'

CHAPTER V

Granite and Getting On

TO the tourist Aberdeen means principally Royal
Deeside; that pleasantly winding entrance to the
Central Highlands is handsome indeed. It has the
brisk, bright river with its dark and salmon-holding pools
and with hills that rise in magnificently rhythmic lines,
pine-dark awhile and then fading off into a bloom of
heather and a dream of cloud. The strath is broad, with a
road to each side of the river, decent townships, and a
rich supply of gentlemen's ' places.' One says gentlemen
rather than lairds, for Deeside is very Anglo-Scottish, at
least from the first run of the salmon in March to the
shooting of the deer and grouse at the summer's end. The
motor-coaches make a nice, smooth run of it up to the
three B's of their illustrious goal, Ballater, Balmoral, and
Braemar. The big hills close in, Morven and Mount Keen
to north and south, then Lochnagar and the Cairn Gorms
which the July snows will be capping while the valley
shimmers in ' fantastic summer's heat.' Deeside is sheltered
by its bulwarks of rock and heather and misses the severities
of the coastal climate. Moreover, the Cairn Gorms often
seem to hold the cloud-mass drifting from the west; I have
crossed the Devil's Elbow from Perthshire on a dark and
dismally wet day and found Deeside bright and fresh in
the sunshine.

Queen Victoria knew what she was doing when she chose her royal building-site under Lochnagar, a site peak-surrounded yet not darkened or depressed by too adjacent crags. In many Scottish glens the narrowness of the defile is such as to cheat the castle as well as the cottage of sun and air; there is a sense of suffocation even in the finest weather; under cloud the lordliest mansion, thus confined by the sheer rock behind, is like a cell in the imprisoning chasm. But Deeside has space and the oxygen is as abundant as it is enlivening.

It has become a seigneurial region with a social atmosphere that is oppressively august in the September season, but the economics of our time are sapping the tenure of the great purses. None the less, if you want to meet, at the end of the summer, the mixture of Mayfair, motor-cars, and tartan, Deeside is the place to look for it. It is the misfortune, not the fault, of Royalty that snobs follow the Crown.

But, if that atmosphere be unwanted, it is only necessary to turn right at Dinnet, as you go up Deeside, and take the hilly road to Strathdon, then swing right to Kildrummy, and right again to Alford. The Don is a different river altogether and Donside, though adjacent to Deeside, is in nature worlds apart. The Irish used the word Ascendancy to describe the Anglo-Irish nobility and gentry and their lands and society. It is not unfair to call Deeside Ascendancy Scotland; the adjectives apply to its magnificent sporting estates with their retinue of competent and courteous ghillies and stalkers, rendering good service and expecting good tips. By the Don you begin to meet the real Aberdeen-shire of a sturdy independence that has grown amid poverty and thrift. North of that again, across the Urie and ' back o' Benachie ' there is the undulant farming country that runs northward to the sea, a nurse of stubborn folk cropping a stubborn land, remote from Highland pageantry, granting ascendancy to no stranger.

It is significant that just north of where the Urie joins the Don is a level piece of ground. Here the fate of Aberdeenshire was settled. It is marked on the map with the crossed swords of battle, ' Harlaw, A.D. 1411.' I like that inclusion of Anno Domini. It reminds one that Aberdeenshire was old and settled before the Roman came, a county rich in pre-Christian civilisation. It abounds in the barrows and kists and standing-stones of the Archaic culture. It was at Harlaw that the lairds and commoners of the north-eastern lowlands faced the vigorous attempt of the western Gaels to win mastery over the whole of the north. Donald of the Isles had gathered his clans from the sea-lochs and the mountains, his Macdonalds, Macleans, and the rest and hurled them eastward at the throat of Aberdeen. Victory would have made the North Gaelic from sea to sea. But not all the Highlanders were with him. The Mackays and Frasers preferred to mind their own business.

But the usual Highland tactic of the charge failed against the solid stand of the farmers and citizens who, with a little Highland aid, came out to defend their own way of life. Moreover the Aberdonians had something up their sleeve: the counter-attack with cavalry. For obvious reasons the men of the mountains were never rich in horses: they lacked the pasture. But their enemy had both the quantity and the manage of horses. No doubt they had also learned from the south the Norman methods of employing cavalry. On the flat open land beside the Urie they were thus at an obvious advantage: there was room for horse-manship to support the obstinacy of the foot-soldiers whom the wild rush of Highlanders did not intimidate. So they kept their town and the north-east of Scotland for themselves and their notions of social arrangement. It was an enduring victory.

They could go their own way henceforward in Aberdeen-shire, partly because of Harlaw, partly because of its geographical remoteness. This has remained a separate piece of Northern Scotland, with a countryside vernacular of its own, and a distaste for being drawn into other peoples' tirrivees. It was not to be lured by Bonnie Prince Charlie. It had its own work to do. So it has acquired and retained a peculiar quality of its own which is neither Highland nor Border Lowland. Braemar is in the county and Braemar may have raised the standard in 1715 and may now be as authentically Highland to the eye as any scene ever put on canvas by Landseer. But only a few miles away the spirit is quite distinct.

Aberdeenshire, as a whole, has been as much severed from Gaeldom as has any other part of Scotland. The Gaels have never concerned themselves with the bleaker virtues of relentless industry, cautious investment, and achievement of success. But Aberdeen has pondered deeply on these subjects and followed thought with practice. It has preferred hard slogging to the flourish of romance, trousers to the peacock finery of the tartan, diligent farming to furious raiding, and a severe Protestantism to the more aesthetic appeal of the Old Faith. The display of ' High-landism ' at the Deeside Games, which culminate early in September with the royal occasion at Braemar, offer the most colourful and the most highly publicised display of the tartan and the sounding of the pipes, but the shire beyond has been a continuous example of austerity in living and of sombrely serious application to the job in hand. The stone of its granite capital is symbolic as well as unique. The Gael on the march, or the charge, was more

terrifying than tough. Stand up to him and he got tired
of you, and the Lowlanders were ever great standers-up, in
the north as in the south. Walls of granite do not collapse
at the sound of a trumpet or fall flat before the skirl of
pipes. Within the city of Aberdeen you can find yourself
on the edge of a gigantic chasm, almost a Grand Canyon.
This is the Rubislaw granite quarry on which the builders
drew. It is as though the city had been thrown up by a
vast eruption, with the granite its lava.

My first memory of the town of Aberdeen is one of early
boyhood. A night-journey from London had ended with
a rose-red morning that flushed the cold North Sea as the
train thundered past Stonehaven and along the cliffs of
what I had learned in school to call Kincardineshire but is
now more briefly and happily known by its old name of
the Mearns. Then, the city reached, there was that sharp
savour of smoked haddocks, an abiding fragrance. He who
reaches Aberdeen by train walks out into a world of fish
and by the time he has tasted them fresh from the sea and
unstaled by any journey of their own he knows that there
are no such fish as these on other urban tables.

Later I was taken to the fish-market where the boats
were belching up every kind of marine curiosity as well as
the serviceable and familiar types of sea-food. It was a
free-for-all aquarium, a parade of goggle-eyed serpents.
Here was a strange world. The bairns with no shoes or
stockings—an economy no longer needed—the nipping
air, the poverty, the energy, the bustle, the clang of horse-
drawn traffic on the granite setts—this was not the bonnie
' land of cakes ' that I had expected. It was a gaunt
metropolis, but the cereal foods were there, great, floury
' bawbee baps ' which made London bread seem like a
flavourless nonentity; there were huge cookies, too, and a
spread succulence of ' fancy bread.' I have always loved

that term, fancy bread, implying that bakers too can be poets.

The excellence of Aberdeen, as I later in life discovered, is to marry town and country. Huge cities inevitably forget and obscure that healthy partnership. London is so vast a sprawl that it actually ignores the sea, the estuary, and the docks which created its being and its power. A careless man could even spend a day or two in Glasgow without thinking about ships. The colossal ' conurbations ' of Southern Scotland and South Lancashire put green fields out of mind. But in Aberdeen you cannot overlook the fishermen and the farmers. It is a promoted market, which is surely the right thing for a town to be, large enough to possess the best of urban amenities and resources, a University and high scholarship, architecture and medicine, theatre and book-shops, the cloistered serenity of the Old Town and the port and commerce of the New, which really is not new at all. Its Press—it used to have two morning papers to serve the shire as well as the town—reported well and commented gravely on the affairs of the world, as well as being properly informative about the crans of herring caught and the prices current for fish and flesh. (Aberdeen is as notable for its beef as for its haddocks.) It draws on the county for brains as well as victuals and enriches the imported talent with its learning and its taste for strenuous competition.

The town does not overlay the county. A well-sized city is one that rides easily on the countryside, assisting, not sapping, the villages. Edinburgh still manages, I hope, to do that, but obviously is in some danger, while remaining a glory, of swelling into a nuisance and of eating up the Lothians. In Aberdeen you may not lift up your eyes to the hills, as in Edinburgh, but there is no danger of submergence by brick and bungalow. It may be impossible to preserve that grey and often glittering unity of granite;

slums must be cleared and new immigrants housed and the craft of building in stone has now become distressingly rare and costly. But Aberdeen will not become a monster of urbanism. Its streets will still be full of countrymen come to market and of fishermen up from the sea, and its shops will cater as much for the country house, the farmer, and the sportsman as for those who make their living beside the clang of Union Street.

The names written up everywhere are not of the Highlands. Mair and Mitchell, Simpson and Sim, Bain and Bissett and Milne—you are not overwhelmed with Macs. The Gordon Highlanders are its pride, but they draw more on the farm-lands than on the glen. Gordonia is a land of cowmen and shepherds. I shall not attempt to guide anybody round Aberdeen; others can better explain and commend King's College and its treasures and the Cathedral of St. Machar. But there is one episode in the antiquities of the town that is not generally mentioned, namely that Shakespeare's company performed and were honourably entertained there: it is possible that Shakespeare was there himself and that the Scottish tour may have yielded direct experience for writing 'Macbeth.' This is surmise, but there are grounds for it, as Clara Longworth de Chambrun has shown in her book ' Shakespeare Rediscovered,' basing her claim on researches in the archives of Aberdeen.

The Aberdeen of the fifteenth and sixteenth centuries had no lack of learning and the arts. King's College was founded by Bishop Elphinstone in 1494. Owing to the gallantry of the principal and his armed supporters the carving in the canopied stalls and choir-screen were saved from the violence of the Reformers who believed graven beauty to be the contradiction of true faith. There may have been University wits as ready to welcome players in Aberdeen, when they

arrived in 1601, as were the Inns of Court men to support
the theatres in London. In October of that year Provost
Cullen drew up an Ordinance of the Dean of Guild, commanding thirty-two Scottish marks to be paid to ' the King's
Servants presently in this burgh who play comedies and
stage plays.' It is explained that ' they are recommended
by his Majesty's special letter.'

That letter from James VI of Scotland, later James I of
England, does not exist: but the Provost's statement makes
it plain that there was a royal behest. There is in the civic
records of Aberdeen a further note of payment:

'Item, to the stage playeris, Inglischman, XXXII lib.
Item, for the stage playaris suppor that nicht they plaiid
to the towne III lib.'

Furthermore Laurence Fletcher, ' comedian servitor to his
majestie,' was made a Burgess of the Guild, a signal honour
for a player. We can fairly presume that the stage players
were an English troupe, although the ' Inglischman ' is
written in the single. (The spelling of the Ordinance has
the capriciousness of the time and the word players is spelled
differently in successive lines.)

Laurence Fletcher was a prominent member of the Lord
Chamberlain's men in London whom King James immediately honoured with the title of King's Men on his accession
to the throne in London in 1603. In the Coronation
Accounts of the Master of the Wardrobe Shakespeare heads
the list of those who were to receive four yards of red cloth
for the Coronation Procession: all the well-known members
of the ' fellowship,' Phillips, Fletcher, Heminge, Burbage,
Condell, Sly, Armin, and Cowley were included in the
allowance and the honour. Phillips in his will left thirty
shillings in gold to ' my fellowe William Shakespeare ' and

twenty to Laurence Fletcher. That was presumably the order of precedence, possibly of affection too.

King James's addiction to the theatre was a very strong one. Even before he ruled in London and commanded many performances by his chosen company, it is proved that he was summoning English players to Scotland and seeing that they travelled as far as Aberdeen. It would be interesting to know with what piece they sang for their supper, a generous one, to judge by the expenditure. Since Fletcher was one of Shakespeare's colleagues and Shakespeare was the chief dramatist of the Chamberlain's Men, the probability is that the piece was one of his.

On the whole it is unlikely that Shakespeare did go to Aberdeen. If he had been there, would he not have been the leader and so the man selected for the compliment of election to the rank of Burgess? (As an Aberdonian devotee of the Warwickshire genius I would love to think that the town of my fathers had thus honoured him.) He took precedence over Fletcher in the Coronation Accounts list and in Phillips's will also. He could have picked up, since he was obviously one of the world's quickest assimilators of fact and atmosphere, enough information from those who made the trip to form his observations about the climate of Inverness and to ask the distance to Forres. I cannot understand how Shakespeare found time for his steady output of plays if he was not only acting and managing but also going on long tours. But there are no certainties. He may have been present in Aberdeen as his fellows certainly were. At any rate there is a proven link between Aberdeen and the Globe Theatre, Southwark. Fletcher, Burgess of Aberdeen, died in 1608 and was buried where so many stage-folk, including Shakespeare's brother Edmund, were laid, in St. Saviour's, Southwark, now Southwark Cathedral, ' with an afternoon's knell of the great bell.' It is at least demonstrated by this occurrence of Fletcher's journey with the players that old Aberdeen was not averse to receiving such folk, although it had also received the Reformation and was to be a stronghold of Puritan doctrine; also we learn that those whom it received in hospitality it fed with generosity.

Remembering that a fine quality in any town is easiness of escape, we may wander northward. That is not to find a spectacular tourists' paradise; go west to Braemar for that. It is to discover the other partner in the fabric of Aberdeen and it is a fair one. Admittedly the eastern and coastal region of Buchan is mostly flat and rather bleak; the wise builders went in for solidity and put sheltering trees to the windy side of their constructions. When I was searching for a house near Cruden Bay occupied by some of my family long ago, I inquired of a farm-worker about the whereabouts and the style of the place. He pointed the way and then said briefly, ' It's in the style of the period —massive! ' You need a certain massiveness of frame and structure in Buchan. The Peterhead quarries yield the granite for such protection and nowhere is shelter more needed. It was not a kindly thought to build a prison there.

The great belt of Aberdeenshire to the west of Buchan can be enchanting to the eye. It is a terrain of smooth ridges that develop an exquisite pattern of colour in the later summer when the crops turn to gold and diversify the rich green of the parks and the neep-fields. It is famous stock-raising country and the Argentines have paid fine prices for its bulls. There are the scattered castles of the eminent, but the staple is the agricultural land and not the sporting estate. One thing that catches the mind as one surveys the map and plans a journey is the sweet music made by the Aberdeenshire names. Shall we go north from the Dee by Echt and the Barmekin hill and Craiginglow to Monymusk? Then north again by Kintore, Old Meldrum, and Fyvie? Or west by Culsalmond to Huntly? It was near Huntly that I lived once as a boy in a house called Cobairdy; one of our excursions was a drive over to Rothiemay. Could a house and a village be more alluringly named?

There are many villages with the prefix Kirk-town. Religion is deep-rooted in the shire and the prefix, while telling you where to worship, adds its own music to the map. Kirktown of Culsalmond surely rings a bell. The great land-mark of the county's southern centre is Benachie; I stick to the old spelling though my map gives Bennachie. Its long, heathery ridge, rising to over 1700 feet, is like a crouching lion, the long barrow of a race of giants. It has attracted legends and ballads in plenty; to be 'back of Benachie' and by the banks of Urie or of Gadie has been the dream of many an exile. The Gadie is a burn in the Garioch, as this region is called. It flows through Leslie to Auchleven and joins the Urie in the woods of Logie-Elphinstone. It, too, is as happy in the sound of its bank-side villages as of its own waters.

> *I gazed an' cast my wandering eye*
> *To get one blink o' Benachie:*
> *It seemed a blithsome sight tae me,*
> *As I did pass it by.*

> *Oh might I die far Gadie rins*
> *Far Gadie rins, far Gadie rins,*
> *Oh might I die far Gadie rins*
> *At the back o' Benachie.*

(Far is the local spelling of whaur or where.)
Benachie is the local barometer as well as the remembered

mountain of those, perhaps more prosperous, who reap the alien corn. It holds the cloud and promises rain.

> *When Benachie pits on her tap*
> *The Garioch lads will get a drap.*

It was common land and occupied by squatters till 1859, when nine lairds divided it and threw out the settlers. Once more the Caledonian, stern and mild, gave way to the greed of the new possessiveness. He could make a song of his sorrow:

> *Oh ye was aince a monarch hill,*
> *To freedom's footsteps free,*
> *But noo, unless their honours will,*
> *We daurna tread on thee.*
> *Alas, the heather on thy broo*
> *Will bloom nae mair for me;*
> *The lairds aroon hae ta'en ye noo,*
> *Ye're nae oor Benachie.*

But songs did not save. The lawyers were always ready to back the lairds. Yet the folk have plodded on; they always believed that plodding meant progress. They sent their sons to the school, the University, and across the seas, to hum the songs of Benachie and Gadie while tackling the business of getting on.

I have a particular interest in 'back of Benachie,' that rolling country of fair summers, hard winters, and hard work. In it lies the village of Rayne, 'the Girnal of the Garioch.' (The girnal was a large box or barrel to hold oatmeal, and so a token of fertility.) My grandfather on the male side was its Free Kirk Minister. Rayne resented the fact that its Minister, the Rev. Alexander Cushney, did not come out in the Disruption of 1843. So it chose to stand and worship in its own unfettered way. It rebelled and raised the money to build a wooden Free Kirk and in 1852 the dissidents had 160 communicants and 300 'adherents.' My grandfather, who had 'come out,' was inducted in 1853 with a salary, raised by the congregation, of £60 a year. He immediately set to work to collect funds for a new and more substantial Free Kirk and this and the Manse were ready and debt-free by 1859.

'Mr. Brown,' wrote Mrs. Beaton in her book on the district, 'Back o' Benachie,' 'was greatly commended for his energy and for getting the bog land around drained and a garden made. He was a vigorous preacher and was untiring in going to outlying districts to preach on Sunday evenings. On these occasions he usually advised his hearers to make all they could, to save all they could, and to give all they could.' He continued this good counsel for twenty-one years and I presume that the £60 salary did a little increase. He had three children to educate, fell ill in 1874, and died in 1876. It seems unlikely that my grandmother had a very easy life. It must have been a severe blow to the wives of the Disruptionists when their men abandoned the security of the Establishment for the risks of an un-endowed Kirk. But they endured, perhaps encouraged. The quality of granite is not strained.

I make no apology for a little detail about family and local matters, because I believe them to be typical of the Aberdeenshire country and its economy, typical also of the stubborn faith in effort, independence, and self-help. Of course that faith has been common all over Scotland, but Aberdeenshire has been especially associated with dour persistence, hard, poor living, trust in education, and profitable escape. It had its bleakness, but it had its backbone.

My great-grandfather was a village carpenter who taught himself Greek. It could hardly have helped him at his craft, but he was able to get his son to Aberdeen University and then into a Manse and it is from the Manse, Established or Free Kirk, that so much of Scotland's energy was to flow outward; there was not a great deal of meat in the larder and certainly no bottle on the shelf. But there were books. Some Athenian graces were there to dulcify the Spartan living. My father went from Raine to Aberdeen, where he graduated as M.D. He took service with the Army, assisting surgically at the battle of Tel-el-Kebir, and also with the P. & O. Line, thus seeing very different worlds from those of the barley-fields and the city of grey granite. Then, observing during one of his voyages that there was an opening for a doctor in Penang, Straits Settlements, he settled there, worked hard and prospered, wrote Honourable in front of his name as member of the Legislative Council in Singapore, and returned at last to Harley Street to specialise in Oriental diseases. It was a march outwards and upwards that might be called typically Aberdonian. He never told me much of his student days except that a threepenny tripe supper on Saturday was his week's luxurious outing.

But what life was like in the eighteen seventies and eighties for the Scottish student from a poor home—and there were many such in Aberdeen since the sons of the lairds went to England—is on plentiful record. Take, for example, the career of the Rev. Sir William Robertson Nicoll, Doctor of Laws and Companion of Honour, an outstandingly successful product of the indigent but book-laden Manse in the Aberdeenshire villages; his life was a notable example also of the hard way up. I have studied the career of Robertson Nicoll with special interest because he was associated with my grandfather. During the latter's illness in 1874 Nicoll, then a probationer in the Ministry and aged 23, took charge of the Free Kirk of Rayne. His

biographer, T. H. Darlow, has recorded that Nicoll found
in the Manse a complete set of Spurgeon's Sermons and
read them all through. (Nicoll had the daemon of bookish-
ness in him; he read and wrote incessantly all his life,
perhaps another quality—or failing—of my native shire.)
The soil of Rayne suited this vigorous young sower of the
seed.

Moody's revivalism had reached the Scottish air. Mr.
Darlow observes that ' During the six months which Nicoll
spent at Rayne he found spiritual interest strangely
quickened all through the countryside. The scattered
population gathered eagerly to special evangelistic services
and enduring results were produced in a number of human
lives. The glow and ardour of these experiences left a
permanent impress on Nicoll himself.' The North East
corner of Scotland usually needs warming up, as any
traveller can discover who journeys into the Buchan end
of it and takes the air at Peterhead. I was once in that
harbour-town when the Aberdeen paper proclaimed a heat
wave and announced that holiday-makers were so overcome
by the heat that they could hardly struggle to the beach
to find cool comfort in the sea. At Peterhead I met its
July North East wind and pulled my overcoat about my
ears, heat-wave or no.

Consequently there is considerable demand for fiery
consolations. Hell-fire and radiance of salvation are very
popular elements of the fishermen's faith and their grey and
windy townships have often been swept by highly emotional
revivalism. The more carnal restorative, whisky, destroyed
two of my forebears, who, having made money sheep-farming
in Australia, most foolishly endeavoured to settle down to
enjoy their gains, after the death of an unsympathetic and
most granitic father, on the coast of Buchan, near Long-
haven. Perhaps they lacked the powerful cordial of

evangelistic religion; certainly they found some inner fire essential after exchanging the Australian sun for the winds of Aberdeen. That was about the time when the young Nicoll was triumphantly fanning the flames of the faith which Moodyism, and possibly my grandfather, too, had so powerfully kindled in the region north of the Don.

Spurgeon-crammed and with a natural flair for making anything popular, be it salvation of soul or culture of mind, Nicoll flourished and was 'called' in the same year to Dufftown in Banffshire, of whose scenery and principal product, whisky, I have already written. The barley-bree was no attraction to the young Minister, who never needed to increase his natural energy. But the size of the population guaranteed opportunities as well as material support and his eloquence was of a kind to lure in the Auld Kirkers as well as the New. The young conqueror of Dufftown's spiritual life was thus described by a local lady with a nice gift of the vernacular. ' A sma'-bookit, mire-snipey bit chielie, gey an' aften wi' a red nose and a gravat aboot his neck, gyan ploit, ploiterin' doon the street to the post-office i' the gloamin' wi' a long, white envelope in's han'.' In other words, a small-framed, snipe-like bit of a lad with his home-work done. The long envelope of the ' ploiterin' chielie ' presumably contained his reviews and articles, for he had practised journalism in Aberdeen almost since boyhood in order to pay his way.

Nicoll came from a Free Kirk Manse at Lumsden, east of Rayne and at the head of Strathbogie; his father, an insatiable scholar, had consistently denied himself in order to pick up bargains in the second-hand bookshops and, though his income never reached £200 a year, he had accumulated a library of 17,000 books. So his son had no lack of reading matter. The pressure in childhood was strong and to be lettered early was expected of all, especially of a Minister's lad. Young Nicoll went to Aberdeen Grammar School at twelve and to the University at fifteen; he graduated at eighteen. As an undergraduate he spent four shillings a week on his bed-sitting room and four more on his food. He had a bursary of eleven pounds a year and some victuals sent from home. I suppose that my father's life and sustenance and those of nearly all the stripling scholars from the county was much the same. It was an austere, melancholy beginning of life's enterprise; small wonder that success was the general goal. At least the air braced them for that escape, out of poverty and often out of Scotland also.

There was almost none of the social and athletic activity that help to make the true essence and the creative pleasures of University years. Nicoll has recorded that ' General reading was strongly disapproved.' What an appalling statement of intellectual imprisonment! The boys, for they were no more in age, read for their special exams with their noses glued to the curriculum. They read narrowly, intensely, and hungrily. ' Many of us,' added Nicoll, ' had our constitutions permanently impaired by lack of good and adequate food. Far too large a proportion of my fellow-students died early.' Far too large! A few casualties, it seems, were to be expected. Success was like an enemy's strong-post in the battlefield. Its capture meant casualties.

It is significant that the first episode in Ian Maclaren's ' Beside the Bonnie Brier Bush,' the now much-abused book which was the first and a very fertile plant in the Kailyard School of Scottish writing, concerns a brilliant scholar of Latin and Greek in the imaginary village of Drumtochty. He was helped by a gifted Dominie and the money of a generous farmer to go and triumph at Edinburgh University. He had no sooner triumphed than he lay back and died. The course of honours was the path to the graveyard. But the prize, so grimly coveted, is dearly and vainly bought if the curriculum be a killer. Even in my own time that sort of sacrifice has continued. When I was working for the *Manchester Guardian* a young and able colleague, who had come from Aberdeen, died suddenly. He looked a large and strong enough fellow; but something snapped. I discovered later that, while at Aberdeen, he had worked as a sorter in the Post Office at night while taking his lectures and doing his reading by day. That was not necessarily a case of cause and effect; but, when we think of Robertson Nicoll's remarks on premature death among his student companions, it well may have been.

Nicoll himself, having graduated in arts at eighteen, went on to the theology course in order to enter the Ministry. He worked persistently at journalism, in which he quickly established himself with the city's papers, and at coaching other students. With this treble life he combined the Aberdonian thrift. 'At twenty I had a £15 bursary, I made £40 a year by journalism, and £50 a year by private coaching and I saved money.' By the time he was twenty-three he had £200 put away. There was then no withering taxation, no threats of a Capital Levy, to discourage such prudent and industrious young investors in the Funds.

His subsequent career was that of the successful Scot of his period, involving the inevitable move to the recognition and rewards, not of Edinburgh, the native capital, but of all-magnetic London. He was 'called' to Kelso after Dufftown and later abandoned the Ministry for publishing and journalism. He became a pillar of the firm of Hodder and Stoughton, helped to found the *British Weekly*, the *Bookman*, and the *Woman at Home*. Lord Robert Cecil said of the *Manchester Guardian* that it made righteousness readable, but Nicoll was no less a master of that art. In his magazines he served Nonconformity, literature, and domesticity. As an editor he was an early discoverer of J. M. Barrie, who wrote for the *British Weekly* under the name of Gavin Ogilvy.

Nicoll, under his own name and with the pseudonym of Claudius Clear, wrote prolifically and was soon a great moulder of middle-class as well as Dissenting opinion. He had a fine house in Frognal, Hampstead, was knighted in 1909, and was photographed complete with silk knee-breeches and sword. He was a powerful ally and consultant of Lloyd George in holding Nonconformity to Liberalism and rallying it to belligerent enthusiasm during the 1914-18 war. He was made a Companion of Honour in 1921, two years before his death at the age of seventy-two. It had been a long way up from Lumsden and stony at the start. Those whom Aberdeen did not wreck it rewarded elsewhere and in the end. First the gritting of the teeth and the tightening of the belt; then prosperity and power, achieved by escape from Scotland into a softer country, easy to plough and to crop. And many a ' brither Scot ' did Nicoll help on a similar climb, J. M. Barrie not least.

That, I suppose, was the start made by my father and thousands of other Scots who left their own country for their own good; it made him an honourable, careful, hard-working man, and impatient of all idle, feckless folk. He spent freely when he thought money should be spent, as, for example, on education. It also gave to him, as it did to so many of his fellow-travellers on the road south, a certain sense of inferiority about Scotland, even a distaste for it. He sent his sons to school in England, reverting to Scottishness so far as to insist that Balliol should be my college at Oxford, whether I got a scholarship to ease the strain or not. This was, he thought, the best thing in education and therefore he was ready to pay the price. But his respect for Balliol was based, no doubt, as much on that foundation's good name as a workshop of successful careers as on the fact that the lady Dervorguilla, wife of John Baliol of Durham and his instigator in educational patronage, was a daughter of Dumfries.

On his holidays from the East he took houses with modest shootings attached to them in Aberdeenshire and in Banff-shire, but as a worker London was his goal and London manners were his model. He liked to think that he had no Scottish way of speech left and, when a friend of his boy-hood turned up to renew old acquaintance in Hampstead and remarked ' You've nae left your accent behind ye,' I remember that a very sour look greeted this observation. He had no nostalgia for Aberdeenshire and would never have composed verses to the green howes where Gadie runs. Nor did he recount pastoral memories of the old folk, the neep-fields, and the rigs of barley.

There was a reason enough for this in the case of many escaping Scots. The childhood in the Manse, the long, bleak Sundays, the constant poverty, the hard grinding at school, a University life so constricted and intense as to make it a travesty of all that the undergraduate's tasting of liberty and the arts should be, were bound to leave grey memories. Scotland was uncouth. Oh yes, the land was a fair one to look at and to fish in and to shoot over when you came back with money in hand. But you did not stay there. Apart from its sports and landscapes, it was deemed remote, quaint, full of things to smile at or to regard with the comfortable sentimentality of one who can leave the place when he likes. Were there not the stories and plays of Barrie to remind the absentee Scot that Scotland need not be taken too seriously? Was it not full of ridiculous Kirk Elders and did not John Shand show the way out and up to London, even if it was the woman who knew most? Then there was Harry Lauder, with his genial caricature of the man in a kilt and his reassuring intimation to the music-hall public that life across the border was all roaming in the gloaming and innocent dalliance with the lassies in the glen. I do not remember that ' The House with the Green Shutters ' was ever in our London house, along with the Barries and the Ian Maclarens and the S. R. Crocketts. That renowned, and now sometimes overrated, attack on Scottish small-town life, with all its greed, gossip, and coarseness underlined, was probably unknown to most Scots of my father's kind.

This is not written in contempt of the so-called Kail-yarders, to castigate whom became later on the common form of the young Scot with a taste for letters. My father's generation liked their easy way of sliding over the harshness and the ugliness and remembering the queer, the couthy, and the picturesque. It was nice to remember in absence that Caledonian nursery of Success, with its grimness gone and its humours smoothed for safe reading and for unexacting playgoing. My father even liked the simplicities of ' Bunty Pulls the Strings,' though his boyhood in Aberdeen-shire must have taught him that the Drumtochty and Lintiehaugh and other Brier Bush villages of the gentle fictions so popular in the library and on the stage were the never-never-lands of romance. But I shall return to this when I reach the Barrie country.

The rigours of the system have been modified now, which is not to deny some continuing and galling poverty in Scottish students who must undertake vacation-work to ease the financial load. But first the huge benefactions and endowments made by Andrew Carnegie for the assistance of Scottish pupils and Scottish Universities and then the increasing intervention of the State and the Local Authority have diminished the desperate nature of the struggle; the death-roll of devoted scholars has diminished. The older Scots of the hard school would have loathed the Welfare State with its handing out of subsidies, its free this and its free that. My father would have called it a Cadger's Paradise and he hated a cadger. But there is the other side to it. The student's life is far more civilised and what is the use of being Dux and Prizeman if you fall dead with all the medals on your bosom and with the laurels turned to a wreath in a grave-yard?

The old type of Dominie in the village school was a personage in his own right, with freedom to teach in his own way, with status in the countryside, and often with great achievements in the fostering of talent. He took enormous pride in his production of Success; he was, it is true, manufacturing exports, for the whole business of the Dominie in Drumtochty was to create the future ' high heid yins ' of capitalism in capitals across the world. But he generated respect for learning as well as for the lucre and position that it was to earn. He wanted to create Professors as well as Governor-Generals and leaders of Industry. ' Professor,' said a small farmer in Ian Maclaren's ' The Days of Auld Lang Syne,' ' is a by-ordinar' word; a' coont it equal tae Earl at the verra least.' It is a remark that might have been actually spoken in Aberdeenshire as much as in Maclaren's Perthshire. There was devout worship of wisdom as well as deep regard for worldly rank.

The old-style Dominie was no form-filling cog in a great machine. Sometimes stern and punitive, he had his heart in a job that was really his own. He was as important as the Minister and liked to be an individual and a character. He remained a poor man whose chief compensation was gratitude and there were Scots in high places and far countries who did remember his encouragement as well as his discipline. The traveller in Aberdeenshire who passes the village-school or the Academy of the small town sees something which procured its results with hard driving, no doubt, but without ingenious or absurd educational theories, without great subvention, and without pretence. It was built not on the system but on the individual teacher, who might, of course, fail it. But, when he did not prove unworthy, his freedom was his strength.

Success is no longer what it was; savage taxation of earned as well as of unearned income has robbed the 'glittering prizes' of their golden quality. If wealth of money be the object now, then to be an acute speculator or the kind of respectable racketeer who keeps just within the law should be the object of ambitious youth. It is the bitter paradox of our brand of Socialism that it pillages industry and the industrious and lets the gambler get away with all he can pick up on the Stock Exchange and the race track. The Scottish view of life was very different and I hope it still is. However, success includes power, which some people esteem beyond treasure; there is still that goal for those facing what is left of the traditional granitic regimen and of the stiff climb up the educational ladder.

It is customary now to dismiss Aberdonian meanness as a jest of local manufacture which was completely unrelated to fact. If by meanness one means prudence and thrift, then the accusation (or rather the compliment) surely holds. For the city of Aberdeen is the superstructure in granite on a county of grudging soil and cold seas. Fishing is always a hard and hazardous life and the farmer in many of the Aberdeenshire acres has had few of the natural endowments given to the tiller of the rich Lothian country in the south. Many of the farms have been wrested from the earth by relentless application to the draining of peaty

acres; where the soil is not heavy it is often thin. J. R.
Allen has given the record of his forebears who, in 1820,
took a nineteen-year lease of 101 acres of which half was
peat-moss and the other half described as ' completely
exhausted and unfit to bear any crop of grain.' The
dwellings were uninhabitable and the byres too bad for
' the bestial.' Yet, within a year, the home and the steadings
were put into order by personal labour; in eight years of
furious industry the wilderness was turned to a productive
holding, with a rich yield from each acre by Aberdonian
standards; to achieve this improvement miles of drains had
to be cut and dug and hundreds of loads of soil brought in
as a necessary top-dressing. Man and horse did this; there
were no tractors then.

In this connection it is worth remembering that the word
manure originally meant working with the hands, manœuvre.
To manure was to hold, to cultivate, to improve. So
manured land, in the old sense, was not earth treated with
farm-yard dung or purchased chemicals; it was earth
larded with the sweat of human labour. Much of Aberdeenshire was thus manured by years of draining marsh and
cutting the reeds and the bushes. The climate, it is true,
usually mitigates perspiration, but the grapple was intense.
Townsmen often think of a farm as something natural;
there is nothing more contrived, nothing more artificial,
especially in parts of Scotland. Take the Aberdeenshire
map and look at the farm-names. The word Moss is very
frequent. So is the word bog. The mire had to be fought
and beaten. Scrapehard is typical; so are Boggendinny,
Crannabog, and Slackbog; Windyhills, Stoneyfield,
Mosside, Heathery Banks—so they sing their song of the
land that was salvaged from the swamp or conquered for
a crop by riving the stone from the earth, the heather from
the hill.

When a region has been thus manured by drudgery the creators of its wealth have a duty as well as a right to be careful. It is naturally instilled into childhood that money is hard to get and easy to lose; so grew the insistence on economy which animated all types, not the farmer only. Thus it happened that young Robertson Nicoll of Lumsden was saving when, taking the long view, it might have been better for him to spend, to sit back a little, to read with more ease and breadth, and to let the world go by. But this kind of care, this self-denying provision for rainy to-morrows, has nothing to do with parsimony. There is no stinting when there is a good thing on which to spend, be it the helping of a friend or a cause or the species of investment that is called education. It has been said in jest that the Jews cannot make a living in Aberdeen; it can be replied in earnest that at least as much charitable Christianity has been practised there as in London. Dr. Johnson was made a Freeman of the City within two days of his arrival, a prompt and proper honour. ' The honour,' he wrote, ' had all the decorations that politeness could add and, what I am afraid I should not have had to say of any city south of the Tweed, I found no petty officer bowing for a fee.'

It is generally agreed that there is no more hospitable county, no city where a man will be more ready with a welcoming dram. It is no niggardly place whose High Teas were reputed to reach altitudes otherwise unequalled in a land famous for its summits of knife-and-forkery around six in the evening. Fish, eggs, sausages, scones, pancakes, and oatcakes were piled on in staggering quantities. Even Yorkshire, taken at its old best of farmhouse feeding, might have ceded sovereignty to the Aberdonian in the quantity and quality, the amassing and absorption, of High Tea with company attending. During our recent years of lean-

124

ness it was common rumour in the South that Aberdeen was the right resort for those afflicted with a painful appetite. Nor would they be put under any financial screw while enjoying their comparative surfeit.

Prices are more or less standardised now so that Aberdeen has less right to claim supremacy as a bargain-centre, but it certainly was once a shopping-town in which everything appeared to be considerably cheaper than elsewhere. I see no vice in wanting value for money and were I rich beyond my dreams I would still resent being swindled. Doubtless that is my Aberdonian blood at work; a millionaire from the Granite City who found himself charged a preposterous price for some such contemptible English driblet as a ' seven-out ' whisky would be the man to raise hell or even to buy the wretched hotel that had so affronted him, as Arnold Bennett's Croesus instantly bought the Grand Babylon in a just indignation because he could not get the meal he wanted.

Aberdonians, like many Scots and perhaps more than most Scots, have long been apprenticed to the social climb. They have had compulsions of poverty, stimulations of climate, the temper and inclination for keen pursuit of purpose, and an urgent tradition of ' getting down to getting up.' Such people are apt to be faulted with material- ism, sometimes unjustly by those who despise success because they will not pay the price of it. The cry

> *'Tis not in mortals to command success,*
> *But we'll do more, Sempronius, we'll deserve it*

is the consolation of the failure as well as a noble sentiment. It does not satisfy the resolute man, who is not to be fobbed off with merit merely.

There are few more tiresome forms of snobbishness than

125

sneering at the man who insists on getting his moneysworth and no sillier form of gentility than throwing money about to create an impression. Sometimes, no doubt, the man who has escaped from a hard childhood and boyhood in spare circumstances and ungracious surroundings, such as Aberdeenshire especially afforded, may become a snob when he finds himself among those of more means and ampler upbringing. The Aberdonian, if he adds up the bill in a fashionable restaurant and questions the items, may look odd in the eyes of his guests, but he is behaving sensibly and courageously; it is either a form of humbug or of folly not to guard against robbery. The child of success who murmurs, in his seat of comfort and of power, that he would he were ' where Gadie rins ' would be there still if he and his parents had not been fairly canny. And does he really want to be by Gadie's banks? For a month in summer, no doubt. But in December—well, he'll think that over. There can be a deal of cant in the nostalgia for the clay of a man who walks delicately on soft carpets. And yet it is so poignant while it lasts. The old names worry at the heart and the burns beckon fiercely to the fisherman.

But take your Southern river that meanders to the sea,
And set me where Leochel joins the Don,
With eighteen feet of greenheart and the tackle running free,
I want to have a clean fish on.

That was written in the heat and dust of South Africa. Getting out and getting on, leaving the granite and the grind for the West End luxury flat and the Chairman's seat on the Board—they demand their penalties.

And all the time the heather blooms on distant Benachie.
And wrapt in peace the sheltered valley lies.

The conquering exile looks at his investment list and wonders—before he decides that it is good. After all, he has a holiday at the end of the summer and then, at King's Cross, the night-train and the ' sleeper ' await him, with Deeside at the far end.

CHAPTER VI

Angus and the Authors

ABERDEEN has not lacked authors, but it has no literary shrine and it is not easy to advise the visitor about the right book for his background or bedside reading. He may pick up a copy of ' Johnny Gibb of Gushetneuk or the Parish of Pyketillim,' but he will not find it an easy matter, despite its vivacity. It was written by William Alexander, a Victorian editor in Aberdeen. Its language is the Buchan dialect of a century ago and, as I have said, that end of Aberdeenshire is an out-in-the-corner place, detached in its practices and with a vernacular very much of its own. The racy sketches, of which it is composed, do, if you can master the lingo, give a vivid and amusing picture of farm-life ' back o' Benachie ' and out to the east and north of it.

It is informative as well as entertaining. The use of Macduff, on the Banffshire coast, as a spa and curative centre, is richly described and one learns that the Aberdeenshire folk were ' hardy dookers ' (duckers) in pursuit of health. This was long before such immersion in very cold waters was popular with our strenuous young who now, on a sandwich or two, walk easily in a day up mountains once regarded as not to be tackled except with immense preparation, guides, ponies, and ample food-supplies. The

Pyketillim men, once at the sea-side, took their marine therapy in earnest; they gulped down sea-water, ate the dulse (sea-weed) and crunched up shells. Maister Saun'ers said of the dulse to Jock Will that it was ' vera halesome.' He then devoured ' a bunch of short, crisp dulse powdered about the root-ends with clusters of tiny shells of the mussels species.' Strong teeth were needed in order to achieve this cure for constipation. But Saun'ers guaranteed that ' shells hae a poo-erful effeck o' the stammack.' No doubt they have, if you can stand up to such medicaments in the manner of a Buchan man.

Books like William Alexander's and Mrs. Beaton's ' Back o' Benachie,' already mentioned, will probably have to be found in second-hand shops: they include ample conversation-pieces drawn from the high-pitched, long-drawn speech of the shire, where the preparatory, dubious, contemplative umph'm and och-aye are frequently the introduction to a cautious judgment. Eric Linklater was at Aberdeen University, but he is an Orkney man who has made Scotland and even America his provinces. Lord Byron sang of his boyhood's Lochnagar, but nobody climbs (or even surveys) that precipitous giant standing sentinel over Balmoral simply for Byron's sake. Aberdeen, like most of Scotland, has its poets to-day. G. S. Fraser has caught in ' Home Town Elegy ' the ' glitter of mica at the windy corners ' and ' the sleek sun flooding, the broad, abundant sprawl of the dying Dee.' George Bruce has sung fitly of the hard coast and of Kinnaird Head by Fraserburgh, the outermost edge of Buchan,

O impregnable and very ancient rock
Rejecting the violence of water,
Ignoring its accumulations and strategy,
You yield to history nothing.

Nothing? There is humility in the Aberdonian; like Banffshire, his county lacks its songs of sentiment and adoration, except in Charles Murrays' 'Hamewith,' whose lyrics in the vernacular were written in South Africa where he in dreams beheld, not Hebrides, but the green Howe (hollow) of Alford and the trout-pools of the Don.

Turning south, the traveller has no lack of required reading. The first two volumes of Lewis Grassic Gibbon's 'A Scots Quair,' 'Sunset Song' and 'Cloud Howe,' are wonderful introductions to the Mearns, the county that used to be called Kincardineshire. Next we come to Angus, once Forfarshire, with its two women-poets, Violet Jacob and Marion Angus, and possessing too the birth-place of Sir James Barrie, who drew on Kirriemuir, his Thrums, for the scenes and characters of his earliest work. Douglas Young, too, that fantastically gifted polyglot, scholar, politician, and native makar, is of a Dundee family and now lives his eloquent, abounding life in Tayport across the water. You can turn to him for the picture of 'Sabbath i' The Mearns,' with its black-clad kirk-attenders among the flowering geans (wild cherry-trees) in the Howe. The Mearns can claim a share too in Robert Burns, whose grandfather and father had struggled as small farmers with the hard soil and even harsher eighteenth-century leases of Clochanhill, in the parish of Dunnottar and not far from Stonehaven. (The Burns name was acquired by a series of abbreviations, which the English jester might attribute to Scottish thrift of ink; Burnhouse becomes Burness, then Burnes—the poet's father's style—and then Burns). It is not to the Highlands that Scotland chiefly owes its poetry: it was from the farms and hand-looms of the east that the stories came. Off the cliffs of the Mearns and the richer straths of Angus song has drifted on the 'roarin', norlan' wind.'

It is good mixed country for wandering. First, moving south, we are in the bleak narrow strip between Deeside and the sea; I stayed once at Muchalls, which is perched on the cliff-clinging main line between Stonehaven and Aberdeen. The roaring express-trains are not frequent enough to destroy peace. I wanted a tonic air and I got it. If you desire to feel that your lungs have been born again, if you crave recreation in the literal sense of a mighty word which has fallen to signify minor pleasures of the dart-board and of table-tennis, then try this sheer fringe of the high eastern cliffs. The reward is a tremendous appetite, a stronger pulse of life, walks along dizzying heights of rock above the sea, to the music of gulls and peewits, and not much else.

Stonehaven itself is a ' resort,' as well as a county town with bay and bathing and the spectacle of Dunnottar Castle, one of the most sensationally sited and toughest of Scottish keeps. But I am no castle-bagger and would rather look at the lands and towns where people made things and fought to enrich life than at the stony prisons where, having fought each other, they gaoled and massacred their kind. The chronicles of castles, Dunnottar not least, include long sieges and gallant defences, but there is a deal of cold-blooded savagery too. The history of Scotland has too much of this cold blood in it to make me enamoured of peering into the murk of rock-cut cells where captive wretches languished through years of deadly night. But the cliffs around Stone-haven have more than old horrors; the golfer hereabouts has the drumble of the cliff-assaulting waves far below him and air straight from Scandinavia to cool the ardours of his climbing. There must be temptation to lift the head, with such sky-scape and sea-scape for scenery.

A spur of the Grampians presses close to the sea at Stonehaven and the railway and the road have to squeeze through; but southward there is more breadth of green levels; here is the Howe of the Mearns, which has evoked abundant praise of its tilth and its parks, so happily propped between the Grampians on the west and Garvock Tap on the east. Some of the weaving-towns that dot the Mearns and Angus are not attractive in general, except for the students of Scottish small-town sociology with its long diversity of economic ups-and-downs, its medley of strict theology and loose living, its grave elders and gossiping wives, its drinking and wenching and bastardy, its geniality below the surface and its grim smile above. This ledge of eastern Scotland, between the high hills where there are only the game-birds to chatter and the harbours, where fish are the argument, is exceptionally beautiful; in late summer there are the purple on the one side, the blue on the other, and the green about one's feet. And what more exquisite green than the larch in early summer, what keener scent than that of pine-woods after rain? The Howe of the Mearns is famous for its skies—' Cloud Howe,' as Gibbon called it —and sweetly fragrant with the smack of the sea working in over the neep-fields and with the Highland airs coming down from Cairn o' the Mount over Drumtochty and Auchinblae.

Angus, as you move down the coast is broader, richer, more towned, a link with the sleek south. Gibbon has the place-name of Blawearie for a Mearns croft and adds the local ' speak ' that a man goes out ' of the world and into Blawearie.' That is apt of the far-flung farms under the Grampian spurs, the Hill of Trusta, and the Braes of Glenbervie. But in Angus you are into the world, not out of it; the way of life becomes more ample and gentle as you work your way down to Perthshire and the land that is rich for the soft fruit, with the miles of raspberry-fields around Coupar Angus and Blairgowrie.

It was at Arbroath in Angus that the lifters of the Coronation Stone handed back in the spring of 1951 the snatched symbol of their country's sovereign rights. Arbroath, which used to be Aberbrothoc, has the ruins of an Abbey that was founded in 1178. 'I should scarcely have regretted my journey,' wrote Dr. Johnson, 'had it afforded nothing more than the sight of Aberbrothoc.' It is not only sacred to God—it was dedicated to St. Thomas à Beckett—but politically significant. For here, in 1320, the Estates of Scotland, with King Robert Bruce present in person, assented to the great Declaration of Independence written out for them by Bernard Linton, Chancellor of Scotland and Abbot of Aberbrothoc. 'As long as a hundred of us remain alive we shall never submit to the domination of England. For it is not for honour or riches or glory but for liberty alone that we strive and contend, which no man will give up save with life itself.' Bannockburn had been won six years before. Eight years after, by the Treaty of Northampton, Edward III's counsellors accepted Robert Bruce as King of Scotland. Later it was from Montrose to the north of Arbroath that the ship sailed for the Holy Land carrying the Bruce's heart. There is plenty in Angus for 'the man of feeling,' especially if he be one of those who feel that the Act of Union destroyed not only a principle but the pride and proper aspirations of a people.

Peace has its victories and they can be sternly bought. It was on this Angus coast, just south of Arbroath, that I witnessed a remarkable English triumph. It happened on a vicious July day in 1937, in an on-ding, as the Scots say, of cold, unceasing rain, that Henry Cotton grimly fought his way to the Open Championship against the American as well as the native hosts. The links there, in the leaden, soaking weather that blows in from the east, can be singularly unattractive to the eye; on the best of days there is no view of serene towers, no hint of the little Athens, none of the enchantment that takes the eye of the golfer who has rounded the Loop and turned for home at St. Andrews. Walter Hagen had given up hope and was taking things lightly, wise-cracking to the crowd in one of his perky and jocose moods. But there was no levity elsewhere.

Henry Cotton, with shoulders bent and eyes dourly fixed upon the squelching grass, seeing neither crowd nor sea-shore nor anything but his immediate purpose, plodded from stroke to stroke, a man in an iron mask, his will commanding a piece of superb physical machinery. He was riveted to what is usually a game. But in such conditions of highest prowess, rivalry, and strain it is nothing but a torturing test of nerve, skill, endurance, concentration, and discipline. His melancholy single-mindedness prevailed. He won. But it does not surprise me, with such conflict in memory, that the reward of Golf Champions is not only the tenure of a rather ugly trophy but havoc of digestion and anguish of duodenum.

If at Arbroath I remember a flamboyant testament of freedom, at Carnoustie I have an image of glum resolution and of a soaked figure in the rain, wiping hands and club on a towel, before he drove again into the downpour. Cotton is of Southern England: but never did a grey Scottish village turn out a figure more resolute to banish all thought of pleasure in the game and take the stress of victory in a sombre stride. Belloc once wrote:

> *There's nothing worth the wear of winning*
> *But laughter and the love of friends.*

Golfers, on their sternest occasions, think otherwise. True, Hagen laughed. But he had abandoned the hope (and the wear) of winning. The links of Carnoustie can be bright with sun and the baked greens kittle in the glare. But I can never associate this battlefield with merriment. Perhaps that memory of Cotton haunts me too much.

Angus has a chain of links up its coast and the holiday golfer, with a taste in scenic back-cloths for his play, has Edzell in the glorious hinterland. To reach it you probably pass Brechin, not a great place now, but considered large a thousand years ago; then it was a sacred city of the Culdees, the Servants of God, who left their signature of piety in a few round and graceful towers. There is one of these in Perthshire, one in Orkney, and one at Brechin, which lies on the main road north and south. Edzell, to the north-west of holy Brechin, is in the Howe below Glen Esk, which runs up into the great mountains south of Deeside. This is the Lindsay country, handsomely watered, and wooded, famous for its beeches of the plain as well as for the conifers of its higher land. The North Esk river here separates the Mearns and Angus, but in quality the counties are not divided: their beauty is continuous, but the latter grows in suavity as you go south to Glamis in Strathmore, where The Queen Mother spent her childhood. The ghoulish legends about the home of the Strathmores seem curiously inappropriate in the comfortable valley of the Dean Water sheltered from the east winds by the Sidlaw Hills and backed on the west by the ridgy lands of the Ogilvies and Barrie's Kirriemuir.

That town is nicely set on its hill, a conspicuous perch, but it modestly keeps itself to itself. There is no Barrie cult, no shrine, no spinsterly coyness of Wendy Teashops, no *modernismus* of a Lady Babbie Cocktail Bar, no show of ' gifties fra' Thrums.' (At least these must be recent arrivals, if Kirriemuir has surrendered to such commerce.) George Blake has recorded in his excellent little book on

'Barrie and the Kailyard School' that Kirriemuir was aloof and unimpressed when Barrie's funeral took place there in June 1937. The B.B.C. and its newsreel men might blazon the event. Ramsay Macdonald might march with Sir Harry Lauder in the obsequies; Edinburgh University might be notably represented, but the locals were asking vaguely what it was all about. 'Barrie!' said a garage-foreman to Mr. Blake, 'Nobody round here thought muckle of him!' But then Barrie had not thought much of Kirriemuir in his years of London fame and prosperity. He rarely returned. He did not give it his summers. He preferred to take a place in the Cotswolds and play or organise cricket with the English. Incidentally Barrie's affection for cricket was not altogether strange in an Angus man. The east coast of Scotland from Aberdeen to Perth and Edinburgh has a summer flowering of the Southern game and plays County Matches with the assistance of imported English, Dominion, or Colonial professionals. Scottish cricket maintains such a standard that it can entertain the Test Match teams from overseas without disgrace. Yet the best of Scottish batsmen in our time was from the West, Kerr of Greenock; he had to score most of his centuries in a city sorely drenched by the rain from the clouds caught up in the Cowal hills across the Clyde and very rarely affording anything but a bowler's wicket. One fancies that he would never have been got out at Trent Bridge or the Oval.

The word Kailyard needs explaining. It became a common term of abuse in Scottish literary criticism, when the young devotees of social realism attacked the older sentimentalists whose pleasantry of descriptive narrative had so profitably taken the fancy of the world in the eighteen-nineties. The term has lingered on and appears to be still in use as a brick-bat by any Scot who wants to break windows in Thrums or to root up the Bonnie Brier Bush and throw it on the rubbish-heap, since he prefers the native Muse to be garlanded with thistles.

It was Ian Maclaren who gave such currency to this Kailyard phrase which was to become a curse to him and his kind. The author's real name was that of Sherlock Holmes's inseparable companion and chronicler, John Watson. He was of Highland blood, born in Essex, educated in Perth and Stirling, and admitted to the Ministry of the Free Kirk; he was 'called' to Logiealmond in South Perthshire, but only stayed in its pulpit for three years. His chief ministration was actually in Sefton Park, Liverpool. Thither he took a good memory and a faculty for remembering the characters he had met, or could imagine meeting, in the pleasant farm-lands of Glenalmond. In 1893 he found that these made acceptable sketches for the English and Scottish market. This was five years after Barrie had done a similar job of sketch-writing about Kirriemuir in his 'Auld Licht Idylls.' Robertson Nicoll became an encouraging editor and Hodder and Stoughton the rejoicing publishers of both. Watson, writing as Ian Maclaren, chose to call his first volume of collected pieces 'Beside the Bonnie Brier Bush' and prefaced it with two explanatory lines from an old song:

There grows a bonnie brier bush in our kailyard,
And white are the blossoms on't in our kailyard.

The word brier can be applied to any thorny bush, but usually signifies the wild rose, which is a common loveliness of the Scottish scene. Kail is a generic word for cabbages and greens and the kailyard is the cottager's patch of kitchen-garden.

My edition of 'The Bonnie Brier Bush' is the fifth 'completing the twenty-third thousand.' In 1895 it had reached its ninth edition and sixtieth thousand. This may sound unimpressive to-day, when best-sellers reach such enormous figures, but book-sales were much smaller then and there could be no disputing the very wide and rapidly increasing popularity at home and overseas of Maclaren's Perthshire pastorals or of Barrie's very similar recollections of the old folk in Kirriemuir which he named Thrums, a term for the cut-off ends of the weavers' warp-threads. Maclaren even became a triumphant lecturer in America on the strength of his brier-scented tales of Drumtochty.

I remember in boyhood the frequent appearance of Ian Maclaren's name on the covers of my favourite London magazines such as ' The Windsor.' For evening or wet-day reading during a holiday in Angus or Perthshire the early Barrie and Maclaren's sketches are agreeable company as well as necessary to an understanding of the rumpus that occurred when indignant youth turned to denounce the sins of the Kailyard School and of its alleged gold-diggers in a bogus soil. Another volume of Maclaren's was ' The Days of Auld Lang Syne.' An obvious and sugary title was no deterrent to him and to his editors and publishers. The books might also be read with advantage by some of those who most raucously denounce them. Some of these, I suspect, are ignorant of their contents. The word ' kail-yard ' became a critical missile readily picked up and hurled at any writer who did not assert that Scottish country life consisted chiefly of incest, adultery, greed, hatred, and all uncharitableness.

The common charge against the Kailyarders, who included another Free Kirk Minister turned story-teller in S. R. Crockett, is that they were sentimentalists, that they falsified the fabric of Scottish life in order to ' sell Scotland cheap' to the outer and richer world, that they deliberately made Scottish character pawky, picturesque, and childishly

' quaint ' so that absentee Scots could think of the home they left behind them with a reassuring smile, while the English and Americans could revel in a Caledonia depicted as an Academy landscape and populated with whimsical non-adults. Certainly there was that kind of response to the idylls of Thrums and Drumtochty and a welcome for such preposterous sickliness as Crocketts' ' The Lilac Sun-bonnet ' and for Barrie's worst descent into unworthy piffle, ' The Little Minister.' There were some sticky and greasy patches in the Kailyard, no doubt; but many of the Idylls were much better than most people now suppose. It was the ecstatic raptures of sentimentalists outside Scotland that did the subsequent harm to the authors' reputations, while it so lavishly filled their pockets. It came to be assumed that anything written by either of them must be false, mushy, and a deliberate betrayal of their country. That is simply untrue.

Barrie's first volume, ' Auld Licht Idylls,' contains much straight reporting done by a young man of rare capacity, drawing on his own experiences of Kirriemuir and still more on what his mother had told him of life there in her child-hood. The first sixty pages describe the town and its people much as Boz described London and its people. There are vivid impressions of the bothy-dwelling farm-hands and of the ' black fishers ' who poached the salmon. There are studies of the Kirk elders of the rigid Auld Licht sect and of their ways of electing a Minister, of their liking for a fierce and combatant moralist, and of their dread of anything or anybody that could be labelled ' Englishy.' There is a similar chapter on ' Lads and Lasses ' and of their grave, repressed courtships culminating in ' Will ye hae's us, Bell,' and a mumbled ' Aye.' ' The only really tender thing I ever heard an Auld Licht Lover say to his sweetheart was when Gowrie's brother looked softly into

Easie Tamson's eyes and whispered "Do you swite [sweat]?"' Is that sentimentalism? Is that love in a brier-sweet garden?

I must admit to finding the successor, 'A Window in Thrums,' with its more personal study of the Hendry family and their concern for the son away in London and yielding to a Wicked Woman to be considerably less astringent. There is much of the wee mother waiting in the wee hoose, the light in the window, and the breaking of hearts. Yet the English critics who saluted this book with such acclaim were not hacks writing in the cheap magazines: they were the men whose judgment counted. 'The Speaker' was a Liberal review with a first-class staff. 'A.B.' who reviewed 'A Window in Thrums' for it was presumably Augustine Birrell; if so, Barrie was being judged by a literary critic of the highest standard and by one of the most gifted essayists of his time. 'A.B.' said of this:

'The author has conceded nothing to the public taste. May he never do so! He has been inflexible and resolute, an artist from first to last. Of Sentiment, that odious onion, not a trace is to be found in these sweet-smelling pages.'

Those who expect their pastorals and small-town sketches to smell of nothing but dung will shudder at the adjective 'sweet-smelling'; but there is that tribute from a high source to Barrie's austerity. No sentiment!

Perhaps 'A.B.' did perceive a danger. That supplication against subsequent yielding to public taste may be the sign of it. There is, for me, a sad descent in 'The Little Minister,' which had reached its thirty-ninth thousand in 1894 and must have piled up many a thousand since. The Rev. Gavin Dishart, when near to death amid the flooded river, turns to his rival Lord Rintoul and says among the screams of the frustrated rescuers and the roar of the waters, ' We must prepare for death and it is for your own sake that I must ask you to tell the truth. Worldly matters are nothing to either of us now, but I implore you not to carry a lie into your Maker's presence.' Here is not a hero who touches either my affection or my sense of probability and as for his winsome dark lady, the so-called Egyptian, I cannot see her within a thousand miles of Kirriemuir.

But there can be no doubt, I think, that both Barrie and Maclaren have been subsequently scolded for offences which they did not commit and for telling some truth that their critics choose to ignore. To put sentiment into a picture of Scotland is fair enough for the simple reason that the Scottish possess, among many other qualities, a rich tincture of sentimentality. When one considers the emotionalism that has surrounded the name of Prince Charlie, the over-sweet tenderness of many Scottish songs, the continual harping on gentle scenery and blue-bell banks in a country far more notable for its grandeur, the wide-spread use of diminutives and of the adjective ' wee,' the yearning for the old home and the roses round the door, is it outrageous to plant a brier bush in the Kailyard? It is nonsense to pretend that Scottish hearts are all granite and are incapable of the melting mood. A writer can tell of tears over the porridge-bowl without being a liar. A picture of the Scots with sentiment left out is not a picture of the Scots. But admittedly the sentiment can be—and was—overplayed.

The Rev. John Watson was, after all, the Reverend John, a Minister of religion all his life, unlike Crockett, who gave up his pulpit for the pen. That Watson wrote of Drum-tochty with his tongue in his cheek I do not believe. He saw the decent struggle of its people to educate their children and set them well on the ladder of success and he approved it; so would any Scot who was not hag-ridden by some Bohemian notion that to be a drunken failure is the way to be a genius. He approved of Domsie, the schoolmaster who toiled and gave of his few shillings to send Drumtochty lads of promise to the University. Domsie is a sentimental name for a Dominie. Furthermore there was a strong vein of rather morbid emotionalism in Ian Maclaren, for whom death-beds and grave-yards and calls to ' Oor Lang Hame ' were oddly magnetic. He was not a great writer, and very far from being as adroit as Barrie, who very soon knew all the tricks of the trade. (Barrie had had a journalist's training which teaches a man to cut the cackle and come quickly to a well-made point. Many a famous author would have been the better for the discipline.) But when Maclaren wrote of the generous way in which the neighbours of Burnbrae rallied round the ruined farmer at his ' displenishment ' (selling up of his farm under legal order) and diddled the ring of professional buyers from the towns, he was, I feel sure, being true to Perthshire's native decency and loyalty and not inventing a happy ending.

He could not, as a Minister, concentrate on the uglier vices of the countryside as raw material for his writing; art, we are often told, is not copying but selection. He selected the better side of his parishioners in order to write of their ordeals by poverty, the hard way of the small farmer's life, and the kindliness of the schoolmaster and so on. I see no cause for flying into a fury with the man who, when he chose his first title, little realised that he was to be magnified into the leader of a School and vilified accordingly. He was more sentimental about the schoolmaster than was Barrie. The latter's Old Dominie in Thrums was a cantankerous despot who clung to his job, fought the

Board, and added to his income by organising occasional cockfights, every scholar to bring a bird and pay a shilling entrance fee. 'The moral of his life came in just as he was leaving it, for he rose from his death-bed to hide a whisky bottle from his wife.' It was not a sentimental Barrie who put this last sentence to his sketch of the master in the red schoolhouse away up Glen Quharity, which you may visit as Glen Clova. Ian Maclaren would scarcely have composed a piece in that vein or ended it thus. But that does not prove him to be a discreditable faker: he had his limited vision, his limited gifts, and he was pleasantly second-rate. Why not leave him so without the uncharitable ' girning ' ?

The case for Crockett is not so strong, because he could produce a rattling tale of adventure and was abandoning a considerable talent when he turned to lilac sun-bonnets and the like. But it is poor Maclaren who, because of his Brier Bush title, has been the target of abuse for thirty or forty years. He probably enjoyed his success, since it is rarely in human nature to dislike it. But he never set out to be important, for good or ill, in the history of Scottish literature; it was an accident that made him that. Let the traveller in Angus and the Mearns acquire some Ian Maclaren and early Barrie from a library or by purchase, if he can. Barrie's Glen Quharity, running due north from Strathmore right up to the high hills that are the buttresses of Deeside, is worth anybody's penetration and should be seen as the tough end of a county that has so much of trees and tenderness in its levels. Barrie, being the better technician, is read with more pleasure, but Maclaren is not easily put aside. No man pleases the myriad without some capacity for his craft, a fact overlooked by those who angrily snarl at popularity in authorship and Kailyarders in general, but it is only fair to establish a sense of proportion in judging a phase of Scottish writing which has been hammered without stint in recent years.

What is strongly resented is the presentation of the Scot as a humorous oddity, with a curious lingo that is only good for smiling at, with a dourness that is funny and a fun that is mainly sly. Pawky is the word usually selected by the English from the Scottish vocabulary and then applied mechanically to Scottish comedy. (Pawky is defined by Jamieson as ' artful,' but is often the epithet chosen to describe ingenuous humours.) I remember James Bridie passionately denouncing the continual description of his plays as being full of this pawkyness by the English critics. The label has stuck and I agree with Bridie that it is time we were rid of it. But, pawky or not, the Scottish drolls of the music-hall used to specialise in a presentation of their people as guffawing curios galumphing round the stage in unbelievable tartans while they songfully courted the bonnie lassies ' mang the hither.' Sir Harry Lauder's technique was beyond question; he chose airs so simple that the least musical could sing them in their bath; he had immense gusto and magnetism: he was a true ' star ' whose light blinded you to the childishness of his lyrics and the element- ary jocosities of his patter. If by Kailyardism is meant betrayal of the Scots as a race of laughable wee men at whom the English could giggle in pleasant superiority, then Lauder, prancing about in the kilt of a never-never clan and brandishing his curly cromach, was indeed the King of the Kailyard. People enjoy smiling in a patronising way at the oddity of animals in Zoos, an attitude repulsive to me. The Kailyard at its worst gave just this Zoo-status to the Scot.

I have enjoyed Lauder's melodies as much as most and have surrendered to his star-quality on many an occasion, even when he turned sentimentally ethical and bade us

' Keep right on to the end of the road.' But as a Scot I could hardly appreciate his incessant portrayal of my fellow-nationals as a band of incurable gloaming-roamers, non-stop tickling Jocks, ' wee-hoose mang the hither ' dwellers, chortling pursuers of the ladies in Tobermory, and ' saftest of the family ' dim-wits. Bridie once observed that the Scot had a remarkably wide range of terms for the fools of the family:

> ' In any railway carriage he can mark his fellow passengers as gaucie, menseful, forfochen, couthie, perjink, cappernoytit, fusionless, dour or douce. It is interesting to reflect what a large proportion of this vocabulary describes character in which mental defect is a prominent feature. The Scots conversation is full of thowless, bloutering nyaffs; of feckless, donnart, doited, havering gowks; of daft, glaikit, foutering taupies, of snuitit gomerals.'

The comedians give us plenty of these last. But the Scots comedians when they stay at home work with homely jest; they do not exploit in Pantomime or Summer Show the kilted absurdity so dear to the English. They draw on the stuff of Scottish town-life in the manner of the English music-hall ' funsters '—to use a term now fashionable on music-hall programmes. They broaden the authentic, of course, but they do not debase.

Admittedly the jester's eternal business everywhere is to make fun of his own: the English hold their own street-corner types up to ridicule, but the Kailyard comics were deliberately going out of their way to create, for alien consumption, a vision of the quaint, wee mannie that was comparable, in its falsity to Scotland, with the ' giftie ' gew-gaws and tartan-garish photo-frames (imported very often from Switzerland) which are still hawked as tourists' delight. Whatever denunciations may be hurled at the Bonnie Brier Bushes and Lilac Sunbonnets of the story-tellers, the latter were not in this line of business. One may question the authenticity of Maclaren's farm-yard philosophers and his omission of the seamy side of rustic morals, but he never turned his folk into contemptible caricatures. His imagined Drumtochty in Perthshire bears at least some relation to the real Drumtochty of the Mearns; it is not a fantasy in garish hues, like the strutting, hoch-ayeing, chortling comics in kilts.

If Harry Gordon or any comparable star is at the Beach Pavilion in Aberdeen, when the visitor is there, he is well worth attention. The matter and patter of the drolls who are favourites in their own country is well-rubbed, familiar stuff and I would not put them above their English parallels. But they are not caricaturists, dressing up a bogus Caledonia in clothes it never wore and offering a mixture of guffawing McKays for whom the Highlands are only an innocent cuddling-ground with the bonnie lasses laid on in droves. I grant that the Scots are nowadays apt to be over-sensitive about this sort of thing; but the protest against 'Lauderism' and the abuse of it by others had to be made. The music-hall Kailyard was the most tiresome of all the 'quaint Scot' forms of nonsense: it did not cease to be nonsense when it was glorified with the infectious genius of a Lauder whose skill in projection of the wee hoose and wee wifie sentiment was beyond question.

But we can leave the 'wee hoose,' as presented in the Palace of Varieties, for the genuine article as visible every-where in Angus and the Mearns. One author, in particular, who knew that kind of building from within, has left his record of it, with 'the wind ablow on ungarmented floors, ploughmen in sodden bothies on the farms out-bye, old, bent, and wrinkled people who have mislaid so much of fun and hope and high endeavour in grey servitude to those rigs curling away, only half-inanimate, into the night.' He knew the other side of the medallion too, the decencies and kindliness interlaced with the harshness and lecheries of the crofters' way of life. And he gave the whole picture, with passion, but with proportion. He knew best, from boyhood experience, the farms of the Mearns uplands, west of Stonehaven, a gruelling land to farm for men of no capital and with few machines, but none the less endeared by its beauty to those who had suffered its buffets of weather and denials of fertility.

I have already mentioned Lewis Grassic Gibbon's trilogy ' The Scots Quair.' Gibbon's real name was J. Leslie Mitchell and he had written many books, especially about Egypt, the Near East, and the development and decay of early civilisations. He had been excited not only by the frequency of Standing Stones and other traces of Archaic Man in his own country but by his experiences in the Near East, where he went as a young clerk in the Army and Air Force. When he settled down to write about his own Scotland, especially the North East, he chose another label. (His mother's name was Gibbon.) He also found a new and larger talent. His memories and imaginings of the Mearns, recollected in London, came flowing out in a vivid, musical prose that at first may strike the reader as affected, but soon seems to suit not only the rhythms of the local ' speak ' but the lines of the country that rolls down from the Grampians to the cliffs and the sea. Neil Gunn has said that in Gibbon's prose you can hear the earth speak: yes, and the cry of the peesies (peewits) in the wind, the teuchats (wood-pigeons) in the trees, and the clatter of the harvesting on the grudging red earth of the hillside crofts.

When he wrote of small farms and small farmers he knew

what he was talking about in a way that Ian Maclaren and Barrie did not. He was born on a farm in Central Aberdeenshire, at Hill of Seggat, Auchterless, but his father had to move south to the Mearns and took a croft near Drumlithie in the Mearns. The boy showed rare promise, went to Mackie Academy in Stonehaven, and thence moved on very early into journalism in Aberdeen and Glasgow. The amount of reading that he crammed into his short life (he died in 1935 at the age of 34) was prodigious. I suppose that he must be counted as another of those casualties of the curriculum and the hard way. Some of his archæology may have been superficial: when he took to writing he dashed into print, working fast and hard. But it is not as Mitchell that he will chiefly be remembered, but as Lewis Grassic Gibbon, of the Scots Quair. This is available with its three books in one volume. It is essential reading for those who pass by the scattered crofts of Aberdeenshire and the Mearns and are curious about their history and their inhabitants. When he drove into the heart of Kailyard life, in a far from Kailyard manner, he did so with authority. He had lived in it, shivered in its winters and sweated in its summers, loathed the bitterness of its battle with reluctant soil, and yet could feel the pride of the peasant in the little victories of grit and grind. Little, that is, in profit, but very large in cost of effort and in pride of result.

There are three stories in the Quair. In the first ' Sunset Song,' the general theme is the passing of the small farmers at the beginning of this century, men working with hand and horse, independent and only dimly aware of the great and changing world beyond. The personal theme is the story of Guthrie, the Aberdeenshire crofter settling down at Blawearie, by Kinraddie, in the Mearns. He is a grim man and a hard father. The heroine is his daughter Chris, a girl who could have been a scholar but who married first a farmer who became a war-victim and then a young Minister who had fought in the 1914-18 war and came back with a vein of Socialism, and a Faith that was far broader than that of the old Kirk; no bumbling of evasive sermons for him.

The second story, 'Cloud Howe,' takes the action to a grubby Mearns mill-town, Seggat, where the young Minister had his next pulpit and carried on his new kind of gospelling; he wore himself out and died. Chris, with her son by her first marriage, a lad with a fire in his heart, moves into the town of Duncairn. The third tale is called 'Grey Granite' and the town has certainly a close resemblance to Aberdeen, though the identity is denied. The boy is swept into social rebellion and Chris, after yet another marriage, goes back to the land. If this be the least successful of the episodes, it none the less contains some wonderful etchings of smoke and stone and of the clang and stir of Scottish city life.

That outline is merely utilitarian: it gives no impression of the rich character of the Mearns crofters and weavers in the narrative or of the breath-taking descriptions of the seasons as they pass over the places of conflict, conflict of man with earth and of man with man. There is coarseness in it, the coarseness of hard-driven men working in a hard climate on ungenerous soil, whose release is an occasional hard revel and the satisfaction of the body's desire. Old Guthrie, sharp of temper, steely of discipline, sadistic, lustful and over-bearing, the victim of his poverty and strain, would not get entrance to a Kailyard story: on the other hand his daughter Chris is a character of high spirit and fine quality; so is her second husband, the Minister. Gibbon held the balance between the sentimental pastoral and the realism of the muck-yard and the slum, which can signally fail to be realistic if it leaves out man's original virtue while it revels in his original sin.

Gibbon was not a balanced man in all things; his politics were a young man's fancy of the Left and his portrayal of the rich could be farcical. But he could take a poised view of the life upon the land; he knew it before he left it. His hands had been blistered with the hoe before he turned he had carted the stuff. He knew the drudgery in the sting them to the typewriter. He did not theorise about manure; of the wind, the lash of the rain that whips a man rawly to the bone. Here is one of his moods, taken from an article on ' The Land ' in a volume called ' Scottish Scene,' in which Hugh MacDiarmid the poet collaborated:

> ' . . . when I read or hear our new leaders and their plans for making of Scotland a great peasant nation, a land of little farms, and little farming communities, I am moved to a bored disgust with those pseudo-literary romantics playing with politics, those refugees from warm parlours and lights and policemen and theatre-stalls of the Scots cities. They are promising the New Scotland a purgatory that would decimate it. They are promising it narrowness and bitterness and heart-breaking toil in one of the most unkindly agricultural lands in the world. They are promising to make of a young, ricketic man, with the phthisis of Glasgow in his throat, a bewildered labourer in pelting rains and the flares of head-aching suns, they are promising him years of a murderous monotony, poverty and struggle and loss of happy human relationships. They promise that of which they know nothing, except through sipping of the scum of Kailyard romance.'

The poor Kailyarders have to be dragged in. They always

are. But there is the reverse of it; earlier in the same article Gibbon had written:

'I like to remember I am of peasant rearing and peasant stock. Good manners prevail on me not to insist on the fact over-much, not to boast in the company of those who come from manses and slums and castles and villas, the folk of the proletariat, the bigger and lesser bourgeoisies. But I am again and again, as I hear them talk of their origins and beginnings and begetters, conscious of an overweening pride that mine was thus and so, that the land was so closely and intimately mine (my mother used to hap me in a plaid in harvest-time and leave me in the lee of a stook while she harvested) that I feel of a strange and antique age in the company and converse of my adult peers—like an adult himself listening to the bright sayings and laughters of callow boys, parvenus on the human scene, while I, a good Venriconian Pict, hearken from the shade of my sun circle and look away, bored, in pride of possession at my terraced crops, at the on-ding of rain and snow across my leavened fields . . .'

Again he wrote of the ploughmen and the peasants:

'They endure a life of mean and bitter poverty, an order sneered upon by the little folk of the towns, their gait is a mockery in city streets, you see little waitresses stare haughtily at their great red, sun-creased hands, plump professors in spectacles and pimples enunciate theses on their mortality and morality, their habits of breeding and their shiftlessness—and they endure it all! They endure the chatter of the city salons, the plannings of this and that war and blockade, they endure the pretensions of every social class but their own to be the

mainspring and base of human society—they, the
masters, who feed the world! '

That states a conflict continually obvious to any spectator
of Scottish life. In the industrial South the squalor created
by the Age of Anyhow during the scramble of the Industrial
Revolution horrifies me the more because of its close
contrast with the splendour of the landscape near by. Loch
Lomond, for example, is only a bus-ride from Glasgow.
So the natural reaction is one of intense surprise that any
man in his senses should leave the straths and the isles to
be immured in the grey hell of ungardened tenements. But
the men and women who have gone out on sleety dawns to
milk and have come back from the fields with frozen fingers
in the sodden dark to long nights of loneliness can hardly
be blamed for thinking fondly of a town lit up, with pubs
and cinemas adjacent.

But my primary subject, my title-theme, is the summer
and you will see the variety as well as the beauty of Scotland
in hue when you seek out the Kinraddies and Blawearies
in their high season of sunlight or stand by the grave of
the author I have quoted in the kirkyard at Arbuthnott.
Better still, for those who would soak themselves in the
colour of the country, is to take one of the many glens that
wind up from Angus and the Mearns, up Glen Esk to
Tarfside or up Glen Clova to Milton and Glendoll.

They lead into a purple wilderness which is not so desolate
as to depress and which is not just another melancholy
aspect of the Dead Vast. The Ancient Mariners, who came
up from the Mediterranean and left in their long journeying
from Spain to Scandinavia their similar, abiding traces, the
hillside terraced for cultivation, the great stone-graves in
the barrows, the Stones in circle or perched in single
solitude, made their abundant mark on this land. They

haunted Gibbon's imagination; he idealised the great adventure of their wandering architects in stone, saw them as carefree and peaceable, unvexed by powers and sovereignties, not yoked to property and war and all the slaughterous raiding and clan-massacre that were to be the hideous habit of medieval Scotland. Perhaps he was wrong; but the sight of a Stone Circle in noble country always compels my puzzled admiration for the men who could manipulate these monsters, chose the sites with such splendour, and left their well-built lairs of rock in the barrows on commanding ridges or in a comfortable nook beside the burn. Matched with the marauding clansmen and theological persecutors and assassins of the coming centuries they must have been far from savage. The Noble Savage is a foolish and self-contradictory term; the Primitive was certainly not a savage in many parts of the world. Savagery was the state to which he sank. There was an original virtue before the discovered sin.

Below you the green land may be steaming in the summer heat and the tractors chugging in the harvest-fields, with the blue of the North Sea a distant reminder of the blessed littleness of our land. In the east of Scotland the scene changes in a score of miles; one is on cliffs that rival Cornwall's, in the emerald foison of the Howe, and away up to the pines and the ridges and the heather beyond in a half-hour or so of motoring. It is all there, the sweet-ness of the Kailyarders' Scottish Arcady, the larches and beech-woods of the sheltered slopes, the bloom of the whins on the uplands of the sheep and rabbits, and then the surge of the beginning Highlands, the pile of the Grampian mass whose lines are so kindly to the eye. It nourishes few but the whirring coveys of grouse in the occasional shelter of the heathered corries and the surrounding nakedness of rock: yet it has a comfortable quality, an amplitude, a richness that is alien to the far west. The clouds ride milkily and golden-edged over the summits on such a day: you can almost imagine a troupe of cherub-angels tumbling out of them, as in the Italian pictures. But I am becoming Kailyardish: to-morrow, maybe, there will be nothing but a swathe of mist and a tyranny of bone-searching rain.

CHAPTER VII

Royal Deeside

BECAUSE of Balmoral and the gaping crowds that it attracts during the season of royal residence, Deeside is apt to be sniffed at by the kind of very Scottish Scot whom I think of as Peevish McKnocker. He cannot see a notice of Highland Games without warning you that the whole business is a racket; he might, I admit, reasonably advise you that a sportive ceremonial, which often begins at 9 a.m. and proceeds until September dusk, is not to be taken whole. Two or three hours of attendance on the pipings and dancings, the running and the throwing, during a fine afternoon, are good entertainment; here is an ancient ritual of a genuine Highland kind. The great Braemar Gathering (the old name of the little town was Castleton of Braemar) was an annual event before Queen Victoria went to Balmoral and was not invented, as McKnocker may try to persuade us, by the Scottish Tourist Board. The Queen and Prince Consort attended the Games in 1849, just after their leasing of the old Balmoral Castle, later replaced by their own adventure in building. In 1850 there was a hillside race, up and down Craig Cheunnich, similar to those still run in the Lake District. It was won in that year by one Duncan, a royal ghillie. But he spat blood after his efforts and so did many others, as the Queen related, and this formidable exercise was discontinued, presumably at her persuasion. Are the Cumbrians, who maintain this kind of contest on their own steep fells, stronger of lung than the Caledonians?

McKnocker, in damning Games and Clan Gatherings, is apt to overlook the fact that the Highlander is a spontaneous showman, that nowhere else in Europe is there, among the males, such a natural delight in dressing-up, that the finery of the clans is indeed fine finery, and that the marching, the piping and the showing of colours may be unaffectedly enjoyed by the participants. If the inhabitants of a country have this sense of *panache*, if they like to go on parade and the visitors like to watch them, there is no ' racket ' about the business, even if a semi-professional element does tour the major Gatherings in quest of the money prizes. Those who want something less elaborate should hunt out a smaller occasion, in a village where only the locals compete. It is less of a spectacle and the cameras will not assiduously click in front of laird and lady; but it may be better, as well as more parochial, fun.

Deeside is called Royal and looks it. It has a sovereign spaciousness. Once the river has escaped from the awesome constriction of the Cairn Gorms, splashed over the Linn, passed Inverey, absorbed the Cluny, dashed under the bridge at Braemar, and won its way past Invercauld to Ballater, it runs through a Strath that is broad enough to accommodate a good road on either side of the water; the mountains here do not loom and glower oppressively, but range away, north and south, with gradual ascents to their curving summits. Lochnagar, it is true, above Balmoral, is sheer and tremendous enough to rank with the bastions of Glencoe, but there is ample breathing-space between it and the Castle. You can always open your lungs in Deeside in a way that you cannot do on a cloudy day in the narrow and confining canyons of the western void. There are long views available as well as a tonic aeration of the scene.

It is one of the disadvantages of the more savage Highland country that one may feel distressingly cramped in a sunless slit among the abrupt menace of over-hanging peaks; some strangers have a sense of suffocation, as though they were more the prisoners than the monarchs of the glen. But Deeside is a land of liberation. By the time the river has reached spacious Aboyne on its eastward course, the view is of a mingled landscape, with pasture and arable, green and gold, to relieve the long blaze of September purple on the hills. It is this diversity of hue and pattern that distinguishes the Eastern Highlands from the Western.

Thus I find the coloured chequer-board of Deeside a very comfortable prospect. Aberdeenshire does not bully you with a frightening beauty or stab the senses with sharp pinnacles: instead, it soothes you with the suavity of its line and tint. The bad weather from the West may be caught and checked on the Central Highlands so that the sunlight can freely warm you and paint the valley with delight: the air is thus keen only a few miles from the massing of the stuffy, murky mist around the summits.

> *Of all that is most beauteous—imaged there*
> *In happier beauty, more pellucid streams,*
> *An ampler ether, a diviner air,*
> *And fields invested with purpureal gleams.*

Wordsworth did not write thus of Banchory or Aboyne; but he might have done. Braemar has more adjacent majesty, Aboyne the ampler ether.

Queen Victoria and her Consort showed much sagacity and real sense of country when they leased the old house of Balmoral in 1848. They had been first enchanted by

157

the Highlands when entertained at Taymouth Castle by the Marquis of Breadalbane in 1842, but, despite her affection for Perthshire, the Queen chose Deeside to be her very own. Old Balmoral was no sooner leased than loved. It was bought outright in 1852 and then began the construction of the new Castle, which was ready for habitation in 1855. The work was done in the towered style deemed proper at the time. That style observed a tradition and those who think that every period must have its own architectural idiom, defying tradition and irrespective of the site, can join McKnocker in his groans about Balmoralism and bogus antiques. Doubtless that style does not suit modern needs of internal convenience, but the tower of the Victorian castle, on that superb site beside the Dee's northward bend to Crathie, need affront nobody. What, by the way, would McKnocker have had the Queen build? Functional cubic stuff? That would ill beseem the natural baroque of Lochnagar's soaring background, or the tartans and the Landseer canvases that were to decorate the walls within.

The emotions roused by Balmoral in Queen Victoria's descendants have naturally varied with their tastes and temperaments. But one thing is certain. In one long life that contained much unhappiness Balmoral was an abode of serene and supreme delight. Here, wrote Lytton Strachey, his irony disarmed, ' her happiest days passed. In after years, when she looked back on them, a kind of glory, a radiance as of an unearthly holiness, seemed to glow about these golden hours. Each hallowed moment stood out clear, beautiful, eternally significant. For, at the time, every experience there, sentimental, or grave, or trivial, had come upon her with a peculiar vividness, like a flashing of marvellous lights.' ' Leaves from our Journal of Life in the Highlands ' and the subsequent ' More

Leaves ' are necessary reading for those who visit Deeside.
These are books of complete sincerity, complete simpleness,
and, up to the death of Albert, complete felicity. There is
no doubt that Deeside continually evoked in Queen Victoria
the word of which she was so fond in her uninhibited,
unpretentious authorship, ecstasy.

There is not so much of deep and genuine rapture in
the lives of those who carry burdens that we can afford to
under-rate its value when we meet it. Deeside was something greater than a place to the Queen; it possessed her
more than she possessed it. Balmoral and its Forest, Glen
Muich and Lochnagar, the bothies, where she had so
Spartanly lodged in her ' grand expeditions,' and the peaks
which she had conquered on foot or with pony and with
John Brown for guide and support, became pieces of her
being. She had to leave it as autumn fell. London and
Prime Ministers and vexing duties called. The parting was
a laceration. The menace of the return southward always
blackened for her the end of the Balmoral vacations. ' Alas,
the last day! I wished we might be snowed up and unable
to move! ' she wrote with the grief of a child at the holiday's
end—and what torment more terrible than that of going
back to a hated school?

Deeside was not only beautiful; it had in abundance
everything that the Highland sportsman wanted, the stags,
the salmon, the grouse. Albert found the scenery agreeably
like that of Switzerland; he also acquired some proficiency
in the pursuit of game. Inevitably the royal example was
followed, the royal tastes and sentiments re-echoed. Deeside
became the centre of great houses, entertaining the eminent
with the most expensive reaches of the river and the most
coveted grouse-moors and deer-forests on the hills. The
Deeside season became the smartest season and the Braemar
Gathering and Games, royally supported, became the high

assembly of the September sports. Queen Victoria was spared the age of petrol which has turned the roadsides of the Dee into Aberdeen's back-garden and a swarming ground of motor-coaches. In these conditions I would hardly recommend the Braemar Gathering as a good occasion for butting in. But all this crowding and peering have happened without royal encouragement, not because of it. McKnocker, who so detests what he calls Balmorality, must turn his wrath against the motor-car. It is the penalty of a monarch's life that, not even in the shadow of the highest Highlands, is a total escape possible. The Royal Family cannot now cross the road on a Sunday to attend Crathie Church, where Queen Victoria had been 'much edified' and given 'lumps in the throat' by the simple eloquence of Dr. Macleod and other Scottish divines, without attracting a crowd of several thousands. It is not royalty that has created Balmorality but the eagerness of its subjects, now able to defeat distance, to be numerous, ardent and intrusive Balmoralists.

So Deeside became symbolic of the Highland Season and the more august kind of Highland holiday. From it, during the nineteenth century, the fashion for Caledonian autumns radiated outwards. After Goodwood and Cowes the southern season ended and Parliament rose. It was then unthinkable that Parliament should rise before there was something to shoot at or remain seated for a day after August 12th, when the grouse were ready for the pellets. So London decanted its wealth and fashion into Euston and King's Cross. Guns, rifles, and rods became the necessary luggage of the English gentry who had not yet taken to golf and were still leaving the cleek and the lofter to their native devotees in Fife and the Lothians.

So began a fine time for the lairds who could either be the centre of high society by their own entertaining or let their territories at such gratifying rentals to those who would a-shooting go. It was a good time, too, for those Highlanders who were ready to assist the chase in menial capacities; the tips, like the rents, ran high. It was a bad time, here and there, for the crofter, unless, of course, he turned ghillie. Once in the way of the sheep, he was now in the way of the deer, a mere nuisance with his petty agriculture in the glen and with his dog, perhaps, running loose on the hill. The game-keeper was a little monarch in his own kingdom and the great birds of prey were trapped and shot and exterminated from the crags and skies where they had soared by natural right. In the nineteen-thirties I remember seeing a deer-forest advertised for letting with an announcement of the number of stags that might be shot and also of the human beings that might be met. The former were many, the latter none. ' No crofters,' was the boasted merit of the place. The ever-growing wealth of the towns poured money into the laps of the land-owners and the servants who provided the brief, fashionable pleasures of the shooting season. After October, when the remaining stags set about the breeding of new targets and the gentry departed for their battues of the Home County pheasants, there was desolation in the glen. This was not so true of Deeside which had a more settled society and more agricultural life than had the forests of the northern wastes. There, as I have said, the sheep had eaten the men and now the deer began to devour the remainder.

Yet the deer-stalker was not to be dismissed as a sybarite. If he really took his ploy in earnest, he had to use muscles and wits to the uttermost, climbing, crouching, crawling in deep, fly-infested heather or exposed to a sudden onslaught of mountain rain. It had not always been so. The traditional chase of the Highlands was a round-up with a massacre to follow. The object was to fill the larder and keep down the deer by the easiest possible means. Strenuous knee-work or stomach-crawling on the summits (with a fair chance for the stag) was not to the taste of the ancient lairds who mingled easy slaughter with generous feasting and drinking. Sport, in the sense of pitting man's wits, skill, courage, and endurance against similar qualities in beasts of the field, scarcely existed for the seventeenth-century chieftain. John Taylor, the London 'water-poet,' has left his 'true Report of the unmatchable hunting in the Brea of Marre and Badenoch in Scotland,' printed 'at the charges of the Author, 1618.' In that year this comrade of Ben Jonson's 'travailed on foot from London to Edenborough in Scotland, not carrying any money to and fro, neither Begging, Borrowing, or Asking Meate, drinke, or lodging.' How then did he manage? This self-reliant voyager had a 'gelded nag' to carry his own 'provant' (victuals), but he certainly seems to have been well entertained, particularly in Scotland. Once there, the jovial foot-slogger worked his way from Perth to Brechin and thence up Glen Esk, lodging in 'an Irish house in the Laird of Edzell's land' and there horribly bitten by 'Irish musquitoes, which have six legs' and, according to Taylor, perform the offices and share the appetite of the louse.

Luckily there was better to come. He entered Mar (as we spell it), 'a large county, all composed of such mountains, that Shooter's Hill, Gad's Hill, Highgate Hill, Hampstead Hill, Birdlip Hill, or Malvern's Hills, are but mole-hills in comparison, or like a liver, or a gizard, under a capon's wing, in respect of the altitude of their tops, or perpendicularity of their bottoms. There I saw Mount Ben Aven, with a furred mist upon his snowy head instead of a night-cap.' Here, too, he met an assembly of Scottish nobles, with hundreds of their knights, esquires, and followers 'all and every man in general in one habit, as if Lycurgus had been

there and made laws of equality.' They wore tartan stockings
and jerkins, with a plaid ' of divers colours ' about their
shoulders and blue, flat caps. They carried long bows and
forked arrows, swords and targets, harquebusses, muskets,
dirks, and Lochaber axes. Lord Erskine, Earl of Mar, took
Taylor to the cottage which was his shooting-lodge, where
were ' many kettles and pots boiling, and many spits turning
and winding, with great variety of cheer: as venison baked,
sodden, roast, and stewed beef, mutton, goats, kid, hares,
fresh salmon, pigeons, hens, capons, chickens, partridge,
moor-coots, heath-cocks, capercailzies, and termagants
(ptarmigans); good ale, sack, white, and claret, tent (or
Alicante) with most potent Aquivitae.'

With this encouraging background, the manner of the
chase was as follows. Five or six hundred men went out
to drive the deer from the Cairn Gorms and surrounding
mountains in huge herds; while their lords, including their
guest Taylor, went and lay down in a valley. ' Then, after
we had stayed there three hours or thereabouts, we might
perceive the deer appear on the hills round about us (their
heads making a show like a wood), which being followed
close by the Tinchel (the beaters), are chased down into the
valley where we lay; then all the valley on each side being
waylaid with a hundred couple of strong Irish greyhounds,
they are let loose as the occasion serves upon the herd of
deer, so that with dogs, guns, arrows, dirks, and daggers,
in the space of two hours, fourscore fat deer were slain,
which after are disposed of, some one way, and some
another, twenty and thirty miles, and more than enough
left for us to make merry withal at our rendezvous. I liked
the sport so well, that I made these two sonnets following.'

The deer-stalker of to-day would hardly call that sport;
Taylor's sonnets paid no respect to the unfortunate prey,

but were the pronouncements of a jolly butcher and a sated trencherman. I must relate, he wrote:

> *How thousand gallant spirits came near and far,*
> *With swords and targets, arrows, bows, and guns,*
> *That all the troop too men of judgment are,*
> *The God of War's great never conquered sons;*
> *The sport is manly, yet none bleed but beasts,*
> *And last the victor on the vanquished feasts.*

The second of his Braemar jubilations ends:

> *Lowland, your sports are low as is your seat,*
> *The Highland games and minds are high and great.*

Well, he had to be polite to such generous hosts, but I can see little judgment, gallantry or height of mind in this almost sedentary massacre of the driven and terrified deer.

By 1850 the Deeside shooting, if we can judge by Queen Victoria's accounts of Prince Albert's adventures with the gun, was both more exacting and more humane. It was not heavily organised: sometimes the Prince would just carry a rifle or a shot-gun while his party made picnic. Occasionally he stalked, but he described that exercise as 'one of the most fatiguing as it is also one of the most interesting of pursuits.' Sometimes deer were driven to him, in which case the peaceful arts could be practised during the waits. On September 18, 1848, there was an excursion to the Balloch Buie forest, which lies south-west of Balmoral. Of this the Queen wrote:

> 'We scrambled up an almost perpendicular place to where there was a little *box*, made of hurdles and interwoven with branches of fir and heather, about five feet in height. There we seated ourselves with Bertie, Macdonald lying in the heather near us, watching and

quite concealed; some had gone round to beat, and others again were at a little distance. We sat quite still, and sketched a little; I doing the landscape and some trees, Albert drawing Macdonald as he lay there. This lasted for nearly an hour, when Albert fancied he heard a distant sound, and, in a few minutes, Macdonald whispered that he saw stags, and that Albert should wait and take a steady aim. We then heard them coming past. Albert did not look over the box, but through it, and fired through the branches, and then again over the box. The deer retreated; but Albert felt certain he had hit a stag.'

He had, killing a magnificent ' royal.' It was an easier way than the long, cautious crawl with its fatigues. It is natural to wonder what Bertie, later Edward VII, made of these outings. In 1859, at the age of eighteen, he had to climb up Ben Macdhui (4244 ft.), after slogging up Glen Derry. His mother noted, ' I and Alice rode part of the way, walking where it was very steep. Albert and Bertie walked the whole time.' It was an eleven-hour day with a lot of mist at times and very cold. The Queen described the occasion as unforgettably sublime. Perhaps Bertie would have sympathised with the groom Batterbury, of whom the Queen wrote, rather tartly, after her first ascent of Lochnagar in a hurricane and downpour, ' He followed me in his ordinary dress with thin boots and gaiters and seemed anything but happy. He hardly ever attended me after this.' Doubtless the Prince was more suitably shod than poor Batterbury, but did he relish those very athletic Deeside holidays?

Among those with no taste for, or even an active dislike of, bloodsports, deer-stalking must surely receive some measure of pardon; it imposes a severe test of endurance and skill on its practitioners and provides the quickest despatch of the prey. The death-dealing missile is the single bullet of the rifle, not a scattering of pellets. Self-respecting owners or renters of forests do not shoot, or let their guests shoot, until they have proved their accuracy at a target; the stag (or later in the year the hind) is not fired at unless there is fair certainty of an immediate kill. This means working one's way within very close range, say a hundred yards, of the deer: and since deer can scent a man a mile away if the wind is coming from his direction, this demands the utmost caution in calculating the wind, which may be a veering one, and in crawling unseen over rough, high ground towards the point where a shot may be taken. If a beast is wounded instead of killed, he is immediately followed and destroyed as soon as possible. The autumn weather in the Highlands may be very hot or very cold and, after sweating from an arduous crawl, the man with a rifle may have to wait long in a cold, wet spot and then, after all, see the stag take alarm and vanish. Here is no pleasure of the flabby or the self-indulgent; they are better served on the kind of grouse-moor where they can be driven close to the butts, there to sit until the beaters have sent the coveys rocketing over them. To hit driven grouse needs a very good eye and a very good hand, but it makes nothing like the demand upon physique and on the endurance of discomfort which is made by deer-stalking. He who gets his venison for nourishment and his antlers for display in this manner has certainly worked for them.

The Scottish red deer are not wholly wild in the way that creatures of the jungle are wild. In the years when feeding-stuffs, such as maize and sugar-beet pulp, were available the herds were helped through the hard winter by the scattering of extra nourishment in an assigned part of the forest known as the Sanctuary. The stock was improved, if possible, by shooting the less powerful and less richly antlered specimens first. In any case, something has got to be done about the deer of the Highlands if they are not to breed too rapidly; high fencing, which is now very expensive, may effectively bar them from over-running the cultivated land and gardens in winter when the 'feed' on the moors becomes very poor. But if excessive numbers are left fenced in on high ground where their natural food-stuff, such as cotton-grass and deer-hair, is limited, some, perhaps many, will die of hunger and disease before the spring. In these years of limited meat supply, venison can be a very useful addition to the larder and the high prices now obtained for it can be set against the heavy cost of maintaining a forest with its stalkers. That the herds should be thinned by skilful shooting with rifles involves less cruelty than leaving them with too many animals competing for too little food. Worse still would be the abandonment of private ownership and preservation of forests, since all and sundry would then claim the right to come in and blaze away with their shot-guns. Poachers, raiding a lonely island for deer or driving them into distant corries and using methods of slaughter similar to those described by John Taylor as fashionable in the Brae of Marr in 1618, are far more brutal to their prey than is any responsible sportsman of the deer-stalking kind.

The sportsman's psychology has its curious kinks. He admires, even adores, the thing he kills. He shoots off the weaker animals in order to preserve, for breeding purposes, the stronger and so to populate his mountains with stags of great weight and many-pointed antlers. The desire is for great heads, with twelve tines or more. (The record head, I have discovered, was one of sixty-six points, but that was a freakish malformation rather than a matter for pride.) Yet all this striving for an ample supply of the

167

best of beasts is linked with destruction in the end. The Monarch of the Glen exists to be dethroned and to crown with his antlers the walls of a castle or a shooting-lodge. Queen Victoria typified this mixture of affection for the animal and delight in its death. After the Prince Consort had shot a stag at Invergeldie she sat and sketched the corpse with rapture. The victim was 'a beauty,' 'a magnificent animal.' Then another, 'with a pretty head,' was killed. 'What a delightful day,' she wrote, 'but sad that it should be our last. Home by half-past six. We found that our beautiful stag had arrived and admired him much.'

The pictures of Sir Edwin Landseer were a great joy to the Queen; so was his company. A complete set of all Landseer's engravings was photographed and set in a nobly bound album after the painter's death in 1873. The Queen, wrote the creator of this volume, ' turned over the leaves of the book as I held it before her, making most interesting comments on many of the pictures. After thanking me her Majesty ordered the album to be placed in her private sitting-room at Windsor. It was afterwards taken to Balmoral where it remained till 1901, when it was removed to the Library at Windsor Castle.' We can tell from the originals what a corpse-parade this album must be. When Beerbohm Tree asked Sir Henry Irving to see his production of ' Julius Cæsar ' and questioned his great guest later as to his opinion of the Senate House scene and the murder of the Emperor, Irving is said to have replied curtly, ' Lot of blood, Tree. Lot of blood.' The Queen might well have murmured, ' Lot of blood, Sir Edwin, lot of blood.'

Landseer, in his self-portrait, with two dogs posed in rapt admiration of what the author is drawing, seems a healthy, blithe type, but his work displays a morbid predilection for the dying agonies of bird and beast and for corpses in rich piles. He gave the world a British version of the Larder School of Dutch painting, a form of art much relished by the Victorians. Here was an abiding expression of the Stag Party spirit, which kills, with a kind of reverence, the thing it loves. The savage and the sentimental commingle. He was probably even happier in the Deeside forests than in the cultural glades of St. John's Wood; success, praise and reward were his in plenty. The hotels at Braemar used to be well stocked with engravings of the famous works of this prolific hand. After occupation by the Services during the second World War, they were, of necessity, redecorated, but I wish they had not been so much stripped of their Victorian character which I had found so fascinating. On revisiting Braemar in 1951 I missed the grand parade of Landseers with their faithful ghillies, stag-laden ponies, and massed cadavers of the successful chase.

Sir Edwin was something of an infant prodigy. Born in 1802, he actually exhibited at the Royal Academy in 1815, was made A.R.A. in 1826, twenty-four being the earliest age at which this honour could be attained. He became a full R.A. in 1831. He was a particular favourite of Queen Victoria's, a guest at Balmoral in 1850 and 1851, and knighted in 1850. He went stalking with the Prince, walked more gently with the Queen, and developed, by tuition, her considerable talent for sketching from nature. He admired the way in which she personally kept the Balmoral Deer-Book, with its details of the place, the date, the stalk, and its result. Whenever a specially well-antlered head had been brought home, the Queen sat drawing it.

Landseer, when he stayed in Highland houses, as he did so often during the season, would busy himself in wet weather by adding murals to the homes of his hosts. I have seen some of these in the house beside Loch Affric; he was a masterly draughtsman, whatever modern critics may think of his work in general. But his love of the noble stag was accompanied by no less an addiction to blood and even guts. At Loch Affric I saw a room packed with Landseer engravings; all of them featured one or more corpses and some exhibited corpses in mass. The artist even found an appealing subject in the ' gralloching ' (disembowelling) of a stag by a ghillie. Gralloching is a complicated operation, since deer have three stomachs with separate functions, but it is done swiftly by the expert before the body is loaded upon a pony and removed to the larder. But I do not fancy having a full, enraptured view of the process hung over my dining-room mantelpiece.

The taste for covering the walls with trophies of the stalk and pictures of carnage and for accumulating a melancholy gallery of stuffed birds looking moodily out of glass cases has declined. The golden eagles that used to be trapped and shot are now permitted to soar over the summits, which means fewer mountain hares and the occasional loss of a lamb or a deer-calf. The eagle's worst enemy is now the collector, who will pay large sums for the eggs. On the wild life of the Cairn Gorms Seton Gordon has written with intimate knowledge and delight, while those who want to see deer-stalking through the eye of the man with a rifle have John Buchan's stories and also a particularly vivid narrative of a prolonged pursuit of an exceptional stag in Neil Gunn's ' Second Sight.' The average visitor to Deeside will never know these ardours and exertions, but they are the background of the mellow beauty of the Strath and of the great mountain-barrier at the west which separates the kingdom of the Dee from that of the Spey.

It is in that barrier that Queen Victoria had some of her happiest moments. There was the First Great Expedition, as she called it, westward from Braemar, by way of the

Geldie and the Feshie burns, across to Grantown on Speyside; this was a trek of more than forty miles and twenty of them were covered on horseback with very rough going, since the carriages called ' sociables ' could not cross this ground. The inn at Grantown gave simple fare to the travellers, who assumed the names of ' Lord and Lady Churchill and party.' One woman did everything at dinner because Grant and Brown, who were to have waited, ' were bashful and did not.' The Queen's use of the word ' bashful' interested me, because of an incident in my boyhood. My father had rented a house and shooting at Glassaugh in Banffshire and one night there was something of a party. The assistant keeper, who was known to be an exponent of the sword-dance, was asked to come upstairs and perform. But it was explained that he was ' bashful.' He had, in fact, been celebrating and was by now incapable of standing, much more so of dancing. Did the Queen signify the same of her two faithfuls who were unable to serve the mutton-broth, lamb, and cranberry tart of the occasion? It was revealed next morning that Grant and Brown had been ' very merry in the Commercial Room.' John Brown was to be pardoned a good deal of this ' bashfulness ' in later years.

Few visitors to Deeside will go over to Speyside by that rough route; there has been talk of building a road that would link the east and west by way of Glen Feshie and so set the cars and coaches pouring through the natural fortress made by the Cairn Gorms on the north and the Ben Uarn mass on the south. At present it is only possible for road-travellers to get from Braemar to Grantown and from Dee to Spey by turning east to Ballater and then making a vast detour to the north by way of Tomintoul or by making an even lengthier journey south over the Devil's Elbow and so by way of Kirkmichael and Pitlochry on to the Inverness Road. Thus Grantown would at last be reached by way of Aviemore. I hope that Glen Feshie will be left alone. Surely in our small island we should leave a few places unapproachable by machinery and reserved for those who will combat nature in the old, hard way. Such a spot is the watershed between the Dee and Spey, ' the scene of all Landseer's glory ' as Queen Victoria described it. The road from Aberdeen to Braemar is as good as any in the Highlands and is extremely hard worked and much enjoyed in the summer. It may reasonably stop at the latter or at least bow in defeat to the mountains when it reaches the Linn of Dee.

CHAPTER VIII

Bed and Board

SO far we have been mainly on the fringes of Scotland. It is time for a look inside, and a drive at the centre. My first, boyhood acquaintance with Scotland, as I have explained, was in the mixed, north-easterly country by the Deveron and the Moray Firth. Discovery of the Highlands came later.

I had been flattered with the suggestion that I had read too much and too long. Pitlochry was to confer upon the over-studious student, sicklied o'er with the pale cast of classic concentration, or possibly by too much Eights' Week, its tonic air and a society which—so I inferred— would be amicably Philistine and genially uncultural. This would relieve of me academic burdens and examination fret. The end was achieved. The sun continually blazed. I had brought some Meredith with me, but soon abandoned Richard Feverel's ordeal for complete vacancy of mind and ease of body. One can be blissfully unintellectual in a surfeit of exercise, victuals, sunshine, and scenery.

This is not to imply that Pitlochry is a sensual sty or a pasture of the low-browed cattle only. Did not Robert Louis Stevenson, staying awhile and writing on the hill above it, find it a ' sweet spot '? Moreover Pitlochry now contains ' Scotland's Summer Theatre Among the Hills ' and in May, 1951, began to regale its residents and

173

numerous visitors with ' Macbeth ' (with the camouflage branches actually plucked in Birnam's neighbouring wood) and with works of varying type and quality by new Scottish authors as well as by Bridie and Barrie. The playhouse itself had to be made of canvas and timber; no permits were granted for a substantial structure. Even the Scandinavians, who specialise in gay pavilions, could not have made a more handsome job of it than did John Stewart, late of the Glasgow Park Theatre, who devotes to the arts the energy and resources which other Scotsmen of like wealth expend upon their sports. Like Norval, in the Grampians he feeds his flock, not with Bard and Bridie only, but with a service of varied catering very different from that usually to be encountered in the grubby bars and foyers of the ordinary theatre.

Pitlochry is largely a Victorian creation with grey-stone, well-gardened villas that rise in tiers of quiet domesticity on the steep hillside above the broad, brown, rapid Tummel. It owed much to the arrival of the Highland Railway, that gallant construction which carved its way from Perth into the heart of Drumochter's lofty wilderness and then swept down to Inverness, providing a journey of continuous and notable beauty in its progress from grass and woodland to heathery desolation and down into the green again. Beside it runs the great central road which surmounts the lofty gap in the Grampians and, like the railway, rises to a height of nearly 1200 ft. at Dalnaspidal and grim Loch Ericht. Here in Pitlochry is the central point of Scotland's central area and roads run left and right as well as up and down. Westward lie Loch Tummel and Kinloch Rannoch and the song-famous road to the isles; Aberfeldy beckons too, and the road to Glen Lyon, a narrow and macabre defile. Here, too, is the road to slim and silvery Loch Tay, and so to Killin, Crianlarich and Oban.

Eastward a less romantic, but no less enchanting journey, awaits the motorist who works over the flank of Ben-y-Vrackie, past Stevenson's high-pitched Moulin, to Kirkmichael and so either south-eastward to Blairgowrie or northward to the Spital of Glenshee and then upwards, tortuously, tenaciously, upwards to the Devil's Elbow, with its ferocious hair-pin bend below the summit, and so down to Braemar and Deeside.

As a motoring centre Pitlochry is unparalleled. Usually in the Highlands there is one road running each way from your base; but at Pitlochry you can turn in all directions and arrange a whole series of circuitous returns. Whichever way you go it is a good way, with splendour after splendour of loch and crest.

But the motoring holiday had scarcely began when I went to the Atholl Hydro at Pitlochry. Where one slept, one stayed; one walked, played games, surveyed the scene, ate and slept abundantly. No gleaming rank of cars stood waiting after breakfast to carry their owners on a 200 mile traverse of central Scotland and whisk them back for dinner. Before the dash-about habits of the petrol age the senior residents and visitors strolled in the woods or practised toxophily. The juniors, disdaining gentle dalliance with bow and arrow, climbed the hills or played golf or lawn-tennis. Their car-owning successors have gained enormously in the range of a Highland holiday and probably lost something in physical benefit.

Now, forty years on, I write under the roof that sheltered me first. It was then the Atholl Hydro; it is now the Atholl Palace Hotel. I do not much care for palatial entitlement of Highland hotels, but the Atholl has sloughed off austerity with discretion and you can be athletic there from golfing morn to after-tea tennis and so on to reeling midnight in the ballroom. Its history has interest, since it is an epitome of Scottish hotel-building and administration.

The old type of Scottish Hydropathic Institution was a curious child of Health and Ethics; it must have been invented, one thought, on the Sabbath Day. It provided an elaborate outfit of baths, pine, needle, spray, and plunge; indeed it was water, water everywhere, since no alcohol was sold. You could import and secrete the latter and even, as austerity dwindled, display your bottle brazenly in the dining-room, being elsewhere provided with a locker for its safe keeping. The sterner Hydros were lockerless, since they would not countenance the wickedness of absorption in any form, but the Atholl was already on the primrose path when I arrived to pursue my mental vacancy.

The Hydropathic Establishment, to give it its full, august title, was a Scottish Victorian invention. It began as a centre of therapy; but soon there was no need to be an invalid in order to qualify for admission. But, if you need not be sick, you had to be good. The Hydropathic, still un-abbreviated to Hydro, became the resort of the new middle-class enriched by the development of Scotland's industrial belt; they wanted a nice, quiet holiday where they could maintain the respectability and decorum achieved in their prosperous and proper suburbs. The Ministers of religion, who could then afford to spend their holidays in good circumstance, were strong patrons of the Hydropathic. They shaped its discipline of temperance and piety. They blessed its ample meals. They led its offerings of prayer.

J. J. Bell, creator of 'Wee McGreegor' (Urban kailyard, I suppose, the angry young Scot would call it now) has left a graphic picture of a Hydropathic holiday in the 1880's. The manager wore a black surtout. The meals were served at long tables; one had to mix with one's fellows and make the necessary genteel conversation. There was a fine, full breakfast followed by a fine, full midday dinner. There was a good plain tea at half-past five, with scones and cookies and ' fancy bread ' abounding. Those who had just arrived, and had missed their dinner, had to be given value for money and so got eggs to their tea or cold meat. At half-past nine a service of milk, bread, butter, and cheese was laid on in the dining-room. Those late for meals were confronted by a money-box into which, for charity's benefit, they paid one penny per (unpunctual) person, thus atoning for sin. There was always grace before meat and at 9.45 prayers in the drawing-room. At ten o' clock or so one withdrew, possibly hoping for a nice read in bed. Vain expectation unless you had brought your own candles! The lights were officially turned off at 10.30.

Smoking was permitted only in the smoking-room, a den discreetly hidden. The drawing-room was the centre of society: it contained a grand piano, locked on Sundays, and a small pipe-organ used for hymns. There was also the Recreation Room; it was there that the rot set in and gaiety began to raise its naughty head. Bell remembered it thus:

' The Recreation Room, which would make a splendid ball-room, has a piano that once was grand, and upon its willing notes a lady " of uncertain age " is performing " The Irresistible Quadrilles," which begin with " A frog he would a wooing go," while no less than eight persons, none older than forty, are gliding through " figure 4." This quadrille business, as many excellent Hydropathists will tell you, is just the thin end of the wedge. In ten years it will be the Polka, and after that the wicked Waltz. What are Hydropathics coming to? Bless their good old-fashioned souls! Well for them that they cannot peep into the future—Hydropathics becoming licensed hotels and subsisting on frivolity! '

The downward glide duly occurred. Before long the Demon Drink had sneaked in at the back door. It was not, of course, stored and sold on the spot; it was sent for. But the runners who supposedly darted to the village and returned from licensed premises with the ordered bottle were sometimes suspiciously rapid sprinters. In Hydropathics, already sliding into more popular status as Hydros —as with Christian names, abbreviation spoke for cordiality —there could be no licence to retail alcohol. But what had been elsewhere, and so swiftly, obtained, could be discreetly retained. The manager in the frock-coat arranged for lockers and keys and there the weaker vessels secreted their own vessels of consolation.

At Pitlochry's Atholl Palace you can still see the stigmata of degeneration, the marks of compromise with Satan. In the billiard room are sixty lockers, forgotten niches each capable of holding two bottles of whisky then purchased at the rate of 42s. a dozen for the best. In my youth Peebles was regarded as the centre of neo-hydropathic joy and still it maintains a high repute for gaiety. On its perch above the Tweed the great Hydro, whose architecture is less winsome than the scenery, invites to sports and dances and I well remember there a Hostess who was fair as a blanched almond and had as much silvery allure as Francis Day herself. What would J. J. Bell's coevals have thought of such a pagan goddess? At the Peebles establishment I have refreshed myself in the Bruce Bar wherein one could mix the consumption of liquor with the contemplation of slaughter. All round the room were most realistic mural paintings of red-headed Scots slashing the English with their claymores at Bannockburn or some other Caledonian triumph. Blood flowed like gin. The many English, who were partaking of the latter, viewed the former undismayed and even unconcerned.

So the Hydropathic became the Hydro and then the Hydro Hotel, even, last step of all, the Hotel, the Luxury Hotel, the Palace. Comfortable beds were installed. Lights were left on for use all night. Graces and prayers were forgotten as the worldly diners settled down to their separate tables. Dancing was encouraged and organised. Hostesses sought out the lonely or the shy and inveigled them to accept introductions, to dance a fox-trot, and to be instructed in the reel. Sunday was made endurable for non-Sabbatarians. Pitlochry's other Hydro became the Hydro Hotel and installed a Cocktail Bar.

The history of the Atholl Palace exemplifies the way of the world. The building of it began in 1874; superbly sited on a sizeable knoll facing Ben-y-Vrackie, it was to be the forerunner of Gleneagles Hotel, the ace-Hydro of the Highlands, serving the grave partakers of an innocent holiday with the biggest and best in its serious, hygienic, economical kind. It was built, massively, of local stone; its landscape gardening was masterly: a rough hill was turned into a throne for summer sessions of the tourist, with forty-six acres of ' policies ' (Scottish for wooded grounds) and trees of every description. It had many financial ups-and-downs. When I was first there, the manager still, I think, wore a frock-coat. But the lockers were in use. The dancing had embraced the sensuous waltz. Sunday was severe, but there was a general admission that those who had come to rest or refresh their bodies need not worry too much about their souls. Shortly after that there was a complete change of management. Luxury, even the Continent, entered in.

' The Company have engaged a Continental Manager well known to the visitors at the Hotel des Alpes, Murren. . . . There is no fixed hour for Breakfast. Buffet Lunch will be served at any time. . . . The Cuisine will be under the direction of a very experienced Swiss Chef from the Engadine.' That was the voice of 1914. ' There is a Hydraulic Lift. A handsome six-cylinder Napier Omnibus is provided for the service to the Railway Station and Golf Links.' ' Whaur are your prayers and porridge noo? ' the old Hydropathicals might moodily inquire. And where your three or four guineas a-week all found? And when the Continental chefs enter the kitchen, will not the full horrors of the Continental Sunday be loosed on the floors above?

To those who grumble about hotel-prices to-day it is interesting to note what the Atholl, thus glorified, was charging in 1914. Breakfast, 4s. Lunch 4s. Afternoon Tea 1s. 6d. Dinner 6s. As the pound was then worth three times what it is now, the breakfast was costing as much as 12s. in our currency with dinner at 18s.! In 1920 lunch rose to 5s. It is that to-day. Dinner was 6s. 6d. It is now 7s. 6d. The all-in weekly rates in 1920 for mid-season were seven guineas to twelve guineas according to room. The charges are now about the same. That may seem quite enough to the father of a family, but the fact remains that, if such prices are deemed high now, they were staggeringly high in 1914 and 1920. Since then we have had a Catering Wages Act. Labour charges in the hotel industry are at least four times what they were in 1920. Complaining parties should take note. Meals may have been rather longer; but they were not better, and now they are certainly healthier for being lighter. There is no need now to announce as part of the Bath Service, ' Liver Packs, 2s.'

The cult of holiday water-therapy has dwindled away. The Atholl used to offer, even in its new status of hotel, Peat Baths at 5s., Droitwich Brine Baths at 2s. 6d., and Aix Douche at 3s. 6d. as well as simpler and cheaper native dips. All these were achieved by a descent to the basement; self-indulgent folk who wanted ' Baths on Bedroom Floors ' had to pay a shilling for their comfort. Now, of course, they pay nothing for what is properly deemed a necessity. Such improvement is general.

It is absurd to generalise about Scottish Hotels. As happens everywhere, they are good if they have a good manager and bad if they have a bad one. A fool in charge can ruin the quality and reputation of an hotel in a few months. With prudence and tact in command, a house with a bad name can be quickly rescued, but the upward course takes longer than the downward. Those who do not like, or cannot afford, the sumptuous can usually find a more homely place. Close to Pitlochry, for example, is the French-looking, chalet-style hotel at Moulin, which, however, has so many faithful friends that it is not easy to get in on a chance call.

Some of the big Scottish houses, with exquisite rooms of the eighteenth and nineteenth century styles and ' policies ' of rare beauty, are now hotels: so too are many of the huge, turreted Scottish Baronial mansions built by the old chieftains in their glory or (in imitation) by the new rich of the Victorian epoch. The latter buildings usually atone for their ugliness of structure by their beauty of situation. The shipping nabobs and iron or jute millionaires had taste, at least in the placing of their castles; in any case, in most of the Scottish straths and glens, with a swift-moving river coursing and foaming amid rocks in front and with a background of larch and fir, it was almost impossible for the builder to miss glory of outlook. Now the coach-parties roll up to enter the old kingdom of the chieftain or the lost preserves of plutocracy.

This new invasion has saved the Highland hotel-industry from the disaster which menaced it when its old patrons became the new poor. The large, comfortable motor-coaches, carrying about twenty in reasonably spacious conditions, make tours of a fortnight or three weeks from the South of England, sometimes shorter ones from the North. The travellers are for the most part elderly, tranquil people who enjoy a day of such travel followed by dinner, bed, and breakfast in a first-class hotel. Sometimes there is a two-night stop with a morning free for an exploring stroll, followed by an afternoon drive round the local beauty-spots before the next move is made. Most of Scotland can thus be visited without worry; the method appeals to tired house-wives who have no shopping to do, no queueing to endure, no rations to consider. It is the most worry-free type of holiday. The tipping is all done by the coach-managers and the total outlay is by no means heavy, since the actual transport costs far less than shifting a number of people by train with the deterrent fares now charged on the railways.

I had thought that it was a passing phase of taste. When the travellers had done it once, would they come again? The answer is that they do. There are varieties of routes to appeal to them. You can see Scotland three times over without much repetition of road. There is also the reunion of fellow-coachers. Lonely people who have made friends on one tour gather together again for another next year. To be thus boxed up for a fortnight with the same company, facing each morning a seven-hour day of torpid landscape-viewing, would be torment to me. But then I am unsocial and a fidget. Very large numbers of people who can afford to spend from two to three pounds a day for a couple of weeks on a holiday of this sort enjoy it enormously.

The hotel-owners enjoy it too. For here are safe, steady bookings which conveniently run through from the end of May to the middle of September. The plague of the Scottish holiday-season is its brevity. July, August, a week or two of September—it is little enough in which to pay the ' overheads ' of a year. Hotels open from April to October have to pay rents, rates, taxes, and upkeep cost through the twelve months. Those who used to patronise the sumptuous hotels have sadly diminished incomes; at their best, they were rather wayward and unsatisfactory customers, all wanting to come at the same time, and often leaving their booking till very late and then possibly discovering that they could not come at all and making last-minute cancellations. What all tradesmen like is the constant and punctual customer and the motor-coaches give the hotel this kind of security. They book well in advance. Their payments are substantial and their cheques do not bounce. The travellers are meek and well-behaved.

At first the major hotels were somewhat aghast at the prospect of Coach Parties. Might not they be full of rough and roystering men in cloth caps, brandishing bottles of Bass and singing ' I've got a luvverly bunch of coker-nuts ' or whatever was, is, or will be the folk-song of the moment? Of course nothing of the sort appeared, only very quiet groups of the new well-to-do or of the recently well-to-do engaged in ' blowing ' another fifty pounds of dwindling capital and determined to see Scotland before they are completely immobilised by poverty. One good service rendered by the Coachers is the breaking-down of ' dressiness.' It is a strange fact that Londoners who do not often parade their gladdest attire in the evening at home will suddenly, in a liner on mid-ocean or in a hotel in mid-Highlands, insist on becoming tailor's dummies and run up huge laundry bills for stiff shirts. It embarrasses those who have not brought their best dresses and finest linen. This tiresome ' snob ' side of the Highland hotel-life has been much diminished by the coach-parties who do not want to burden themselves with a lot of luggage and I thank them for it. In the long and exquisite summer evenings it is ridiculous to be hampered by your clothes from taking a late stroll.

The other prop of the hotels is the Business Conference. These affairs are conveniently arranged for the beginning and end of the season, when ordinary clients are few. Their solid bookings in May and at the end of September make all the difference to the balance-sheet. If a hundred and fifty tycoons of the Neo-plastic Industry arrive (with liberal expenses paid by their firms) there will be not only the usual charges for ample board, but parties, Gala Nights, Sports Competitions, and all the activities which go to the promotion of the good thirst that is killed by costly kindness and the care-free opening of purses. Not all Conferences are equally convivial; I shall not betray the names of those renowned for carousing most and conferring least.

In the morning, as a rule, the ballroom is set out with chairs for solemn occasions in which, no doubt, a paper will be read on the latest development in this or that phase of the industry or a discussion held on the folly of retailers —unless it is a retailers' rally, in which case the folly of wholesalers and manufacturers will be the theme. This is followed by discussion, followed by refreshment, followed by lunch, and then by golf, tennis, or motoring, and followed at last by the Gala Dinner with dancing under or amid such etceteras as paper-hats and balloons. This will be followed by friendly gatherings at which there is agreement with Shakespeare's Sir Toby that ' to go to bed at midnight is to be up be-times.' The Conferrers and their ladies are apt to sport ' full fig ' at nights, especially on Gala Nights, with white ties, long dresses, and all things handsome about them. They arrive with cars luggage-packed. But as I said, the Coach Parties, should they be there at the same time, restore the balance and do not so bedizen themselves that it is impossible to benefit by a nocturnal walk in the near-midnight sun of a Scottish June.

The Business Conference can be a rather elaborate and boring piece of pretence as far as the official sessions go. I myself shun Conferences of all kinds: they tend to be a Bores' Carnival and occasions for exhibitionism by those who think they are undervalued and overlooked and are itching to get their word in. If I agree with the resolution before the meeting I have no desire to sit for hours on a hard chair listening to platitudinous orations in support of it: least of all would I want to do so on a bright day in one of the better parts of Scotland. However, each to his taste. The informal meetings, private discussions, and ' contacts ' thus obtained can be very useful; a good time may be had by all less fidgety than my self and certainly bad times are averted by the management and shareholders of the hotel.

The anti-Kailyarders and more prickly Nationalists will grumble that the hotels put a bogus Scotland for sale. The fetching of local pipers and the serving of frozen venison out of season is the kind of service to strangers which they do not like. But the strangers like such things very much; they think that they are being cheated if they do not get ' atmosphere.' And to be summoned to the ballroom by a kilted piper is a piece of *panache* which they greatly favour. There may be a menu with Gaelic attachments instead of that preposterous hotel-French which writes ' New Potatoes à la Menthe.' Here is one such bill of fare and it sounds a very good one to me:

DINNER

BROCHAN BUNTATA AGUS UNNAN
(Scotch Leek and Potato Soup)

BRADAN BRUICH
(Boiled Tay Salmon, Sauce Hollandaise)

MARAG, SNÈP PRON
(Haggis, Mashed Turnip)

CEARC BRUICH
(Boiled Chicken Suprême)

FIADH RÓSD
(Roast Venison, Redcurrant Jelly)

BUNTATA RÓSD AGUS BRUICH
(Roast and Creamed Potatoes)

PESSAR BRUICH
(French Beans)

DEARCAN AGUS BÁR
(Raspberry Melba)

SPOINSE AGUS BÁR
(Scotch Trifle)

ARAN AGUS UBH
(Scotch Woodcock)

Kailyard books were very much loved by overseas Scots and such people, returning, are the first, as I have noticed, to welcome the Gaelicised menu. They were asking the chef to sign the one which I have printed. Fortunately the chef was a Scottish cook and not a distinguished *Maître de Cuisine* imported from Murren or Le Touquet.

You can have what you like in Scottish hotels from the lavishly exhibitionist to the genially local. The trouble about the smaller hotels is that, if they have a good name, they are likely to be full in high season; advance inquiries are essential. Country house hotels, with their lawns, walled-gardens, and a fine girdle of trees, can be very delightful, but their rooms may all have been sold out in advance to the coach-tourists just when you need them. I stayed at a beauty of this kind near Lockerbie on the road up from Carlisle and Gretna Green. But I could not book a return visit because of big coach bookings. You cannot blame owners for the long-term arrangements which make them secure. They experienced a very hard time before the Coach Parties became general, frequent and popular.

The Scottish countryside hotels have worked their way up from nothing. In the eighteenth century, outside the cities, the courageous traveller took a chance of hunger as well as of squalor in the Highlands.

'Of the provisions the negative catalogue was very copious. Here was no meat, no milk, no bread, no eggs, no wine. We did not express much satisfaction. However, we were to stay. Whisky we might have and I believe they caught a fowl and killed it. We had some bread and with that we prepared ourselves to be contented. . . . We were now to examine our lodging. Out of one of the beds, on which we were to repose, started up, at our entrance, a man black as a Cyclops from a forge. Other circumstances of no elegant recital concurred to disgust us.' Thus Dr.

Johnson of his stay at the inn at Glenelg. A kindly neighbour called Gordon, hearing of unknown strangers present and knowing the poverty of the place, sent them in a gift of rum and sugar. 'Sleep however was necessary.' The Doctor lay on a bundle of hay in his riding coat. 'Mr. Boswell, being more delicate, laid himself sheets with hay over and under him, and lay in linen like a gentleman.'

Fortunately Johnson and Boswell had excellent entertainment, as a rule, at private houses. But, when they lacked this convenience of claret, cleanliness and conversation, they had often to bed themselves down in 'circumstances of no elegant recital'—superb phrase! Nor did Dorothy and William Wordsworth, when, with Coleridge for part of the way, they explored the Highlands thirty years later, find anything better. The occasional hospitality of a kindly crofter was varied with rough company in inns and wretched paucity of victuals. Of the King's House, in Glencoe, Dorothy wrote of conditions that 'concurred to disgust us,'

'Never did I see such a miserable, such a wretched place,—long rooms with ranges of beds, no other furniture except benches, or perhaps one or two crazy chairs, the floors far dirtier than an ordinary house could be if it were never washed,—as dirty as a house after a sale on a rainy day, and the rooms being large, and the walls naked, they looked as if more than half the goods had been sold out. We sat shivering in one of the large rooms for three-quarters of an hour before the woman could find time to speak to us again; she then promised a fire in another room, after two travellers, who were going a stage further, had finished their whisky, and said we should have supper as soon as possible. She had no eggs, no milk, no potatoes, no loaf-bread, or we should have preferred tea. With length of time the fire

188

was kindled, and, after another hour's waiting, supper came,—a shoulder of mutton so hard that it was impossible to chew the little flesh that might be scraped off the bones, and some sorry soup made of barley and water, for it had no other taste.'

The sheets were wet, the peat was not dry. ' Nothing wanted to make it a place of complete starvation.' Small wonder that the scenery was not appreciated. Their ' expectations of grandeur ' were disappointed. It was ' a dreary waste.' One must feed and sleep and have no fear of the lesser vermin if one is to enjoy a Highland holiday. If the Palaces be too palatial for some, at least they permit ' elegant recital ' of their comforts and fit the traveller to view the scene in a good temper. Nor, in my range of Scottish country catering, are you likely to lie dirty. It has been an upward climb from 'Highland scab and hunger ' to the liberal table and pleasant appointments of the Hydro turned Hotel, a climb in whose middle reaches lay the ethical severities and very temperate living of the Hydropathic in the eighties.

CHAPTER IX

Perthshire and Power

'WE passed Pitlochrie, a small village, Faskally, a
very pretty place of Mr. Butter's, to the left,
and then came to the Pass of Killiecranke,
which is quite magnificent: the road winds along it and
you look down a great height, all wooded on both sides;
the Garry is rolling below it. I cannot describe how
beautiful it is. Albert was in perfect ecstasies.'

Thus Queen Victoria, describing in ' Leaves from the
Journal of our Life in the Highlands,' a visit to Blair
Atholl in September, 1844. Prince Albert was frequently
ecstatic among the mountains and the Queen was always
in similar bliss, rain or fine, amid ' my dear, dear Highlands.'
On this occasion they had further cause for ecstasy, having
been primed with Atholl Brose shortly before reaching
Pitlochrie. (It is a pity, to my mind, that the old spelling
has yielded to that of Pitlochry.) As for Atholl Brose, ' Put
a pound of dripped honey in a basin and add enough cold
water to dissolve it (about a teacupful). Stir with a silver
spoon and when the water and honey are well mixed add
gradually one and a half pints of whisky. Stir briskly until
a froth begins to rise. Bottle and keep tightly corked. If
liked, the old fashion may be followed of pouring the liquor
over a little oatmeal from which it is afterwards strained.'
The ' silver spoon ' is nice. So is Atholl Brose.

Pitlochrie is no longer a little village and Faskally has given its name to a man-made, but notably good-looking, loch above the great dam and power-station opened in 1950. Now Killiecrankie collects the motor-coaches and Blair Atholl, the historic stronghold of the Murrays, Dukes of Atholl, is open to the public and ready for them with tea and scones, massed antlers, a considerable armoury, and all the relics natural to one of the most famous of Scottish castles. Its sentinel site on the road from Inverness to Perth has given it more chronicles than are owned by most great houses of the Highlands. To listen to the pipers here is to hear the echoes of a thousand years.

At Blair Atholl the strenuous walker can turn north-westward up Glen Tilt to attempt the passage along the bridle track to Braemar, a matter of nearly thirty miles. Queen Victoria and Prince Albert made the journey in October, 1861. It was part of their 'Third Great Expedition.' These major tours made in part on foot but mainly by pony and carriage (the latter called a ' sociable ') were severe and exacting undertakings and few now appreciate the hardihood of the young Queen in achieving them. But the Great Expeditions brought their genuine rewards and satisfactions. Not only Albert was ' in perfect ecstasies.'

On Tuesday, October 8th, they drove West from Balmoral (fresh horses at Braemar) beyond the Linn of Dee for 18 miles. Then they mounted ponies, in pouring rain, and the Queen rode with an umbrella and water-proofs, crossing the Geldie burn into Glen Fishie (now usually spelled Feshie), and working steadily upward along the flank of Cairn Toul and the Cairn Gorm mass. With the weather clearing lunch was taken. A hut with Landseer frescoes was visited. At last the carriage track was found, carriages were waiting, and they drove to Kingussie,

Newtonmore, and at last Dalwhinnie. This was 29 miles from where they left the ponies. It was now a quarter to nine with the weather cold, wet, and windy. Despite the royal nature of the party there was very little organisation of comforts in advance. They stayed in Dalwhinnie at the inn ' which had only tea, two miserable, starved Highland chickens—without any potatoes. No pudding and no *fun*.' (What exactly was the Queen's missing (and italicised) *fun*?)

Next morning, in brighter weather, they were off again and drove south to Dalnacardoch on what is now the great main road to Perth: they paused at Blair Atholl, where the Duke of Atholl entertained them with coffee, but not for long. On they must go, and at half-past twelve were entering Glen Tilt for the long, rough scramble to Braemar. They could drive on a stony sort of road eight miles up to Forest Lodge and there meet their ponies which had been brought across the hills to meet them. Often it was all walking and riding. At two o'clock the cavalcade moved off, with two pipers ahead of them. At three o'clock they lunched at a spot called Dalcronachie: then they forded the Tarff where the water was up to the men's waists: John Brown, who had for some time been the Queen's favourite attendant, looked after her passage of the rushing stream. The Duke of Atholl walked all the way and offered to lead the Queen's pony, but her faith was in John Brown. ' I like best being led by the person I am accustomed to.' When they reached the County March, where Perthshire and Aberdeenshire join, whisky was taken and toasts drunk. Then came three miles more of pony-transport to the Bainoch, reached almost in darkness, at ten minutes to six. There were carriages available again. The Duke of Atholl turned back, returning over that rugged and desolate route with no moon and showers falling. The Royal Party drove on and reached Balmoral at a quarter past eight. ' We had travelled,' wrote the Queen, ' 69 miles to day and 60 yesterday. This was the pleasantest and most enjoyable excursion I ever made. Did not feel tired. We ladies did not dress and dined *en famille*; looking at maps of the Highlands after dinner.' Ecstasy indeed!

The driving in the ' sociable ' was over very rough roads: the pony-work was over stony and steep tracks. ' Brown constantly could not walk next to the pony, but had to scramble below, or pull it after him.' The vigour and endurance of the Queen, in pursuit of her mountain pleasure, were astonishing. I have never myself been farther up Glen Tilt from Blair Atholl than a couple of miles beyond Forest Lodge: the defile is superb. There is a glorious chasm where the Tilt is tumbling between Carn Chlamhain (3159 ft.) and the vast mass of Ben-y-Ghloe, whose highest ridge is 3671 ft. The snow lingers in early summer on the northward corries and flecks the dark landscape with its flash of white, while the precipice burns brandish their foam with glittering flourishes of silver. The young people who now foot it up Glen Tilt from Blair Atholl to Braemar are taking on a job that has its ample rewards: they will wonder surely at the ' sheltered Victorian womanhood ' which faced it, with pony and sometimes scrambling on foot, as the second afternoon's portion of a journey which had started after breakfast the day before and covered nearly 130 miles (many of them over wilderness tracks) with only the most starveling dinner and two picnic lunches. And then no fatigue was admitted. The Royal Party settled down to traverse its mountain-journey over again with outspread charts and joy renewed.

I share Queen Victoria's affection for Perthshire as well as for Aberdeenshire. It has no advantage of the sea, none of the surprise views, that meet you in the West when, at the summit of a climb, suddenly the bright shaft of a sea-loch is met and the isles lie summoning beyond its silver tip. But its inland lochs, especially of Tay, Tummel, and Rannoch, are exquisitely set, Tay under the great broad shoulders of Ben Lawers, which just misses the 4000 foot mark. The splendid cone of Schiehallion is ever coming into view, a grenadier on guard. There are not the jaunty, almost insolent, sky-stabbing peaks that you meet in Wester Ross. It is all smoother and friendlier. The beauty is of the curve, not of the pyramid. At evening, in the lingering light, it is a wilderness at peace, reassuring, not appalling. There is no better place to see a Perthshire sunset than on the road running east out of Pitlochry to Kirkmichael. It climbs through Moulin over the flank of Ben-y-Vrackie and then, as you reach the crest and stop to look west, the whole of the central Grampians are outstretched in their browny-purple bloom, with the mountains of Glencoe, eased into serenity by distance, nicking the sunset far away beyond the monstrous summit of Lawers and the soaring ridges, almost as mighty, of Glen Lyon.

Of course you can find more sensational panoramas among the prickly, serrated edges of the western coast and of Skye, where the birth-pangs of Nature's primeval writhings are still manifest, still menacing, as it were the testament of geology in torment, the jizzen (Scots for child-birth) of the rocks. Here in Perthshire the shapes have the maturity, the athletic grace, of a strong and easy adolescence; the growing-pains of landscape are over.

The villages, too, have a ripeness and security; they have had their troubles, the passing of broken armies, the departures of men marshalled to far, unmeaning wars. But they have out-lived them and matured and settled to the rhythm of peace and its labours. Moulin itself is a captivating little place. Small wonder that Stevenson—there is a plaque on his hill-side lodgment, Kinnaird—was warmed with affection for his perch. I have spoken of its much-liked Hotel, with its homely courtyard and enfolding, hospitable look. The Kirk is the work of 1834, erected on the site of an older building of dateless age. The old tomb-stones have their graven reminders that we owe God a death (' My Lot This Day, Your Lot To-morrow ' and ' Death is a debt to Nature dew, I've paid the price and so must you '). Two of the flat stones have incised swords and one of them has also a Maltese cross, which has caused the belief that the Black Castle of Moulin, now a smallish ruin, was once occupied by a Knight of St. John or that a Scottish crusader went out from and returned to Moulin. You touch Europe as well as Perthshire in this well-seasoned hamlet overlooking the rich vale of Atholl. Its very name recalls the French influence and the Old Alliance.

The ancient road from Perth to Inverness ran by it, climbing the slope and dropping to Killiecrankie and Blair Atholl instead of taking the Tummel valley, as the new road and the railway were to do. There was little of Pitlochry then; Moulin was the parent and it has been a nice touch of local humour to give the name of Moulin City to the village football team, which surely cannot find it easy to raise eleven men on all occasions. Young Pitlochry continually spreads. Old Moulin abides.

And so too abides twelve miles away to the east, past the big houses of Tarvie, Straloch, and Enochdu, neat little Kirkmichael, where a man might drowse away a long vacation and study an everlasting silence by the banks of the pattering Ardle burn. The gauntness of so many Scottish villages is not to be seen in this peaceful bend among the lesser Grampians, but you can find all that a glutton for the grim could desire by turning north on that absurdly courageous road that goes switch-backing up to the water-shed above Spittal of Glenshee and Dalmunzie

195

House (the latter now a trim hotel with a special appeal for shooting parties), and then sweeps down beside the tumbling Clunie Water to Braemar. Here is the naked truth of Grampian majesty, with the great bare skull of Glas Maol (3502 ft.) on your right and a bony skyline poised away to the east until it meets the hill of Mayar and dips to Glendoll and Barrie's beloved Glen Clova. Motorists who take this road will have to stop for their views, for driving is a riveting job, a full-time watch upon the dips and turns. On a day of pewter-coloured cloud the skeleton of central Scotland stands up with only mist for its winding-sheet. Even in sunshine it can be austere enough to be menacing.

But at the Devil's Elbow, with its terrifying hair-pin bends, we are into Aberdeenshire and this is Perthshire's chapter; so let us turn backward and southward to the Vale of Atholl, which has kept the name of Vale—unique in these parts—instead of Strath, presumably because Strath Atholl would be too awkward a mouthful. It reaches, broad and green, down to Dunkeld, with the Tummel, which has devoured the Garry, becoming itself consumed in the broader Tay. Here is a gentle gap in the severity of the middle Highlands and it is all the more beautiful for its contrast with the surrounding nakedness of summits.

The Vale of Atholl has a splendid variety of timber. With the late spring of the Highlands, Perthshire's June is like Southern England's flush of May. The woods touch every note of tender greenery in the great diapason of bursting leaf and the rivers, usually of umber tint, may be astonishingly bewitched by a radiant day and assume a Technicolour blue. It is a common silliness to sneer at such scenery and to dismiss it as Nature in a picture post-card mood. For my part, Perthshire can be as close to a Victorian Academy landscape as it pleases; those who want

Nature to scowl murkily are satisfied only too often. I am not going to grumble churlishly when the Tummel insists on being sapphire or when the hills wear as bonnie a purple as ever sentimental tenor sang about to a cosy audience in the lounge of a Grand Hotel.

The peak on guard hereabouts is that of Ben-y-Vrackie, which, though no giant, is so nicely proportioned and so happily sited that it is always taking the eye on the busy road from Dunkeld to Blair Atholl. It is in places a twisted, narrow road, inadequate to the great north-south traffic which it now has to carry; the sooner they get on with the widening and straightening the better, for the driver will then get more sense of the Vale's rich quality without risk of a disaster. So grand a strath has long deserved a wider road. Away to the west there is the gentle roll of the hills above Errochty, whose water has now been turned to utilitarian purposes. Kinloch Rannoch leads to the great Moor which frightens with its vast nakedness in winter but gives long, heat-quivering views away to the Western peaks in high summer. It is a fisherman's haunt and above all this county looms Schiehallion, almost as high as Snowdon, but by no means so rugged, a lovely, pensive peak that seems to stand in maiden meditation. (Its name is explained by some as Maiden's Breast.) It always lifts my heart to see its lonely grace as one rounds a wooded corner in the steep and timbered country round Loch Tummel. That loch, as every purchaser of a picture-postcard hereabouts soon knows, has the famous Queen's View, where Her Majesty paused 'in perfect ecstasy' looking west. She was right to be entranced. The Queen's eye for a vista was as sharp as Dr. Grace's for a cricket-ball. The Tummel view will be a little affected by the enlargement of the loch by the Hydro-Electric Board: a wooded promontory will become an island, which may be to better part of Nature's best. But the famous Falls of Tummel have been flattened out; one must, of course, lose something when the engineers get to work. On the other hand they often provide the public with far better roads than were there before they came and so give access to views hitherto unobtainable except by strenuous pedestrians. Central Perthshire now provides a chance for those who dreaded the arrivals of dams and turbines to assess the losses and the gains of this aspect of Progress.

Perthshire has become one of the chief operating areas of the North of Scotland Hydro-Electric Board, whose kingdom ranges from Ultima Thule to the Clyde Belt. The rivers of the county are no longer scenery alone; driving a turbine is increasingly a national necessity: would that we could extract all our industrial energy from the clean tides and torrents of our coasts and glens and so were able to close up the dark and death-dealing mines for ever. But, while that is impossible, we can at least develop the ' white coal ' of the heavily-watered mountains to the best of our resources and ability. There can hardly be comparison, for safety and amenity, between the life of a coal-miner and of a power-station operative in a Highland glen. True, some very hard and occasionally dangerous navvying and tunnelling have gone to prepare the harnessing of the waters; but once that job is done, the accumulation and release of water-power is a civilised occupation for the man who goes to work in the machine-house from a home under the hills and beside the swirl of waters.

The Board has a Gaelic motto, *Neart nan Gleann*, which means Strength of the Glens. It is a phrase shrewdly chosen, albeit from the language of simple men who knew nothing of amp, volt, and watt when they spoke thus of the natural energy of their territory. Really what the modern engineer is doing is to practise in his own way and medium the kind of faith which scholars of comparative religion call animism: this creed saw a spirit in all the elements, in the wind or the rock, the river or the wood. The ancient Greeks conceived Nature to be thus animated by almost personal powers. The Oread was their nymph or daemon of the mountains, embodying the wealth and potency immanent in the rocks. The Dryad was the similar genius of the trees; when a man cut timber to build he was in debt to this vegetable spirit. The Naiad might be called the Lady of the Lake; she is the vitality and vigour of the stream viewed as a spirit-person. The geologist has been the servant of the Oread; in her temples were his metals. Perthshire, to the benefit of its looks if not of its treasury, has never been a mining county. But the Oread has been successfully, if not beautifully, courted at Fort William to the west. Her presence there is in the form of aluminium.

Afforestation lures the Dryad-haunted forest from the bare hillside. The Naiad is the presiding goddess of the Hydro-Electrician as he tames a river to his purposes or tunnels the hills in order to convey the power of a mountain-loch to the service of a dam. When he has completed his collection and canalising of water, the Dryad then answers to the press of a button and serves the citizen, local countryman or far-off town-dweller, as Ariel served Prospero. A word is flashed to the control-room of a Power Station, the waters come crashing through the opened dam, the turbine does its job, and the lights come up and the wheels are turned in village, town, workshop, and factory.

Let me admit that, when one of the greatest of the North of Scotland Hydro-Electric Board's schemes was put forward, I was among the many angry protestors. Was a filthy mess to be made of the glorious Tummel? Was that proud torrent famous in history to be cowed into the

199

submissiveness of a mere canal? Was sweet Loch Errochty to be made a navvies' battle-ground? Were Pitlochry's gracious old Clunie Bridge and its mellow field of sports and games to be submerged to make a mechanics' pond? We campaigned. We were granted an Official Inquiry. (But those of us who knew anything about Official Inquiries were well aware what the answer would be. The Official, especially under Socialism, always wins.) Still, we thought it was worth a fight. We lost and now that most of the dreaded work has been done, it is not what we feared. The initial stages were bound to be ugly, but the finished article is seemly as well as serviceable; I think we are nearly all ready to confess a victory for the innovators in a task which now we would not have undone. They have exploited the wealth of waters without defiling them.

An artificial loch sounds dreadful. But now, if you sit outside the Green Park Hotel in Pitlochry, on the shores of the new Loch Faskally, and survey what has replaced the old recreation-ground and some of its wooded banks, you are more likely to be charmed by the resulting views than offended by man's surgery of the natural scene. The Pitlochry dam and power-station do not offend; they seem to ride the glen with natural poise. The generating stations at Pitlochry and Clunie are not alien giants garishly or clumsily imposed upon the water-scape. The Oread has been called in to work in harmony with the Naiad and pre-cast slabs of Aberdonian granite gleam, bright but not too brilliant, over the impounded waters and these in turn do not reveal any bleak air of imprisonment but lie at ease, waiting the call to work.

The Board, incidentally, has done something to stop one of the saddest features of the new Scotland, the decay of the stone-mason and the inability, through growth of cost and lack of craft, to build in the traditional material and manner of the country. The change to brick and other substitutes for local stone has frequently set an ugly pink rim round the grey towns; pink, perhaps, is too mild a word for the hideous, blatant red employed in some of the suburbs; Edinburgh's edges have some ghastly slashes of colour which are wounds upon the surface of the city. Accordingly I particularly welcome this statement in the Board's Report for the year ending December, 1950:

'The Board by making use of local stone as far as possible in the building of generating stations, sub-stations and staff houses, have contributed to a revival of the Scottish stone quarry industry in the north and the craft of the stonemason.

'These buildings, while adding to the amenities of their surroundings, will, it is hoped, draw public attention to the fine building stone available in the North at prices which compare favourably with the cost of other building materials which have to be transported to the North of Scotland.

'The Board's orders have resulted in quarry masters modernizing their plant and it is gratifying that some local authorities are considering making greater use of local stone in their housing developments.'

Welcome, too, is the further announcement:

'The Board are building all their main groups of staff houses of stone: at Tarbet, Loch Lomondside, 27 houses for the staff of the Loch Sloy scheme, 33 houses on two sites at Pitlochry for the staff of the Tummel Valley stations and 17 houses for the staff of the Affric scheme at Cannich, Strathglass.

'The Board have also decided to use local stone for

a number of other stations which are under construction or the construction of which is about to begin.

'These measures have provided the quarrying industry with hope for the future and recruits are now being obtained into the masonry industry for the first time for many years.'

Many who have regretted the usurpation of splendid Scottish sites by English-style bungalows and villas will find these to be very comforting statements. Especially in such places of surpassing beauty as Loch Affric, which lies south-west of Inverness and north of the Great Glen, it is most reassuring to hear of traditional building applied to the usage of this piece of water; it is not a great deal visited, but is beloved of those who know it. Now it will be more available, with better approach. When I was there in the autumn of 1948 it was suffering from the inevitable initial upheaval: but news from recent visitors confirms my hope that the final results will increase the visitation and enjoyment of a scene, on the whole, unspoiled.

Some apprehension had indeed been justified by the unsightly operations of the early Grampian Electricity Supply Company round Kinloch Rannoch. This previous adventure of private enterprise, now absorbed in the North of Scotland Board, was useful not only in its provision of power but as an example on which to improve. That the lessons have been well learned is, by all I have seen and by all reports I have heard, proven in the numerous operations of the Board all over the North. The one disconcerting feature is the spidery trail of the pylons as they radiate out over the moors, carrying the precious product of the generating stations. It would be impossibly expensive to carry the load by underground cable: repair-work, as well as the construction of subterranean wiring, would be difficult to execute and costly beyond endurance. So we must have the pylon-chains and they are not an addition to Highland loveliness. But the Highlands are large and the pylons are not very many. If they cannot be forgotten, they can be forgiven for their indispensable part in preventing waste of waters. In the case of islands and some lochs lines are being laid under the surface.

Only too often do we curse the driving, day-long rain of the Highlands. Since we must ' bide the pelting of this pitiless storm,' shall not we use the water which it too often discharges to the affliction of the crofters and the frustration of our holidays, if it can be made to ease and enrich the work of man? At Loch Sloy, the loch dammed for electricity in the mountains to the west of Loch Lomond and serving the inoffensive power-station on Lomondside, the recent rainfall has been over 150 inches a year. (The Londoner is used to a rainfall of about 25 inches.) A bit less than half-an-inch every day of the year! And half-an-inch is a soaker. Appalling, but not so bad if you can make the nuisance your benefit and the tyrannical downpours your slaves. Here, at Loch Sloy, is a Naiad indeed and now the goddess is on duty, a factory lass all the time as well as a spoil-sport on too many occasions.

In the Tummel-Garry catchment area the rainfall has been at the sixty- to seventy-inch annual level. This is far less of a curse to the tourist than the cataracts of Sloy, especially as the early months of the summer in mid-Scotland may be almost rain-free. None the less the drench can be turned into a drudge—and has been. The burns that pour off the Perthshire hills are no longer running wasted to the Tay and the Spey. Moreover water-power can be used twice over, as coal cannot. What has passed fruitfully through one dam, may be set to work again at another farther on. Coal is burned out; water continues.

Great Tay through Perth, through towns, through country flies,
Perth the whole kingdom with her wealth supplies.

The thirteenth-century rhyme proclaims a new truth.

Moreover the Board has its eyes on other nymphs than the Naiad. At Costa Hill, in Orkney, it is experimenting with improved and extended harnessing of Aeolus, god of the winds, a very potent deity in those parts. The little wind-wheel run up for working a water-pump or for gathering electrical power may be developed into an Aeolian Hercules, labouring in large measure on man's behalf. The spirit of the earth is manifest in the huge peat-fields of the Highland moors. Here too man has new plans and hopes. If peat can be coaxed into firing gas-turbines, a great blessing can be brought to the Highlands, where the Board is also working at the drying of hay by electricity. When the crofter can be released from the ruin wrought by soaking rains after his crop has been cut, one of the chief curses of his life will have been removed.

It has been feared that one very popular source of Scotland's wealth and nourishment, the salmon, would be frightened out of his course and denied his spawning-grounds by the creation of the necessary dams across his favourite rivers. Very great care has been taken to provide ladder-ways round the obstacles and that these are being used by the fish can be seen whenever there is a ' run ' of the salmon up-stream. At Pitlochry there is a fish-pass 900 ft. long, mounting by easy stages to the new Loch Faskally. Not only can the salmon be watched as they move up this convenient passage-way, but at the top there is an observation-chamber, available with an easily obtained permit, in which the salmon can be seen through glass as they proceed or take a rest on that urgent drive of theirs to the shallow, highly aerated waters that are their marriage-beds and journey's end.

The number passing through is checked by day and night invigilation. Some 750 went up the Pitlochry ladder in May, 1951. I myself watched a very handsome fellow swimming meditatively round the pool behind the glass; there was also present an unwanted brown trout who was suspect of devouring some of the parr or tiny new-born salmon on their way down to the sea. But I suppose he would do that in the river or loch in any case; two spawning salmon beget myriads of parr and the infant mortality is always very heavy. But one getting through to the sea returns a sizeable fish in future years and in turn helps to create a prodigious family. The aquarium provided at the top of the ladder can be a fascinating spectacle when there are fish about and adds to the interest of Pitlochry as a tourist-centre.

Furthermore, salmon-fishing which, in the best water, is usually a private monopoly with very heavy rents for the fishing tenant, is now made open to the public by the Board at reasonable rates. A boat on Loch Faskally costs only half-a-crown an hour in the evening for one rod and three-and-sixpence for two; a whole day, from 8 a.m. to 6 p.m., costs a pound for salmon and fifteen shillings for trout; the fisherman can keep his trout, if he gets them, free; if he takes a salmon he has to pay a pound for his fish. When I was there, an eight-pounder was caught and, at the prevailing price of salmon (fifteen shillings a pound in London at the time), the twenty-shilling fee plus boat charge left its captor very well in pocket. But I learned later that this was rather a lonely catch; most of the salmon hurried on. The Board has now in its possessions fishings and shooting-grounds of considerable value and, if this policy of fixing easy fishing and game charges is continued, the old, expensive Highland monopolies will be shared out in a way that many will appreciate.

The careful invigilation at the observation chambers may in the end help us to the solution of the salmon-mystery. Why does this astonishing fish force his way up the river of his origin, after some years on ' the Atlantic shelf,' to breed in its topmost and often tiny waters? Is he, as some suppose, struggling always, when bent on mating, to find water of greater aeration? A flood of cold, bubbling water off the high hills usually seems to evoke a good run of salmon up-stream. Does he never feed en route? He is always, they say, caught with an empty stomach. If so, does he snap at a fly out of irritation or curiosity? In that case, why does he prefer one kind of fly one day and another on the next? And would a fly be worth-while nourishment for a fish of eight or ten pounds or even of far greater weight? Or does his stomach empty itself with extraordinary speed?

Volumes have been written on these problems and fishermen have argued them incessantly. Possibly the close watch on salmon, which the fish-ladder and the aquarium at the summit facilitate, may bring new evidence. Certainly, where the ladders are provided, the salmon are having a much easier journey than they had of old. But perhaps they do get a sporting pleasure out of the battering they receive when they hurl themselves at a fall in spate. On the Garry, up at Struan, beyond Blair Atholl, one used to have a magnificent view of salmon engaged with what seemed to be impossible odds; the great curved body flung itself, as though from a catapult, at the torrent crashing over the rocks and, after several defeats, the fish would usually achieve his leap—or wait till the water was descending with less quantity and violence. The Hydro-Electric schemes will not abolish this battle of fish against flood; countless water-falls will remain. But some parts of the salmon's journey will be eased on certain rivers.

The mathematics of electricity mean very little to me; but they are extremely important to the nation. The Board's work is still only beginning and here are its 1950 figures. 'The 877,979,479 units generated during 1950 were disposed of as follows:

	Units Sold	Percentage increase (+) or decrease (−) compared with 1949
Units sold in Board's Area ..	586,578,058	+ 14.8
Units sold to British Electricity Authority ..	135,936,400	+141.8
Units used in the construction of hydro-electric schemes	19,000,000	− 29.6
Units lost in transmission and distribution	136,465,021	+ 17.9

The amount of ' juice ' mislaid may strike the uninformed reader as considerable. As Wilde's Lady Bracknell said, ' To lose one parent, Mr. Worthing, may be regarded as a misfortune; to lose both looks like carelessness.' But electricity is, I understand, extremely perishable matter; like the salmon-parr, its rate of mortality is high and I would not dream of attributing negligence to the engineers whose enthusiastic Chairman is the Rt. Hon. Thomas Johnston, generally regarded as having been the best of Scotland's Secretaries of State and certainly, since he refused the salary of his office, the least self-regarding of our politicians. The Board has been very much his creation and remains his care.

The Highlands are, and will remain, in debt to the enthusiasm and pertinacity of this Lowlander. His late deputy Chairman, Sir Edward MacColl, brought in a Highland name and an engineering genius. I am the more bound, and the more happy, to acknowledge these things now, since once I regarded these invaders as a couple of vandals and denounced them as menaces to the places that I loved. I have now to confess my belief that when all their multitudinous schemes have been completed and tidied up, they and their colleagues will be remembered as designers of something great and new rather than as destroyers of what was beautiful and old. There are those pylons that smutch a moorland, those harnessed falls that tumble no longer in the old foaming freedom that we knew. But the Board's architects and the Amenities Committee have been better guardians than we expected, while the continuing disasters of the coal-pit and increasing need of power stress the folly of letting dynamic waters run to waste.

The capital expenditure has been high. You cannot tunnel mountains and impound waters on the cheap. If the work had been done in our years of plenty and cheapness, instead of in our years of scarcity and high prices, it could have been done at a quarter of the cost. The Board had, by 1951, been permitted by the Government to borrow eighty million pounds for the execution of existing schemes and the development of new ones; 'capital cuts,' imposed owing to the general economic situation and Rearmament needs, were in 1951 interfering considerably with the future plans. But, within reasonable time, the waters of Scotland will be effectively exploited to warm and to lighten the lives of those living beside them as well as to bring new power to the factory worker's elbow in the industrial areas. It need not be feared that the taxpayer will be bled for this transfusion of water-power. Compared with the forty millions muddled away by ill-considered schemes for ground-nuts and hen-runs in Africa this investment in the neglected home-lands and long over-looked riches of the rivers is sane in policy and will almost certainly be remunerative in practice. Subsidies will not have to flow in to keep the power flowing out. Once a Hydro-Electric scheme is past the building and engineering stage its running and maintenance costs are very low, man having arranged that the Naiad should be his hand-maiden and that in her untiring person Nature should do the work.

So those who take a Perthshire holiday will find the riparian scene slightly altered, sometimes for the worse and sometimes for the better. The Highlands are enormous as well as various. If you do not like what has happened to one glen, you can turn to another. (This will not be the case if Snowdonia, which is a tiny paradise compared with the region from Loch Lomond to the Pentland Firth, is submitted to drastic man-handling; North Wales has far less alternative wilderness to offer the devotee of solitude and of Nature untarnished. Parallels between the two countries are dangerous.) The string of Grampian pylons may distract the eye, but the new power-stations and the homes of their workers will not offend and may positively please.

Awake my Muse! Portray the pleasing sight
That meets us where they make the Electric Light.

Thus Mr. Belloc's Mr. Lambkin, competitor for The Newdigate Prize at Oxford. Mr. Lambkin's eyes were turned to Osney, in the Seven Bridges Road. Now the Muse, under similar invocation, can turn to Caledonia and especially to its central Perthshire rivers; I see no reason why poetry should be silenced by what it thereabouts must see.

> *Shall I describe the complex Dynamo*
> *Or write about its Commutator? No.*

I agree with Mr. Lambkin's firm negation. The detail can be left to the specialist. For most of us it is sufficient that the rivers are used, not abused. And the lesser ones, a thousand strong, the tiny servants of the great, are untouched. Let those who resent the occasional confining of the Tummel and Garry, take the old royal example and make one of the Great Expeditions: if they can ride or walk from Blair Atholl to Deeside, as Victoria and Albert did sixty years ago, they will find the Tilt untamed, the hills unpyloned, the track true Bridle Path, and the wildness of scene unparalleled. The old 'perfect ecstasies' are guaranteed, at least for solitudinarians. And this not in one famous glen only. There are plenty such. From Perth to Pentland Firth there is beauty indestructible.

CHAPTER X

Sands of Pleasure

THE Kingdom of Fife is for St. Andreans, both golfing and academic, the kingdom of heaven on earth. It has, like most desirable regions in a crowded land, a certain remoteness. Since both the great Firths of East Scotland have been presented with railway bridges and denied road ones, the motorists' approach involves the delay and cost and nuisance of a ferry or a long drive round. St. Andrews itself is defended from easy railway approach by the barrier of Leuchars Junction. The old entry by sea vanished long ago. The Kingdom is not far from being a peninsula. So Fife remains an individual, unassimilated region. With only slightly different geography and a road bridge over the Forth and Tay, Edinburgh and Dundee might have overwhelmed it and turned St. Andrews into a dormitory and a week-enders' camping-ground. But that has not happened.

As things are, it is chiefly Fife that invades Fife, that is when the mining and industrial towns of the east and south of the county send their hundreds by motor-coach to strip and sport on the great sandy crescent beyond the St. Andrews links and even to kick a Sabbath-breaking football on the deserted fairway of the First Hole. The intrepid enter the swimming pool which I take to be one of the most

211

cunningly devised traps for a cold wind ever invented. The sun may blaze on St. Andrews, but in the pool there will be a whistling draught. People sun-bathing there lie about with immense bravado in the nearly nude developing more goose-flesh than tan. This pretence that the coast of Fife is the south of France may be heroism, but it is not sense. Yet along the sands and away from that temple of the east wind one can abundantly bask.

A strange and comforting felicity seems to beset everybody whom one meets. St. Andrews is a place in which no person in good health can possibly be in bad spirits, provided the rain from the west slinks away over Angus to the north, which it so often very kindly does; provided also that the whole shore is not blotted out by a haar (sea-mist) which is pestilent when it occurs but is not too common. Even in this Age of Anxiety, when youth is afflicted by National Service, the uncertain future, and the soaring prices which make the student's income utterly inadequate to exploit in purchase, travel, and hospitality the scope and freedom of his newly discovered adult status, St. Andrews has struck me as the happiest University of my acquaintance in these times. The air is as keen as that of Oxford and Cambridge is sluggish. The victuals are better.

The dingy black gowns that are a shabby disgrace to the great English Universities, which should surely sport their different blues for academic dress, are replaced by the flush of the red robe. This, gladly and generally worn by the undergraduates, makes ' the old grey city by the sea ' a study in scarlet and a flower-bed of the Muses with none of that funereal look assumed by the English Universities when there is a large move to the lecture rooms. The summer term ends so early that most visitors miss seeing the streets of St. Andrews in proper hue. This is a pity.

The grey, so handsome in the great wide avenues that are the streets of the shops as well as of the Colleges and so poignant in the ruins of Cathedral and of castle, is beautifully relieved when thus incarnadined by the symbols of a scholarship that proudly hangs out its flags instead of seeming to mutter its woes in mourning garb.

St. Andrews, it may be said, is what the Irish would call an Ascendancy Town. It is, if not Anglicised, Britannicised. The University, in some recent years, had more than forty per cent of its students from over the Border or over the seas. (And why not? Is it not the business of a University to admit the Universe in person as well as in learning?) St. Leonards, the famous boarding-school for girls, also draws on the south and could hardly be called a typically Scottish academy, though its pupils may do their reading in rooms once occupied by Mary the Queen. Henry Cockburn, writing in 1874, said of the town that it was full of 'retired Indians,' by which he presumably meant Anglo-Indians. The more prosperous natives to-day are certainly not the kind who would go shopping in a kilt or cry loudly for Scottish Home Rule. Perhaps that is why George Scott-Moncrieff, in his otherwise admirable book on 'The Lowlands of Scotland,' gives only a chilly nod to St. Andrews, despite his delight in the mingling of Scottish architecture and Scottish scene. Or it may be that he is saddened by the reverence paid to golf, a secular exercise from which he averts the eye, being as neglectful of its glories on the Lothian coast as on the links of Fife. He may even hate it as much as he hates Calvinism; but that would be difficult.

But, before we become trapped in the bunkers—or 'faces' as St. Andrews used to call them—of golf, it is necessary to look more widely at all this southern half of Scotland's eastern coast. The Kingdom of Fife has much of everything that is not Highland although its chief hills, the Lomonds, have a proud and Highland-sounding name. It is, like its principal game, royal and ancient. It has two palaces, Dunfermline and Falkland, assorted castles (more, less, or totally ruined), a range of fine country houses, and a prosperous agriculture which appropriately has a place called Ceres at the fair heart of it. I suppose we must accept the view that this is St. Cyr's town and not the altar of the Roman goddess of corn, but the latter derivation appeals to my sentimental fancy. The place-names of Fife, incidentally, are a collector's treasury:

> *Largo, Blebo, Dunino*
> *Into Europe seem to go,*
> *But plainly Scottish we may deem*
> *Auchtermuchty, Pittenweem.*

A conspicuous feature of all this country is the doo-cot (dove-coot or pigeon-roost), standing like a handsome grey beehive in the Big House grounds. The pigeons gave a welcome change of flesh in the old winters, when they varied the monotonous diet of salted meat and fish.

Fife has, in the west and south, abundant coal and the mess that goes with it; it has fishing, harbours of varying vitality and similar beauty: it has in Culross as good a reminder of medieval Scotland as remains and there are also new-model, unmessy coal-pits thereabouts. Fife's little towns with their crow-stepped gables and attractive church-spires (note those of the two Anstruthers) make one feel that this is the parallel to England's Cotswolds; the harbours indenting a rocky coast remind one of Cornwall while happily avoiding the self-conscious quaintness that has latterly infected some of the Cornish fishing-ports. At Crail you can feel a mellow history in the tingling air, but people take their vacations there naturally and without the guide-book too much in the studious hand. Its coast is a favourite for family holidays but without excessive invasion. The sun shines far more than in the West. But there are smoke and bustle of industry too in this genial container of diversities. Linoleum and oilskins are some of its more noted productions in the service of Scottish homes and climate.

With the exception that harbours are scarce on the coast between Berwick and Edinburgh much the same might be said of the counties, Berwickshire and the East and Middle Lothians, which compose that battle-scarred shore, where Scots and English have so often swayed to and fro, battering and besieging, charging and receding. The castles show their wounds, but the fields of war are not conspicuously honoured. I have often passed through Prestonpans where Johnny Cope was routed, but I am not sure exactly where this stramash took place. There is less industry than in Fife until you get to mid-Lothian, whose face is mine-pocked and bing-pimpled. The land, with which many generations of skilled and diligent farmers have mixed their labour, is a model of clean cultivation and grand use of rich soil. There are hills and moors of moderate height which go loping away to the south with a soothing rather than a striking beauty. The eye is taken by fine plantations which offer good shelter from the east wind as well as a good source of timber-wealth. When Scotland was at last rid of its wars, the lairds availed themselves of their new security to plant and they planned their work for posterity with the hard woods instead of cultivating only the less handsome, quick-growing conifers with their quick return on capital invested. The great country houses are fine statements of their period's confidence and grace. And here too is golf and yet more golf.

The enemy and blessing of the south of the Firth of

Forth has been sand. It has at times been a destroyer, as on the Moray Firth, by monstrous and drifting accumulations. The town of Gullane lost its church and now stands cautiously back. Leith lost its historic golf-links and the race-course celebrated in Fergusson's poem. Musselburgh was the gainer. But the sand has also blessed the coast by creating the play-ground of the children and, with a fine grass coverlet, the links for the golfer. North Berwick, which the English must realise is forty miles from the Border's Berwick-on-Tweed, is a typical East Lothian town. Most of it is set well back from the sea, like Gullane and castled Dirleton between the two. The menace of sand-burial has enforced these cautionary tactics.

North Berwick had solid development for solid families at a time when building had nothing gim-crack about it and the Edinburgh lawyer or banker or business man could tuck himself cosily behind grey walls of weather-beating, as well as weather-beaten, stone and plant a fine walled-garden to give him privacy as well as lawns and fruits. His children had access, across the links, to a perfect play-ground, a safe sandy shore with enough diversity of rock, a harbour for small craft, boat-trips round the Bass Rock, sea-fishing, and a climate notably keen and dry.

By the sands of Fife and East Lothian golf is not just a week-end extra or a gentlemanly exercise tempered by a few concessions to ' artisan ' golf. It is a piece of life. This may be intensely distressing to non-golfers. But there it is. The small boys by the wayside are practising their swing as you pass and almost every adult is an addict, if not an expert. (Considering how much golf is played in Scotland, I am always surprised to see how much hacking and hewing continues on municipal courses.) Most of the courses are available to all and sundry at popular prices. There is the holy ground of Muirfield, however, where you have to be ushered in with a passport of influential introduction, but as a rule the social and financial barriers are down. So those driving down from Edinburgh to North Berwick will pass a chain of admirable links, especially in the region of Gullane where they play without cease in the wind and the rain and probably go home to play in their sleep. And now that the motor-car has crashed its way through the Scottish Sabbath, at least in the south, there is a seven-day week on many courses.

All devotees of a sport or a game are bores to those outside their circle; the golfers may take high rank with the fishermen as the leading hotel pests when there is company not sharing their passions. Yet, for my part, there is a curious attraction in a place with but a single thought. Even the grimmest educational mandarin, if he had any humanity in his composition, would not want the children of Newmarket to regard the horse, in Mr. McChoakumchild's way, only as 'a graminivorous quadruped.' One expects the sons of Pudsey and thereabout to have Yorkshire cricket in their marrow. And it would be a poor product of St. Andrews or Gullane who does not feel the shiver of ecstasy down his spine when, at a desperate moment of the match, he sees a perfect iron-shot soaring dead on the pin and dropping obediently to lie beside it.

The Scottish culture of golf is more than five hundred years old and has soaked its way into the after-dinner choruses and even the set pieces in the heroic manner. The clubs had their famous laureates as well as their after-dinner baritones. As a Carnegie on my mother's side I am naturally proud to think that it was Carnegie of Pitarrow (1800-1851) who wrote 'The Golfiad.' He was not an inspired poet, but he realised that his darling sport was a social influence and a promoter of trade and resolved to state the fact in the measure proper to a classically educated, if somewhat dissolute and spendthrift, gentleman:

> *Ball, clubs and men I sing, who first, methinks,*
> *Made sport and bustle on North Berwick links,*
> *Brought coin and fashion, betting, and renown,*
> *Champagne and claret to a country town.*

Reflectively Pitarrow pursued his song of praise:

> *Had Mecca's Prophet known the noble game*
> *Before he gave this paradise to fame,*
> *He would have promised, in the land of light,*
> *Golf all the day—and Houris all the night.*
> *But this is speculation; we must come*
> *And work the subject rather nearer home.*

After this he accurately observes:

> *The game is ancient, manly, and employs*
> *In its departments, women, men, and boys.*
> *Men play the game, the boys the club convey,*
> *And lovely woman gives the prize away.*

He would now have to amend his last couplet, owing to the introduction of the go-cart for carriage of clubs and the unchallengeable prowess of the one-time weaker sex. I would suggest an emendation:

> *Men play the game, machines their clubs convey,*
> *Their daughters give them strokes—and win the day.*

'The game is ancient, manly.' It is familiar knowledge that Scottish kings of the fifteenth century strove to suppress the golf-playing on the links in order to promote an armaments drive instead and to get the men from the tees to the archery butts. James the First tried to legislate against 'able-bodied idlers in Fife,' but perhaps he was not thinking of golfers. The extended use of gunpowder, with cannon fired by specialists in ordnance, made the conscription of archery-recruits less urgent later on and golf was then pardoned for its sins. The Stuart kings were attracted by the game. James the Sixth of Scotland and First of England appointed William Mayne to be his club-maker in the same year that he appointed William Shakespeare and the others of his fellowship to be his play-makers. James Melvill was appointed maker of the royal golf-balls. Golf-balls, then constructed of feathers with a leather covering, cost three shillings each, a tremendous sum in those days. The poor presumably had to rely on a keen eye for the lost ones and a certain shrewd ability not to find them till the players' search was over—an aptitude not unknown to some caddies ever since.

The game was played, as was early cricket, for high stakes; twenty guineas on a match then would be the equivalent of two hundred now. The notorious Captain Porteous, of the Edinburgh Civil Guard, matched himself for this sum at Leith against the brother of that Lord Balmerino, who died for the Stuart cause on Tower Hill in 1746, and the struggle was followed by Dukes, Earls, and 'a vast mob of the great and little besides.' Duncan Forbes of Culloden, Lord President of the Court of Session, was an insatiable player. ' This day,' he wrote on November 1st, 1728, ' after a very hard pull, I got the better of my son at the gouf on Musselburgh links. If he was as good at any other thing, as he is at that, there might be some hopes of him.' Other fathers must since have felt the same when youth was more ardent for the links than for the books.

Betting and big money prizes were continued. In 1849 £400—or £200 each for two of a foursome—was great wealth to a poor man. Yet for that sum the invincible

Allan Robertson and Tom Morris of St. Andrews played the two Dunns of Musselburgh. There were three matches, at Musselburgh, St. Andrews, and North Berwick. The Dunns won easily on their home ground: the St. Andreans, less easily, on theirs. So the Dunns came to the neutral territory of North Berwick with a big lead in holes. With eight to play they were four up and, humanly speaking, all was over. But Robertson and Morris got their heads down and their spirits up; they actually won four and halved two of the next six. All square and two to go. Allan and Tom won both—and £400. This purse, interpreted at to-day's value, is the kind of prize at which even American champions would not sniff.

The gentlemen golfers of Fife and Lothian were combatant first and convivial after. As Carnegie of Pitarrow has told us, claret and champagne, as well as fashion and betting, were the cups of victory or consolation. They were also the medium of paying for lost wagers or breaches of club rules. Claret was more precious than port. In the record book of the Honourable Company of Golfers it was set down in 1782 that 'Port and Punch shall be the ordinary Drink of the Society, unless upon those days when the Silver Club and Cups are played for. At those Meetings Claret or any other Liquor more agreeable will be permitted.' In 1837 Mr. Wood, of the Society, was fined two 'tappit hens' (a 'tappit hen' is a vessel holding three quarts) for appearing on the Links without a red coat. For a similar offence, but committed five times, Lt. James Dalrymple of the 43rd was 'fined only in Six Pints, having confessed the heinousness of the crime.' 'At his own request he was fined of Three Pints more.' At St. Andrews in 1825 'the present Captain, having imposed on himself a fine of a Magnum of Claret for failure in public duty, imposed a similar fine on all old Captains present.' The evenings

usually ended with ' harmony and melody.' The Bruntsfield
men sang

> *Wi' a hundred golfers and a' and a'.*

Golf was taken both to create a thirst and to remedy the
too enthusiastic slaking of it.

> *When in the dumps with mulligrubs*
> *Or doyte with barley bree, boys*

the counsel was

> *Then don your brilliant scarlet coats*
> *And your blue velvet caps, boys,*
> *And some shall play the rocket shots*
> *And some the putting paps, boys.*

' There's no disease we cannot cure,' sang James Ballantine
to the air of ' Let Haughty Gaul.' And there is abiding
truth in it. An old friend of mine who used to go with
the Hoylake men for matches with the Lothian clubs told
me that there was a dinner every night of the visit, at
which a bottle of whisky was set before each man and
finished during the evening. But all were early and steady
on the tee next morning, not doyte with barley bree,
prepared alike for accuracy with the rocket-shots or putting
paps. I presume that a rocket-shot was a high one meant
to drop ' dead ' on the green.

The games began with royalty, nobility, and gentry.
King Charles I, who played at Leith, was pictured with
a horse beside him on the green and close to the hole.
There was no fuss about perfection of turf. As golf became
more popular and cheaper, the quality of the grass and the
greens was steadily improved. Now a good player is
indignant at a bad lie on the fairway and must have a
billiard-table surface in which to make his ' putting paps.'

The heavily watered green with its grass rendered artificially lush with dressings of chemical has entirely altered the approach to the hole, since a ' rocket shot ' will fall dead instead of scampering beyond the mark and the run-up shot, which was the special pride of the old Scots golfer, has been well-nigh abolished, because so difficult. The professional who wants to go round in under seventy has everything in his favour as well as his uncanny skill: perfect fairways, a tamed ' rough,' graded steel clubs that demand the same stroke with only a difference of strength, a far-flying ball, and a nice, moist cushion of green on which to descend with the minimum of risk.

Of course all courses or links have not been robbed of their own natural and baffling qualities. Not, I think, St. Andrews, which is one reason why some of the leading professionals do not like it. Dare I call them craven-hearted? Certainly, on the whole, there is no sense in comparing the old game of golf, even the golf of forty years ago, with the golf played to-day. Played? Worked at, very often, and not by the professionals only. The amateur is often the most careful, calculating and slowest of all players now. In a ' needle ' match he will take four hours over what ought to be done in two-and-a-half, with his spying out the line, practice swings, and infinite calculations before a putt.

A booby like myself, ' rabbiting ' happily round, has no right to discuss the various links in terms of the excellence demanded by the great. I cannot dissociate the game from the place and that is why a sunny morning on Gullane Hill has often seemed to me the most enchanting of all adventures in exercise. Seaside courses are usually on the level and over-browed by sand dunes; but at Gullane one is both at the sea-side and on top of the world. It has all the merits of a marine turf, dry yet springy, combined with the views proper to a mountain course. To the north the Firth of Forth is a broad blue ribbon between you and the Kingdom of Fife. The Pentlands to the west stand guard in a gentle haze over Edinburgh's Rock and towers. To the south the Lammermuirs rise to the crest of their long heathery wave. The scent of thyme is in the salty air; the earth you tread is resilient and untiring; you may play like a fiend, but you feel like a god.

That happens, of course, when you are out beyond the wall at North Berwick or turning the loop at St. Andrews and facing back to its little grey acropolis of history and scholarship rising behind the first tee and the last green. But in those cases you are down to sea-level and your first visit to St. Andrews leaves you a little shocked at the squalor of railway sheds as you near the end. But at Gullane you are a climber. I know that the second hole is a long tug, but say not the struggle naught availeth, the panting and the puffs are vain. On the top you are rather more than a mere swiper of a small ball: you have the freedom of a mighty coast, the enfranchisement of an islanded channel, and the liberty of the outspread Lowlands. The true golfer will say that he wants a links, not a gazebo or a belvedere; he dislikes the temptation to lift his eye from the ball or take his thoughts from victory. No doubt, but I am not a true golfer. I am a holiday hedonist who would gratify all his senses at once beside the sands of pleasure. So give me, first and foremost, Gullane ' smelling April and May.'

Incidentally, one of the best places from which to see the central coast of Eastern Scotland is from Dundee Law. Dundee, Aberdeen's rival in size, has been too easily dismissed as far from bonnie, mainly by people who do not go there. It has been censured for misuse of an unquestionably fine site on the southward facing bank of the

Tay. But that was not the only fine site misused in what Baldwin once aptly called ' The Age of Anyhow.' It is true that the jute industry, which was built up round the harbour used by the Dundee whalers because whale oil eased the coarseness of the jute fibre, has created gaunt-looking mills and soaring chimney-stacks; but smoke drifts across the town rather less than it did, its new light industries make no mess, and on a day of little cloud a stance on the Brae or beside the War Memorial on the Law gives a glorious survey of sands of pleasure on the shores of Angus and of Fife as well as of the mountainous core of mid-Scotland.

It is a pity that Dundee is now less used than it was for passenger traffic by sea. Queen Victoria's first entry to Scotland was made this way; she had travelled up from London by steamer and came in by ' silvery Tay,' to use the adjective so dear to Dundee's poetic curio, the strolling player and wandering minstrel, McGonagal; his solemnities in a species of banal rhymed prose have been laughed at for their constancy in sinking. But there is something likeable in a bathos so honest, so unqualified. James Bridie did well to give the man some honour in a play, ' Gog and McGog,' based on a figure fairly identifiable as McGonagal; the latter's astonishing minstrelsy is worth the purchase in a Dundee book-shop. He was proud of his town and so are Dundonians still. It suffered terribly from a slump in the jute industry between the wars, but now its economy is stronger and better balanced. It is not a city for a holiday, but from its northern slopes there is a panorama of inviting beaches and of Scotland's most famous links issuing their invitations to old Pitarrow's ancient, manly, and employment-yielding game.

CHAPTER XI

The Conspicuous Town

THIS chapter can deal only in general impressions. It would be ridiculous to write more concerning the detail of Edinburgh when so much has been written and so worthily about its panorama of Nature's architecture and man's, its aroma of history, and its splendid capacity to be vividly modern amid all its cluster of old bravery. James Bone, with his vivid, human touch in 'The Perambulator in Edinburgh,' George Scott-Moncrieff in his expertly architectural book on the city, and Moray McLaren in his fascinating study of Edinburgh's folk, climate, and social being, 'The Capital of Scotland' are three of the city's lovers to whom I am most indebted; and finely have they declared their passion. They have spoken with experience and devotion about the quality of the city's building, the variety of its skies, the shifting music of its light, and the whole personal richness of this astonishing town. Edinburgh, as I find it every year, is like Shakespeare or Dickens: whenever you turn one of its corners, or one of their pages, something new and shining and superb confronts you. You have already walked the street, or read the passage, a score of times, but you missed a beauty —and here it is. Of course that is true of many places, of London not least. But it is especially true for those who start once more to meander north or south of Princes Street.

The first thing which must strike any stranger is that Edinburgh is both by natural ordinance and man's contrivance a Capital. It was made to rule; it did rule; and it was robbed of its command. Its kingdom was absorbed. It became the head-place of a province. When a genius in the arts has gone out of fashion and lost his acclaim in the onsweep of a new ' school ' with its novel jargon and its new aesthetic battle-cries he wears his majesty still for those who have the eye to see it or the ear to hear it and are not bullied by the thrust and clamour of the fashion. In the same way the disasters which history so capriciously inflicts can submerge a capital in matters of title and power, but the essential authority abides, like a presence in the air. Prague, for example, has remained, through all its vicissitudes and subjections, a capital. You can see at a glance that Edinburgh was meant to put its stamp on Scotland, not to take its orders from London. In appearance it is sovereign to the heart of its stones.

In this book I do not intend to be drawn into Scottish politics; the arguments for and against the renewal of a Scottish Parliament can be read elsewhere. I deny myself a fascinating subject. But, if the claims of the senses be admitted, if the fabric and feeling of a place be allowed their due persuasion, then the very look of Edinburgh is an overwhelming argument for Home Rule. That a city so beautifully mixing the fortress of Nature with the forum and the courts of man should be anything less than self-governing in all matters of national concern seems a lamentable defiance of propriety. Few Scottish Home Rulers want a drastic separation: the movement is anti-Whitehall, not anti-English. Only a fanatic denies the community of British interests in the international sphere: unity of defence and foreign policy are granted. What seems to be against all reason, when you see the regality of Old Edinburgh from the Castle to Holyrood and sense the senatorial gravity of the New, is to accept a humble, small-town function for such a place. Is this to be a scene of national sway or just a recipient of dictates from Westminster, rubber-stamping the by-laws of an alien bureaucracy?

True, Scotland has never lost its own system of law, as it has never lost its old masterly good looks, and Edinburgh is the high temple of Scottish law; but it dwindled, under the Union, to be an accepter, not an issuer, of political and economic policy. A certain amount of Civil Service deployment from Whitehall to St. Andrew's House beside the Calton Hill is welcome and that kind of change increases; but this does not abolish the central and obvious fact. Here was meant to be the seat of decision by a sovereign people, not the lodging-house of an administrative devolution. If it be culpably sentimental for a Scot to speak thus, then the blame is mine and the alleged Scottish vice of sentimentality is rooted in me. Of course I have heard all the contention that, on the executive level, Home Rule will create more trouble than it is worth; but this is no occasion to enter on that tangle, on which I shall hold my own Covenanting opinions without obtruding them or pretending that no contrary pleas have value. For the moment I assert merely an aesthetic consideration. If it be claimed by myopic politicians and desk-bound bureaucrats that aesthetics have nothing to do with economics and administrative problems, I can only disagree and leave it at that.

To me it is incredible that ancient Athens can have been what it was without looking as it did—and does. The Scottish Athens proclaims itself to me as a natural centre of dominion—in its country's own affairs. It wears a crown and, short of utter destruction in some future war, it will remain a courtly and a Parliamentary place. Partition of kingship nobody but a crazy zealot would demand, but recognition of Scotland's own rulership of its own concerns in a united British democracy is urged by every impression and sentiment upon all who are susceptible to the impact of an urban scene which is matchless in our isles. Glasgow is far larger and has its own magnificent traditions of industrial enterprise in the use of its river, of its adjacent minerals, and of its craftmanship of all kinds. So Glasgow may, in its proper pride, ask ' Why not I? ' But I do not think that a sensible Glasgow Nationalist would, on reflection, deny Edinburgh the claim, based on history, architecture, and civic atmosphere, to be the Washington of to-morrow's Scotland, while on the Clyde remains its New York.

But let us leave the politics and turn to other facets of its appearances. Edinburgh can have few rivals for closeness and urgency, even violence, of contrast. The stranger encounters several ages, a dance of periods, and a medley of chronicles. The Old Town, for example, has such menace, the New such confidence and promise. The former seems to have been built when a Scotsman's home was indeed his castle and when every man might expect to be murdered in his bed if he did not live at the top of a tiny, curling staircase and bar the stout door at the top of it. The great mansions of the High Street are dourly, defensively handsome. The imprisoning ' wynds ' and soaring ' lands ' around the Royal Mile make you shiver for the spirit of Mary the Queen when she came out of France, to this grim hub of her turbulent and slaughterous kingdom. France could hold its own, no doubt, in crimes and counter-crimes, passions, persecutions, and revenges. But Paris can never have had quite as macabre a mask as medieval Edinburgh.

It struck me as strange, when I was walking down the sinister grey canyon towards Holyrood, that Rizzio lived as long as he did. Death took few holidays hereabouts and his wings still beat in the air.

Moreover the place was long dirty after it had ceased to be dangerous—and so, in another way, it was dangerous still. Hygiene penetrated very slowly into this fortress of established squalor. Sir Walter Scott's father was a genteel, well-set lawyer, but, living in College Wynd, on the site of that Kirk o' Field where Darnley was killed in 1567, he had, in John Buchan's description, no home of health or spaciousness. 'The house stood in the corner of a small court, the flats were reached by a foul common stair, and the narrow windows looked out on Wynds where refuse rotted in heaps, pigs roamed as in a farm-yard, and well-born children played barefoot in the gutters.' Out of Mr. Walter Scott's first eight children six died in infancy. His young Walter was lame from the age of eighteen months owing to some form of infantile paralysis and was lucky to survive. Fortunately the family moved into the light and air of George Square, a beautiful piece of Scottish urbanism for which not only Edinburgh should be thankful since it probably saved the life of Scotland's greatest novelist.

What a contrast with the New Town where Craig planned and the Adams and their colleagues were to build as though space was nothing! Here was everything denied by the Old Town, broad acres, fresh airs, and a sense of security, a scene set for a ballet of graces and a high comedy of manners, not for a tragedy of fitful fevers and of bloody conclusions. The new builders designed a majestic domesticity, where all is open as the future. They put aside that past of the fortress-homes and of the man-made cliffs. They looked out not only to the country and the water, but to an age of serene existence in which law was to prevail. It was natural for the Highlanders and romantics to scoff at this new Edinburgh of writs and parchments, but it was a better place for growing Scotland than the old Edinburgh of riot among refuse.

The New Town was built as the token of a new age in which life was to expand, with the living not threatened or jostled or driven to perpetual thought of self-protection. Its creators turned the old stone from bartizan to salon, from lofty sentry-box to broad and seemly domesticity. The last disenchantment of the blood-soaked Middle Ages was faced across the old loch (and later smoke-pit) by the airy confidence of the pacific age of Reason. There is the frown of Fear in the Old Town, the smile of Hope in the New. Malignity lurks in the one, benignity walks openly in the other. Not that the lords of justice, who made their solid homes there, were fountains of Christian charity. Read ' Weir of Hermiston ' for a reminder of that. But, matched with the Royal Mile, Charlotte Square and Heriot Row breath tolerance and even mercy.

I find the New Town an essentially inspiriting place. Especially in these years of cosmic apprehension does it console. When there is so much agreement with Gloucester in ' King Lear ' that we are fallen from ' the bias of nature ' and that ' we have seen the best of our time; machinations, hollowness, treachery and all ruinous disorders follow us disquietly to our graves,' it is a powerful comfort to move in this grandeur of civic development where still the huge terraces, crescents, and squares proclaim a faith in the spacious, sedate, and civilised survival of mankind. ' Change and decay in all around I see.' Elsewhere, no doubt, and abundantly; but in the New Town of Edinburgh change and decay are exactly what you do not see: there is no craven hint that cities are made to crumble. The seigneurial society of Law Lords and Land Lords and Bank Lords that made this its refuge from the cramped violence of the Old Town has suffered economic decline; mansions are partitioned into maisonettes; the old potentates are gone or must rub elbows: milord must join milady in the labours of washing-up. But the place proclaims its belief in the permanence of the decencies and in the abiding grace of life. It has equanimity: it is as far from hysterics and bustle as any town can be. It suggests a world in which people think over what they are doing and, having thought and chosen, believe that it can be done. Philosophy is in this larger air. There is mind-room as well as elbow-room.

Lower down the hill that looks north over the Firth, in Princes Street, especially when the summer visitors are there, one may expect to be modernly jostled; this pressure arises not out of incivility but from sheer number of wanderers and window-gazers. But up in George Street you can walk as though crowds were not and never would be. It is the obvious assumption of the New Town that space is a natural feature of a city, that roads and pavements should be calm channels of passage, and that you can have a whole window to yourself when you meditate on the stately display of what we have now so drearily to call 'consumer-goods' and select a garment, a book, a fishing-rod, or a piece of furniture. The largeness of the lay-out makes one believe that dignity and leisure and a slow-paced, contemplative approach to the business or the domesticity of life have not gone from our day's trafficking. I find it hard to be a pessimist in Charlotte Square or to be in dismal tune with the melancholics or the petulants of modern literature when I take a dander among the book-shops of the New Town.

Moreover, this is a single town with many views. It is not part of a confused 'conurbation.' Once on a height— and heights are plentiful in Edinburgh—you can look over and out. Have peaks in Darien much to set against the

231

prospect from George Street, either southward to the Old Town ridge, its spires enlaced with the haze, or northward across the dip to the Firth, behind which lies Fife, 'afloat upon ethereal tides'? Even should the chilly haar, the sea-mist, seep in from the east, it is not all a dismal loss. I remember a nocturne on the Castle Rock with the marchers and dancers of a Tattoo moving like wraiths in a filmy tangle of cloud silvered by the flood-lights. It would have been cosier certainly with a clear, hard sky; the haar has a searching clamminess. But for the weaving of magic, when man's illuminations are at grips with nature's curtain-spread, it can be grotesquely captivating. At times the performance that I saw was like a coven of witches: then there would be a lift of the gauze, as it were the raising of a transparency in the old scenic dramas. There followed a sudden definition of the soldiery in all their intricate device of drill and dance. You are never at an end of Edinburgh's visual tricks. Cleopatra's 'infinite variety' is hers. Enobarbus had the word for it, when he described that Queen of Egypt. Not to have known this city is 'to have left unseen a wonderful piece of work, which not to have been blest withal would have discredited your travel.'

Well did Marjorie Fleming call it 'The Conspicuous Town.' You see it from the country surrounding as well as from its own sheer hills. It is the natural capital of a divided country, since it embodies both Highland and Lowland; the Castle Rock might have been carved out of Glencoe, yet the Lothian coast has as serene a tilth and as sweet a set of links as ever cried out for a plough on the one hand and a golf-club on the other. Poised on its own ridges it is, as James Bone has said, 'less the handiwork of man than a rearrangement of Nature.' And that is what a fine town should be, a marriage of the natural with the

232

invented. Yet it caters solidly for all needs, not the aesthetic
only, and has a particular knack of making all that it offers
for sale look even more attractive than it would do anywhere
else. We live in an age of standardised goods: no doubt
any other large city can supply in its shops of quality much
the same stuff at much the same prices. Yet in Edinburgh
something seems to be added—I am not referring to the
costs of a shopping excursion—and your appetite for buying
is strangely quickened. It is the genius of the place to raise
ordinary things to a higher power.

Having absorbed and revelled in the contrasts of squares
and terraces as sedate and affable as those of Bath and of
streets that climb and tumble like those of precipitous
Malvern, having tasted the darkness and the light of
Scottish history, the stranger who has come for the annual
Festival of the Arts can settle to his relish of the present
not only in the concert halls and theatres but in the shopping-
streets. It is easy to strengthen the inner-man (or woman)
with cake and cookie and ' fancy bread ' of a richness and
variety undreamed of in the bakeries of England or to
adorn the outer, if you have the funds, with the haberdashery, Highland or otherwise, so handsomely on parade
behind the plate-glass.

I must confess that I grow weary of those thistle-prickly
Scots who natter away at any kind of Scottish salesmanship.
Let me grant that the tartan mementoes and nicknacks on
view in sundry windows are often tawdry and hideous. They
are gimcrack Kailyard stuff, if by Kailyard, as I have defined
it, we mean a school of writing that put Scotland on the
market as merely quaint, picturesque or absurd. The true
tartans themselves are not this kind of ridiculous rubbish
and saleable fudge; they are a good and genuine thing and,
if people like to look at and even buy them, why should
they not?

Any mention of tartan, which Edinburgh displays in plenty, and, in my view, rightly, provokes endless contention among the learned in the ample and engaging letter-columns of *The Scotsman* ; there is constantly some high debate about the origins and authenticity of the weaves. I once complained that the Carnegie tartan was rarely on view and that, since my mother was a Carnegie, I much wanted to see it. In fact I had neither the purpose nor the funds to order a Highland Gentleman's Outfit. I was promptly informed by one of the sages that ' unfortunately Mr. Brown cannot wear it. He can only do so if his mother, who was a Carnegie, was an heiress, without brothers, and if he assumes the name of Carnegie.' I do not qualify. My mother was no heiress and she did have brothers. And, though Carnegie is my third pre-nomen, I shall not change my simple Aberdeenshire name of Brown in order more augustly to enkilt myself. But to be put thus out of court is not to be put out of laughter. I find this sort of heraldic hocus-pocus more amusing than irritating. Such high, pedantic talk only makes me want to be a Complete Caledonian Cad and strut about in an unjustified Carnegie kilt. So, when I see the Festival strangers surveying that generous list of ' septs ' with all its tartan-entitlements, I wish them joy of any colourful purchase which they are coaxed to make.

Surely the Scots do well to let the world know and share their own invention, an invention which has the true blazon of their hills, proper to their climate and scenery, based on their own wools and dyes and skill at the loom, usually handsome and gloried with heroic memories. No doubt many of the old clansmen were cattle-thieves and ' quick on the draw ' with a claymore in any marauding brawl. But they were honourable warriors too; they served in Britain's foreign wars with rare valour and endurance. The strangers

who buy a famous tartan for a travelling rug or a woman's
skirt—few are for the kilt—claim an honour. As long as
they realise the nature of this claim and are not con-
descending with a smile to something quaint, I am all for
accepting their custom without any pulling of sour faces.

It is true that the tartan business was organised by
salesmen during the nineteenth century. Why not? There
was royal encouragement. (George the Fourth contributed
to this good fashion, as to many other aspects of elegance.)
There was the skill of the workers: there was a European
vogue. Paris had broken out in tartan patches after 1815.
Queen Victoria continued to favour the Scottish tradition
and taste in such patterns. There was the sheer merit of
the sturdy cloth. A tartan rug is not just good tartan: it is
a good, wind-cheating coverlet. It is possible, I know, to
smile at those Guides to Highland Dress that so conveniently open wide the doors This has been done by
drawing up enormous lists of 'septs' (defined by lexico-
graphy as sub-divisions of clans) whose members are tactfully
credited with tartan-rights. Even if I abandon my right to
the Carnegie weave, as advised by high authority, I can
still make claims as a mere Brown. I discover that I am
entitled to a Lamont kilt with dark green base or to the
gaudy Macmillan weave with red upon a yellow foundation.
Are you a Clark, Clerk, or Clarke? Then, says the obliging
book of the rules, you can parade as a Cameron, Mackintosh,
or Macpherson. The Blacks can draw upon the tartans of
Lamont, MacGregor, or Maclean of Duart. The Ruskins
are well in; the great John, I read, could have worn the
Buchanan, but he might well, as an art-critic, have declined
the honour, for the Buchanan wear has a lurid yellowness
among its reds and greens which has powerfully suggested
to one irreverent commentator on kilts the optical vagaries
of a hang-over. The Taylors qualify as Cameron septs, the

Wilsons as Gunns, the Sandersons as MacDonells of Glengarry, the Shaws as Mackintoshes.

And so, multitudinously, on. I have never met anybody called Warnebald, but, if I did, I might find him, according to the book of rules, to be lawfully accoutred as a Cunningham. The film-star Donlevy is apparently entitled to a Buchanan outfit, while another in that firmament, Mr. Niven, can emerge as Cumin, Mackintosh, or MacNaughton. I am old enough to remember that the Nottinghamshire cricket-team once had a demon bowler of the name of Wass; he was said to specialise in that rarity, the fast leg-break. Had he chosen to propel these deliveries from above a kilt it would properly have been that of Munro. They make it easy for us all to have a claim on the clan-colours. Few common English names are omitted from the list of ' septs ' with these gay tartan rights attached. I am sorry, however, for the Smiths; they appear to have been left out altogether. The Robinsons could scrape in as Robiesons, with a Gunn entitlement, and the Gunns, warlike Nordic Thanes of Caithness and Sutherland, have a very handsome colour-scheme in green and black with a thin red stripe. Since my grandmother was a Manson, probably the Scottish form of Magnusson, and since according to the book, Mansons are also Gunnish, I can have my eye on that one as well as on the Lamont and Macmillan, if not the forbidden Carnegie. It is an accommodating industry.

But not, for that reason, to be mocked. Scotland is a country of limited resources: it does certain things extremely well, one of which is to use its flocks for food and clothing of the best, to design cloths with ingenuity, and to weave them with warm, enduring results. There is no shame in taking to market a good article which performs its function and gives pleasure in doing so. The abuse of tartan is not to promote its sale for proper uses, but to put it to idiotic purposes, such as the covering of booklets or photograph frames, and the bedizenment of fatuous keepsakes.

Edinburgh was first in the field with the after-war Festivals of the Arts. It took the brave line in 1947 and was rewarded with brilliant weather (not, alas, always repeated) to welcome the leading musicians, singers, dancers, actors, and other notabilities of world-wide repute. If Edinburgh is essentially a capital, it is also, in itself, essentially a stage and a setting for all things of glory. The background is a large contributor to the pleasures on any such occasion. The Festival is primarily international, but the Scottish element has tended to increase. The Glasgow Citizens' Theatre has been responsible for some of the best of the theatrical elements, both in native authorship and in lively performance. The difficulty has been to keep the Festival balanced between the top international standards and the just claims of native pride. This has been achieved by the uniting of the visiting artist with some officially recognised Scottish items and with much local and unofficial activity on the fringe. There have been admirable exhibitions of Scottish crafts, furnishings, paintings, and so on in the famous public buildings and private mansions of the city, with the Saltire Society always revealing some aspect of Scotland's legacy or present workmanship in its tall and typical Edinburgh house of the Old Town, Gladstone's Land.

The assemblage of opera, orchestras, ballet and play-acting of all kinds, of Highland Games and Military Tattoo, as well as of manifold displays and excursions to famous country houses and gardens, has become so multifarious that no visitor can hope to keep up with all of it. That is a trouble common to all Festivals. One grows faint with pursuing. The wise are those who practise a discreet selection, choose what is their own best, and then limit their activities; it is no sort of junketing that only produces 'Festival Foot,' with its corns, puffy ankles, and fallen arches, sight-seer's neck, and the malaise of cultural surfeit. In any case Edinburgh is a city which asks for time and leisurely perusal; it is nonsensical to try to 'do' it in a day or two, Festival or no Festival. Considered elimination of what not to see is most necessary to proper relish of the chosen thing. One must have time to sit back and let the influence soak in. Great cities are not to be snatched at, but absorbed.

I have spoken of the setting. What more breath-taking entry to a play than to walk from the Mound up the stairs to the Assembly Hall in the Old Town where 'The Thrie Estaits,' Sir David Lindsay's medieval riot of Scottish satirical and panoramic comedy, has been given on several occasions? The fretted sky-line proclaims the ancientry of the piece; and then there is a vast open platform with ample scope for the pageantry and blaze of colour in Tyrone Guthrie's vital massing of crowd-tumult. Guthrie has served the Festival finely, both there and in the Royal High School, whose eighteenth century hall was the apt frame for Allan Ramsay's Scottish pastoral, 'The Gentle Shepherd,' candle-lit and mellow in its midnight sessions. (The late hour was compelled by the fact that many of the devoted and industrious players were working elsewhere in the evening.) 'The Thrie Estaits' has a wider public appeal and, though the old Scottish speech in which it was written has its difficulties for ears unaccustomed to the dialect, it is so vivid in Guthrie's production, with its miming so graphic and revealing, that nobody need be deterred by its seeming strangeness or deem it to be 'blasted with antiquity.' The fact that it can be so often renewed is the proof of its wide appeal and demonstrates the range, as well as the force, of its impact. Place and performance are partners; it would not be the same if it happened outside the time-honoured façade of the Old Town.

We shall miss with feelings of poignant regret the presence of Dr. O. H. Mavor, more widely known as James Bridie. This wayward genius of Britain's theatre, as well as of his native Glasgow's, collaborated with Edinburgh to the full and from the first. The Glasgow Citizens' Theatre, of which he was the founder and the guide, has contributed splendidly to the Festival and also to breaking down the notion that Glasgow and Edinburgh are poles apart and by nature unco-operative. Bridie was the Scot first and the Glaswegian second.

Moreover, since he made life his feast, he was the perfect Festival man. He preferred enjoyment to scolding, which is uncommon in these times. Though he wrote prolifically he gave time to the drudgery of committee work and organisation, from which the creative artist may naturally flinch, although he depends so much on its efficiency. His enthusiasm seemed to raise the temperature in any gathering which he entered; he was at once gentle and cantankerous, mixing the dour and the droll; his impatience of fools was masked by his courtesy; he never paid heed to critics or made obeisance to what the public wanted; he was sweetly obstinate. He went everywhere during the Festival and, with his muttered speech which never flaunted, indeed almost wastefully obscured, the many good things that he had to say, he was the welcome, the indispensable centre of all the genial activities and quickening discussion that are the good companions of any good Festival. It is now up to Scotland to find another Bridie: it will not be easy.

England has sent the ' Old Vic ' to Edinburgh in several ventures and provided Henry Sherek's world-première of ' The Cocktail Party.' This keenly divided opinion wherever it went after starting its triumphant career in Edinburgh. There is a school of thought which holds that a Festival play should have some august and solemn quality, that it demands costume, poetry, and history, and that the provocation of uproarious laughter in Festival-time is like brawling in church. It is not an opinion that I share and I was greatly diverted by Eric Linklater's modernising of Ben Jonson's ' The Alchemist ' in ' The Atom Doctor,' which some found too funny to be festive, too high of spirit to suit the high of brow. Another Scottish item was Home's ' Douglas,' an eighteenth-century tragedy in the Shakespearean manner which made history and scandal in its day and was suitably revived as an Edinburgh curio. It was so well directed by John Casson and played with such skill and integrity by his father and mother, Sir Lewis Casson and Dame Sybil Thorndike, that its antiquity did not creak. Its derivative nature was concealed. It emerged with an air of spontaneity.

These are but few of my memories and they exclude the greater part of the Festival, which is musical and operatic, with ballet as an extra. The reason for this is simple. If one goes to Edinburgh with a special eagerness for one of the arts or with a special commission to see the plays, there is little time to see and hear much else. But those not so confined in their activities can dally with one Muse after another and have enduring memories of all. But, as I said, they should be careful not to be lured by all the dishes or by the bounty of beauties, if exhilaration is not to be turned into exhaustion.

So each year, at the end of August, Edinburgh opens its gates, invites the stranger, and disproves the absurd superstition that it is an aloof city, with the sneaping winds of its winter still lingering to nip its summer courtesy. The first impression that the visitor must surely get is of a generous and affable salutation. I have not forgotten a sweltering summer morning during that first Festival when I stood in the Old Town just below the Castle, looking the very model of a perspiring, rubber-neck tourist, a meet subject for derisive cartoon. I had in my hand one of the illustrated books on the city and was applying its architectural lore to the buildings about me in order to remedy my ignorance. There strode towards me a Senior Military Officer in uniform. I surmised that perhaps I ought not to be where I stood, that I had trespassed on some holy ground, and that I should be reminded of the fact and moved on. Instead the high officer asked me what I particularly wanted to see and could he help me? You could have knocked me down with a sabre.

My own Festival memories centre chiefly in the theatre. But they include many happy meetings and encounters in the city's famous clubs and in the special and temporary Festival Club, whose home each year is amid the Georgian elegance of the Assembly Rooms in George Street. There have been festive encounters, too, in the Masonic Hall, in the restaurants, and as far out as Muirfield and North Berwick. Among the best features of any Festival of the Arts are the chance meetings and midnight sessions; to see and hear challenging things is only half the pleasure; subsequent discussion crowns the delight. It can, of course, be as exhausting as it is tempting to sit and talk, let alone to drink and smoke, too late. But the Edinburgh atmosphere is one which, as a rule, happily defies fatigue. You can undertake a good deal more amid its tonic qualities than in places of less stimulant and nimble air: here is a place where you start 'two whiskies up,' even before you have had any whisky.

I suppose that the artists themselves enjoy it least. They arrive in a rush, harassed with past rehearsals, hag-ridden by 'first night' fears. They lack the time to look round and, if they have the time, they are perhaps too tired or perhaps too intellectually lazy to do so. It always astonishes me that actors, who in their course of work have to visit many strange and fascinating places, rarely bother to go outside their hotels or their stage-doors. Very few spots are a tenth as exciting as Edinburgh, but no place is dull or wearisome if you have curiosity and care to fathom its secrets, to taste its humours and, by reading a little in advance and then by wandering a little when you get there, to appreciate the variety of character and of social being that our British towns possess. I remember one famous company in Edinburgh which had a few days off between performances. Its wealthier members rushed back to London as though they were escaping from a desert of brick and a barbarian society. Incredible blindness! It is easy to be bored by bores; but it is ridiculous to be bored by places. Such tedium is a symptom of human inadequacy: it is permissible, no doubt, to morose isolationists yawning amid the dead air of hotel lounges, but why stay in these prisons? Festivals are meant to get you out of them. I fail to see how anybody who has an eye in his head or any appetite for the oddities and splendours of the human achievement or the natural scene can possibly be bored in Edinburgh, the Conspicuous Town.

CHAPTER XII

Ayr and Song

BEFORE we move across to the sister-city of Glasgow, it will be agreeable to take the country air again. Opposite the Sands of Pleasure, and with notable Pleasure Sands of its own, is the shire of song, the Land of Burns. There has been a prodigious cult of Robert Burns in Scotland and beyond Scotland; the English-speaking world sings the Scottish-written song on New Year's Eve wherever hands are joined at midnight; on the Burns Birthday there will be oratory and toasting in circles of Scottish Reunionism round the globe. But there has been no considerable development of a Burns Industry.

This must surprise some of the English who regard the Scots as devoted money-makers and persistent takers of the main chance wherever offered. Yet the English, while proudly and properly observing the Shakespearean rites, have built up a far more flourishing Shakespeare Business than the supposedly greedy Scots have ever constructed on the soil of Burns's Ayrshire. Scottish enterprise has, it is true, squeezed out of some genuine (and more invented) tartans a trickle of profit by selling hideous ' gifts frae yont the border ' to the less judicious tourists and the same enterprise has produced some little ' memento ' editions of Burns's most seemly and enduring songs in a garish and bedizened form that might be described as ' Caledonian Plus '; these would be powerful competitors in any international Tournament of Bad Taste. But the Scots have not made Ayrshire a notable centre of pilgrimage with Mauchline a Mecca.

A dramatist, of course, is much more easily honoured in public by performance of his plays than is a lyric poet saluted by recitation of his lyrics. But, even so, more might have been done by Burnsian commerce if the Scots had set about it with relentless avidity. Fortunately the Scots are not so rapacious. You can tell by the number of hotel-beds available in the Burns County that few travellers settle there, even for the night; nor do a great number flit through the various villages which own poetical associations. The English tourist's concentration on the Highlands and his reluctance to dally in what is, except for the single-minded Burnsian, ordinary country, sweeps him straight to the Trossachs. Those who journey by air and land at Prestwick are immediately hurtled away by road or by another flight.

The landscape around Ayr is not sensational; it is not even, by commercial standards, romantic; it is not, in any exploitable way, ' traveller's joy.' The visitor finds a utilitarian farming landscape, much improved in productivity since Burns's time, workaday Lowland pasture and tilth with uplands that do not soar with any spectacular uppishness. A frieze of summits may be descried across the Firth of Clyde in glorious abundance, but Ayrshire, as a centre of visitation, lives by its famous golf links of Troon, Prestwick, Turnberry and the others on the coast and by the modest gaieties of a ' resort ' which the town of Ayr itself presents to the workers of the Industrial Belt; these may, like so many Scots, be ecstatic Burnsians on January 25th, but are not otherwise concerned to be pilgrims, bowing the knee at a Memorial or musing in reverence by the banks of a burn ' famoused by song.'

Furthermore the chances of the Burns Industry are hampered by the dispersal of the sights and shrines. Shakespeare rendered an inestimable service to his birth-place when he also bought property, died, and was buried there, all within half-a-mile. He almost certainly went to school in Stratford-upon-Avon and there certainly his children were born, grew up, and married. He acquired the Big House there and, despite long periods in London, he was essentially a citizen of Stratford and of no other place outside London. Since London has lost all the streets and buildings with which Shakespeare was most closely associated, Stratford has taken from London the profitable status of the Bardic Mecca in the eyes of the venerating pilgrim. Burns, on the other hand, comparable with Shakespeare in the passionate loyalty of his addicts, though certainly not comparable in range or depth of genius, is remembered in various places between Kilmarnock and Dumfries; these are not much more than fifty miles apart, it is true, but far more wandering is involved if all the relics and tributes are to be ' covered.' If only Burns had lived and died in Ayr, as well as being born close to it, all would have been well for the Industry.

Ayr, though Defoe described it as decaying daily and sunk from the fifth best town of Scotland to be the fifth worst, has defeated his pessimism. It has not only its mellow antiquity, its historic bridges, Wallace Tower, and Auld Kirk: it has an admirable sea-beach, separated from the town by a handsome stretch of green; it has the amenities of race-course and theatre, and it is a town that makes holiday reception one of its chief concerns. Its northern coast-line is dull, except for golfers, to whom it is Paradise; but southward it soon acquires a wilder quality as it sweeps round by Girvan to Galloway. So, if Burns had concentrated his life in Ayr, the happy travellers could have poured in and ' done ' the shrines promptly and properly in neat rotation, all linked with a paddle on the beach, if not in the burn. But the poet strayed too much and died in Dumfries. His remembrance is not to be pinned to one place.

Robert Burns was born at Alloway, on the banks of Doon which runs down from Loch Doon in Galloway to create here and there the sylvan riparian scenery which the poet so much preferred to austere grandeur of landscape. So he is first remembered in the cottage where he was baptised, with punctual celerity, on the day after his birth in January, 1759, being vowed to righteousness by as sombrely righteous a father as ever begat a brilliant but ' a rovin', rantin' lad.' The family stayed at Alloway till Robert was seven and then moved, to their misfortune, to bare Mount Oliphant, between Ayr and Maybole, hard land for a farmer who was always under-capitalised and ill-equipped. The next move, taken when the boy was 16, was to Lochlie, which made Tarbolton, a weaving centre for linen, cotton, and silk, the centre of his young society. It had a rowth, as the Scots say, of lusty bachelors and their natural prey. Here, at Lochlie, the poet's good, glum father died, worn out with the ill-rewarded toil of a farmer for whom there were no subsidies, no social services, and not much more beneficence of Nature than of man.

The sons then moved to Mossgiel, which made Mauchline their target for commerce and for gay adventure. If we are to judge by the bawdy hilarity of Burns's somewhat phallic ode ' The Court of Equity,' Mauchline did not lack the rough pleasures of small-town gallantry and seduction. It was then a comparatively busy and a bustling place, where roads met and ' drouthy billies ' too. It had a brisk tavern life; to this a nefarious slut called Poosie Nancie contributed with a market-side inn which received the lowest and wildest company. Later, in 1788, came the move to Ellisland, forty-six miles from Mauchline; there followed another farming failure and the employment of Burns as Excise Officer at Dumfries, his dwindling of health (endocarditis, not drink the cause) and his death in that town where he had begun to relish the clash of politics as well as the favours of the barmaid at the Globe.

Hence the memorials are scattered. Alloway has the birthplace and its own Monument, a Corinthian cyclostyle with cupola. But the Auld Brig o' Doon, with the banks and braes about it, and the Kirk where Tam o' Shanter had his memorable encounter are more powerful mementoes of genius than are cupola and museum. The National Memorial, as well as Poosie Nancie's establishment, are at Mauchline; Kilmarnock, away to the north, has its own tributary edifice and collected ' Burnsiana.' Ayr has the two Brigs of which Burns wrote with passion and a tavern now almost sacrosanct. Dumfries contains the Globe Inn, the death-place in the Old Mill Brae, now Burns Street; the grave, with classical mausoleum, is in St. Michael's Churchyard, and the statue is in High Street.

Of course a motor-car can ' do ' the Burns Circuit in a day and by some it is done; but I have never felt in visiting the shrines that I am doing much more than pay a formal call. About Stratford where Shakespeare was all his life a permanent influence, though long, to the world's benefit, an absentee in London, about Stratford to which he retired to find a prosperous peace, there is a settled Shakespearean feeling which no amount of superficial sight-seeing by myriads of transients can destroy. But Burns had no such

247

resting-place: he lived so rapidly, moved so much, lacked municipal attachments, and was never, as Shakespeare was, essentially a rooted citizen; so his genius has to be sought, if that be a possible quest, on the fields, in a few taverns of the gangrel folk, and above all in the gentle hollows where the Ayrshire rivers run among the rowans and the thorns, where the birds sing in May, and there is a little shelter in black January from all the various tyrannies of weather.

The traveller to-day will see in good heart land that was in very poor fettle when the Burns family shifted from one unprofitable holding to another. The agricultural improvement was not for a long time so conspicuous or so rapid and thorough in Southern Scottish life as was the swift industrial revolution which both enriched and befouled the central belt. But, coming far more slowly, it has vastly altered agricultural method and turned life on the hillside steading from a desperate drudgery into a reasonable investment for the industrious and careful men of Kyle, Cunningham, and Carrick. One has to look at Mossgiel or Ellisland to-day with imagination if one is surely to apprehend the places as they were while Robert ploughed, read, and wrote with an industrious application only relieved by the surrenders of the other sex to his charm and importunity.

The most exciting thing about the Burns Country is the view out of it. Hard by, to the west, are the lovely reaches of Clyde's lower Firth, with Ailsa Craig to the south and the sensational façade of the Arran peaks directly facing the farm-lands of Mount Oliphant and Mossgiel. Yet Burns, as far as his poetry is evidence, was little impressed by the sea-scape and sky-line which are so impressive to us. His heart was in the hollows, not the Highlands: his later travels to the mountains never moved him as did the song-resounding glades by Cluden and by Doon. In the parlour

of the Inn at Taymouth, which lies at the exquisite eastern
end of the long, slim loch below the huge Ben Lawers, he
was moved only to indulge his classic vein:

> *Th' outstretching lake, imbosomed 'mong the hills,*
> *The eye with wonder and amazement fills;*
> *The Tay meandering sweet in infant pride.*
> *The palace rising on his verdant side . . .*
> *Poetic ardors in my bosom swell*
> *Lone wand'ring by the hermit's mossy cell . . .*
> *Here Poesy might wake her heaven-taught lyre*
> *And look through Nature with creative fire.*

Might wake, but did not. When a natural singer of the
banks and braes talks of ardours in his bosom and heaven-
taught lyres, you know that he is feeling almost nothing.
Burns found fifty times more inspiration ' amang the rigs
o' barley ' and among the cushat-sounding, milk-white
sloes than ever he discovered under the vast majesty of
Lawers. Again, at the torrential Fall of Foyers beside the
savage melancholy of Loch Ness, he found refuge in the
classical couplets that were but a memory of the English
convention:

> *Prone down the rock the whitening sheet descends*
> *And viewless Echo's ear, astonished, rends.*
> *Dim-seen, through rising mists and ceaseless showers,*
> *The hoary cavern, wide-surrounding, low'rs.*
> *Still through the gap the struggling river toils*
> *And still, below, the horrid cauldron boils.*

A clever school-boy could churn out this competent pastiche
of eighteenth-century heroics. It simply is not the real
Burns. By Bruar Water, near Blair Atholl, a cascade now

harnessed by the Hydro-Electric Scheme, he did, indeed, compose in his own idiom and metre. But his purpose was only to protest against the Duke of Atholl's tree-felling in a jingle of some charm but of little strong or well communicated emotion.

Farther west, amid the splendours of Loch Fyne, it may have been an inhospitable landlord who provoked him to register his opinions of Inveraray thus:

> *There's naething here but Highland pride,*
> *And Highland scab and hunger:*
> *If Providence has sent me here*
> *'Twas surely in an anger.*

His own Lowland pride, a fiery quality, and his early Lowland hunger hardly gave him the right to sneer thus at the Campbell country. Regard that jest as lightly as we may, we cannot find in Burns the devotee of the Dead Vast; his own romanticism was far removed from that of the English Lake poets, who felt mountains to be the pith of the sublime. His taste had been formed on the earlier rhapsodies of eighteenth century English poetry, and the first impact of Nature on his rejoicing consciousness was the 'impulse from the vernal wood.' His affection was for the gentle breeze so frequently called a zephyr, since it was then obligatory with intending poets (and it often remained so with Burns) to link the terminology of Greece with the scenery of our own shires. He long preserved, amid the racy bawdy of the taverns, an addiction to calling a lover a swain and the 'cauld blast' Boreas. Always enjoying a posture, he had to chose a classical name for his Edinburgh wooing and elected to be Sylvander. At times he would mix the alien and native idiom without concern: 'The Lass of Ballochmyle,' for example, mingles such honest simplicities as

Give me the cot below the pine,
To tend the flocks, or till the soil,
And every day have joys divine
With the bonny lass o' Ballochmyle

with wanton zephyrs, country swain, maiden fair, and
' Nature's vernal smile.' These had little enough to do
with Ayrshire and much with the reading of his boyhood
under Dominie Murdoch.

On the farmlands he did indeed slave at the plough,
though he was never the unlettered ploughman. His father
had seen to that: it is no rude yokel that has a share of a
private tutor, is master of trigonometry at sixteen, and a
year later has worked through Locke ' On the Human
Understanding.' On the farmlands he looked across,
whether he liked it or not, to what rivets the eyes of any
Burnsian now at large there, the serrated rim of the Arran
mountains which soar up with such conquering theatricality
across the Firth. As the clouds so often shrouding Cir
Mhor, the Castles, and Ben Nuis suddenly lift and the
infinite blue breaks open, the island of Arran seen from
the Ayrshire coast is a breath-taking spectacle. It has given
me beauty's shiver of delight often enough: it is a view
enchantingly various. There is a sudden hardening into
spears of rock of what had been a wisp of delicate vapours
only a few minutes before. There is a restless play of colours,
now dark as thunder, now glittering with the sheen of
naked stone. These may follow the majesty of a roseate
sunset behind the great façade. Given a poet of genius,
of a genius intermittent but overwhelming in its use of
simple words for simple feelings, you would expect a score
of unforgettable lyrics to have sprung from this panorama.
But they did not spring and the dying Burns was dreaming,
in Dumfries and in his pathetic and fatal condemnation to

251

a sea-water cure in the cold waters of Solway, of quite
other comforts of the eye and of the recollecting fancy:

> *In gowany glens the burnie strays*
> *Where bonnie lasses bleach thir claes,*
> *Or trots by hazelly shaws and braes*
> *Wi' hawthorns gray*
> *Where blackbirds join the shepherds' lays*
> *At close o' day.*

That was the view before his clouding eyes.

Those who wish to be good pilgrims, loyal to their man,
in Ayrshire must prefer the rivulet in the meadow to the
great surge of the Galloway hills and moors so close at
hand or to the view of the Arran miracle across the water.
The merle and mavis, as he long preferred to call them,
were far more to him than the muircock or the soaring
buzzard. The odd thing about the idol of Scottish song is
that, as far as scenery counted, he would have been completely at home in Surrey.

> *Still o'er these scenes my memory wakes.*

What scenes ? It is so often the same. The buds are always
bursting, the choir of the thicket is always in gentle voice,
the time of day is always evening, the worker's play-time,
the work-time of the lover:

> *Ayr, gurgling, kiss'd his pebbled shore,*
> *O'erhung with wild woods, thick'ning green;*
> *The fragrant birch, and hawthorn hoar,*
> *Twined amorous round the raptured scene;*
> *The flowers sprang wanton to be prest,*
> *The birds sang love on every spray—*
> *Till too, too soon, the glowing west*
> *Proclaim'd the speed of wingèd day.*

252

All streams ran sweetly in the gloaming.

> *Flow gently, sweet Afton, among thy green braes,*
> *Flow gently, I'll sing thee a song in thy praise;*
> *My Mary's asleep by thy murmuring stream—*
> *Flow gently, sweet Afton, disturb not her dream.*

Such lines could have been written in any bosky and well-watered countryside. Ayrshire is only particularised by Burns in its speech, when he abandoned traditional 'poetese' for the vernacular, and in his people, when he forgot his education and remembered his mates. Perhaps that is one reason why Burns won so wide a worship. His poetry transcends locality; is not of any single shire or country. His lyrical home is wherever Nature softly pleases.

The Scottish Burns Cult has been the subject of ridicule and even of scorn. It is frequently said that the members of the Burns Clubs, who maintain with such fervour and such constancy their annual rites of oratory, toasting and drinking on the Birthday Night, think far more about the liquor than they do about the lyrics. It is said that they are ill-read in the poems and ignorant of the poet's life, with the added hint that more realistic knowledge of his behaviour would mitigate the idolising of their hero. It is claimed, chiefly by the English, that the Scots are obsessed by Burns, over-estimating what they have because they have so little else. It is replied, I think with more justice, by the Scots, or at least by those Scots who take an interest in poetry as well as in Burns, that this Burns Obsession has been a literary nuisance as well as a necessary tribute, since it has blinded the eyes of far too many to the work of Scottish poets both before and after Burns. These are points which must occur to anyone who is a guest at a Burns Night, who includes an Ayrshire journey in his visits to Scotland, or who is interested in the psychology of national and racial symbolism and of heroes and hero-worship in general.

Of the quantity of the Burns Cult there can be no question. Sir Alexander Gray, when introducing his admirably fresh and characteristically acute Anniversary speech to the Scottish Arts Club of Edinburgh in January, 1944, put it thus:

'. . . I have a theory that a Burns speech is like matrimony—while it is a task to which every man should brace himself once in his life, a wise man should have very good reasons before risking it a second time. When you think of it, a Burns speech is something of an ordeal. To-night, on the 22nd, we are ahead of the crowd; but in normal years, on the appointed night, the earth whirling on its axis at the appointed hour rouses unwilling speakers from their chairs in Calcutta, in Cairo, in Cape Town, and in Cardiff. It is a solemn thought that in these islands some hundreds of speakers may simultaneously be sweating the juice of haggis while groping for the elusive word. Six hours later the flood of oratory—a greater than the Severn Bore—sweeping past the Statue of Liberty breaks upon the shores of America, and traversing the great plains dies away in rippling waves in California. It is, I say, a devastating thought . . .'

Those who have either proposed the Immortal Memory themselves or listened to others, less gifted than Sir Alexander, performing that office, understand the full meaning of that devastation. All over the world, as well as all over Scotland, the Burns Night brings dutifully forth—the duty to be later relieved by libation, song and dance—myriads who never look at or think about the writings of their darling for the remainder of the year.

Is that merely a form of humbug? I think not.
Thousands go to Stratford whose knowledge of Shakespeare
is trifling and whose appreciation of him is perfunctory or
a matter of cultural routine: but there is something credit-
able, or at least something better than nothing, in public
obeisance to a writer of genius instead of to yet another of
the athletes, charlatans, or divas of the screen and of the
gossip-column who are the popular idols of every day. If I
am not to sneer at the crowds gaping beside the Warwickshire Avon during a summer week-end, I am not going to
deride the haggis-eaters and dram-drinkers who pay the
poet the compliment of speech-listening as well as self-
indulgence on the night of the annual salaam.

Shakespeare and Burns have one great thing in common.
They give to every one, simply and superbly expressed, the
sentiment that he wishes to hear. There is no attitude to
life, to morals, and to the pursuit of happiness that both
did not express with felicity. Because Shakespeare was a
dramatist he could put these contradictory sentiments into
the mouths of his characters, leaving us in constant doubt
as to his own private opinions. Burns voiced all this variety
of mood himself: many of his songs are new, and wonderfully improved, versions of the old. But the work is signed
as his and, if he is alternately on the side of God and Devil,
that is his affair. Since Burns praised lavish drinking and
wise restraint, free loving and the domestic virtues, railed
at the ' birkie ca'd a lord ' and cried up the Stuart cause
whose success would certainly not have resulted in the
equalitarian and democratic republic at other times so dear
to his heart, he can reasonably be called Mr. Facing Allways.
But he was, in my view, not so much a hypocrite as an
impulsive, impetuous person, innocent and childlike in his
notions of society. He responded to bright and generous
things without pausing to co-ordinate his verdicts. Charlie

was a brave and bonnie loser: therefore salute him with the tribute of a sigh. Liberty, equality, and fraternity are brave and bonnie, if incompatible, notions; so give them, too, the tribute of a rousing song.

In a similar way the author of the frankly licentious ' Court of Equity,' not usually printed, and the charitable singer of the ' tousie drab,' in lays deemed more presentable, could sincerely praise the conjugal virtues:

> *The sacred lowe o' weel-placed love,*
> *Luxuriantly indulge it;*
> *But never tempt the illicit rove,*
> *Though naething should divulge it:*
> *I waive the quantum o' the sin,*
> *The hazard of concealing;*
> *But, och! it hardens a' within,*
> *And petrifies the feeling!*

He himself, through plentiful experience, knew well enough the ' quantum of the sin ' and the hardening thereby of sensibility's arteries. He frankly declared the ugliness of such corruption and uttered warnings fit for the sternest of pulpiteers.

> *When ranting round in Pleasure's ring,*
> *Religion may be blinded;*
> *Or if she gie a random sting,*
> *It may be little minded;*
> *But when on life we're tempest-driven,*
> *A conscience but a canker—*
> *A correspondence fix'd wi' Heaven*
> *Is sure a noble anchor!*

Adding elsewhere:

Reader, attend—whether thy soul,
Soars fancy's flights beyond the pole,
Of darkling grubs this earthy hole,
                    In low pursuit;
Know prudent, cautious self-control
                    Is wisdom's root.

The gravest Minister could not give graver counsel. While
he was far from a faithful husband and treated his women,
by our standards, callously, he could yet be on the side of
the domestic angels:

> *To make a happy fire-side clime*
> *To weans and wife,*
> *That's the true pathos and sublime*
> *Of human life.*

That put him right with the Kirk whose servants, even the
holiest of Holy Willies, could rub their hands and take
their place, unabashed, at a Burns Celebration. That piety
could quote him to its own purpose does not prove the loose
liver that he was to have been an intolerable hypocrite. It
does prove him wayward in judgment, as in mood, now
lured by the discipline of decency and now by the call of
liberty, in love as in politics. Burns, with all his occasional
brutishness, was too big to be a brute. Consistency is a
fine thing in logicians, but poets of genius are to be excused
its obligations. Burns was a fiery particle whose sparks
flew in all directions: we can properly be warmed by all
his radiations without censuring his inability to blaze only
up the chimney of a single and a virtuous home.

In Ayrshire one should, of course, have a volume of
Burns for company: it is not necessary to carry the whole
'corpus.' Few writers gain more by being read in selection:
stick to the Scots poems, with glossary, and all will be well.

Some of the Anglicised compositions, using the classical 'poetese' of the eighteenth century, are frightening.

Tho' something like moisture conglobes in my eye

is as dreadful a line as ever was written by a man who should have known better. Yet it came from the pen that wrote 'Ae fond kiss.' With the selected Burns, I advise two recent books, the Life by Catharine Carswell and 'There Was A Lad' by Hilton Brown: both are as frank about his failings as they are warm with affection for his greatness. Other useful additions to the portable library are the poems of Robert Fergusson, on whom Burns drew so much: the Saltire Society's edition, published by Oliver and Boyd of Edinburgh, is slim and light and useful. It is only fair to add, for balance, another reasonably sized volume of contemporary Scottish verse, say Maurice Lindsay's anthology, published by Faber. This has an excellent introduction briefly describing the decline of Scottish poetry in the nineteenth century and its resurgence in recent years. That will get Burns into proportion, as a derivative poet, as a creative poet, and as a too powerful influence that had to be overcome. I do not think that the moderns need be afraid of comparisons. Scotland to-day is rich in poets and the last thing Burns would have wanted would be to get in their way.

With the lives in hand, one is tempted to link the loves with the localities. At Mount Oliphant was Nelly Kilpatrick, first cause of his affection's Muse.

> *She dresses aye sae clean and neat,*
> *Baith decent and genteel;*
> *And then there's something in her gait*
> *Gars ony dress look weel.*

Some of Robert's later 'flames' were to be neither decent

nor genteel, but for a while a pleasant idealism ruled his
heart. At Kirkoswald, below Mount Oliphant, was Peggy
Thomson (' We'll gently walk and sweetly talk '). Lochlie
brought Tarbolton's charmers to his ken, Annie and Jennie
Ronald and Alison Begbie. (' I'll ne'er forget that happy
night, Amang the rigs wi' Annie '.) Miss Begbie would
not have Burns in marriage; but there were consolations.
At Lochlie he got his first ' bastart wean ' by Lizzie Paton
the servant-girl. The move to Mauchline and Mossgiel
brought Jean Armour into the heart which she was to hold
longer than did any other: she married him twice over, if
the first document was binding: she bore him two sets of
twins and other children. Mortality ran high. Of the
quartet of twins but one member survived.

Then there was Highland Mary, a Miss Campbell of
Dunoon, who probably had (and lost) a child by Burns. In
Edinburgh there was not only Mrs. Maclehose, Clarinda
to his Sylvander, but May Cameron and Jenny Clow on a
much lower level of society. The Ellisland and Dumfries
periods bring us to Anna Park, barmaid of the Globe, who
gave him a daughter, and Jessie Lewars, probably the most
platonic of his affairs. It is a little strange, after all this,
to find Hilton Brown, who has charted Burns's loves most
carefully, asserting that he was not promiscuous. ' If we
neglect the mere utilities—the Clows, Camerons, and Parks
—the number of love-affairs in his life was probably below
the ordinary male average rather than above it.' But can
we thus write of ' utilities,' especially if they have borne
children to the user? It is an odd doctrine of ethics that a
man's animalism in sex relations is dismissed as irrelevant
to his moral character.

It cannot be denied that Robert Burns was as coarse and
callous at one time as he was tender and sensitive at another.
The worst thing in his life was the appalling letter to Ainslie

259

in which he boasted of the 'thundering scalade that electrified the very marrow of her bones,' administered on some dry horse-litter to Jean Armour when she was eight months gone with child. 'And how much harm,' adds Hilton Brown with justice, 'was done to his unfortunate twins who were to appear in three weeks and die in four?' It is best to face the facts before we start the excuses.

The excuses lie, I suppose, in the prevailing opinion of the time. 'It was na' adultery,' pleaded one arraigned by his ethical betters, 'It was just plain forni.' 'Plain forni' was accepted by the young men and women of the countryside. Burns's own mother, wife of the godly William, would sing the old Scottish lilts to her children: and they were not songs for saints:

> *Kissing is the key o' love*
> *And clappin' is the lock,*
> *And makin' o's the best thing*
> *That e'er a young thing got.*

That, to say the least of it, is provocation.

The Kirk was severe, but it was not sovereign. It scolded, but it could not check. And the very severity merely increased the enticement of the forbidden thing. If, as Cyril Connolly has said, inside every fat man there is a thin man crying to get out, there is no less a hedonist inside every Puritan demanding a passionate release. Calvinism has begot a myriad Scottish bastards in its time and made the Scot, when drinking, inclined to drink bestially. If a man is to be damned for entering a pub, he soon decides that he may as well have his money's worth on this road to Hell. If the Sabbath is so strict that there is nothing to look at out of church except the other sex, then Sunday is likely to be the solvent of much virtue. The

Scots of the villages had long combined an iron-clad theology with a lax morality. The young women whom Burns so easily fascinated took both the pleasure of the fall and the penalty of pregnancy for granted and there was no commonly accepted atmosphere of heinous sin about the getting of bastards by servant-girls and barmaids in ' plain forni.'

That is the kind of moral (or a-moral) climate which the traveller to Mauchline must imagine as he tries to reconstruct Burns's life and see the poet plain. Then against the shocking callousness and ' the quantum of the sin ' he must set the unaffected beauty of tenderness with which Burns could invest his sunset songs of love among the birdsong and the barley. The songs could never have been written in a mood of mere fudge. Sometimes, of course, it seems intolerable that a man who could be so compassionate to the pelleted hare and the frightened mouse, so tormented by the sportsman's breach of ' Nature's social union,' should have paid so little reckoning to the consequences of his seductions and ' scalades.' Yet that man had such a grace of vision and so sincere a hand to portray it that he defies our indignation. Even his ' tousie drabs ' drew some of his finest verses. The petrifaction of the feelings never destroyed the generous authenticity of his lyric love. ' A thought ungentle canna be, The thought of Mary Morison.'

It is now commonly agreed—and Hilton Brown confirms the point—that Burns was no reckless soak and did not drown his genius either in ' tippenny ' ale or the stronger ' usky ' of the day. He took his drink with others and may have carried it less steadily. It is to be noted that he continually praised ' the social glass,' since a drink to him was the companion of fellowship, conversation, and hilarity: he does not sing of it as the anodyne of solitary melancholiacs. The glass warms and it stimulates. He was, in his cups, not running away from life, but going to meet it.

> *Leeze me on drink! it gies us mair*
> *Than either school or college:*
> *It kindles wit, it waukens lair,*
> *It pangs us fou o' knowledge.*
> *Be't whisky gill, or penny wheep,*
> *Or ony stronger potion,*
> *It never fails, on drinking deep,*
> *To kittle up our notion*
> > *By night or day.*

This notion-kittling may be an idealistic version of what once went on in the Ayrshire taverns where now the occasional motor-coach stops for more physical bracing. But it is the Scottish equivalent of Hilaire Belloc's Heroic Poem in Praise of Wine:

> *Wine, true begetter of all arts that be.*
> *Wine, privilege of the completely free,*
> *Wine, the recorder; wine, the sagely strong:*
> *Wine, bright avenger of sly-dealing wrong.*

Burns would have been glad to write that of his own barley-bree.

He dramatised himself, a practice often the defence of the lowly and the rising man. In Edinburgh he stressed his early ploughmanship. 'I was bred to the plough and am independent.' That was true: but he was also much more than an untutored hand and it was dramatic to conceal, before the nobility and gentry of the capital, the fact that he was better schooled and more widely read than they were. In the same way he flaunted his flowing cups and posed occasionally as a maltworm of tremendous application to the bottle. But there seems to be no doubt that it was rheumatism, with its damage to the heart, and not alcohol, with its damage to the liver, that broke him so early. Modern medicine, in all probability, could have lengthened his life far beyond the thirty-seven years of his ardours, triumphs, and disappointments. Travellers by the Solway Firth, while remembering its brightly coloured history of estuarial smuggling and adventure, must also look on the dark side of its famous tides; they were accessories to the medical murder of Robert Burns.

He was ordered to take not only the chalybeate waters available at Brow Well, but a course of sea-bathing—and that in a cold July. Sea-bathing in Scotland is a considerable plunge for a strong man. (To judge by the crowded beaches and swimming-pools even in east-windy summer weather Scotland has plenty of such gallants—and plenty of strong women too.) For an invalid it is homicidal. Each day, as Mrs. Carswell described the cruel discipline of the doctors, ' he waded slowly into the chill water that he might stand obediently up to his arm-pits until it was time to drag his aching joints out again and slowly dry himself and sip his allowance of port.' Icy water first and port for a restorative! It was a bizarre cure for acute rheumatism. That picture makes Solway a name for ever shiversome to me.

Devotion to Burns has not made Ayrshire a world-renowned scene of cultural festivities. Possibly if Burns had been born at mid-summer instead of in January the red, red rose of June and the little white rose of Scotland would have been carried to his birthplace in ceremonial processions and an annual Ayr Festival not only of poetry but of drama, for which art Burns was preparing his Muse at the end, would have drawn the faithful from far and wide. As it is, while Shakespeare-worship has been increasingly centripetal and has drawn ever greater crowds to Stratford, Burns-worship has been centrifugal. It has worked so far outwards that on January 25th you would be as likely to hear the Ode to a Haggis recited in Alaska as in Ayr itself. Had Burns been a Highlander, born and dying in Perth or Inverness, celebration would have drawn the many. (Consider the available scenery for additional attraction.) But if Burns had been a Highlander he would not have been Burns.

He became the symbol of Scottishness since he had worded so well the multitudinous and conflicting moods of his nation's piety and of its licence. He had spoken for the honest worth of poverty and his poems have been part of the inspiration of nearly every reforming leader and of the Labour Party pioneers. Yet he was smooth enough to the gentry of the Caledonian Hunt to atone in their eyes for his more frequent egalitarian sentiments. Though his voice was untuneable and his ear nearly tone-deaf, he had a rare feeling for a melodious line and, when he wrote in his vernacular, his verses flowed like the rivers and burns that he so adored. 'He has the semi-miraculous power,' wrote Edwin Muir, 'of making any Scotsman whether generous or canny, sentimental or prosaic, religious or profane, more wholeheartedly himself than he could have been without assistance: in that way perhaps more human. He is a comforting, a necessary figure.' That is a wise judgment. To reassure the common man and to be essential to his confidence and comfort is the function of all National Myths, the attribute of all worshipped heroes. To that heroic status Robert Burns has been appointed and Ayrshire is the more honoured.

Despite some unromantic qualities and unheroic deeds of self-indulgence, Burns has justly been elevated to a niche in the great line of National Presences. The Immortal

Memory is annually toasted at a thousand tables, but the libation is a compliment paid to many others whose abiding is much more in question. The singular thing about the Burns Toast is that the man has had immortality thrust upon him without question. The phrase that I chose to use, National Presences, applies accurately to Burns, for wherever there is a stir of Scottish life or the calm of evening with a dander of lovers by the burn there is he. He has said all there is to be said on the elements of Scottish toil and pleasure and said it in a way that the common memory can hold with ease and with affection.

You may go to Ayr and Alloway in search of him; but his spirit is ubiquitous. It is odd that a man so bound to one corner of Scotland, so limited a traveller—he never entered England—should be so unlimited, so unlocal, in devoted recognition. I am not trying to deflect the visitor from Ayrshire. It is a piece of representative Lowland that has well earned its keep with or without benefit of poetry; it gave Scotland a wealth of ability in industry and science, especially from its northern and more urban end. It is richly castled as well as sweetly rivered. And it has that coastal view to the great Firth from which Scotland has drawn so much of her wealth and Britain so much of her maritime security.

Burns had a mind to sail to the West Indies, but he never did. The world of his direct experience was a very small one. Except for the Edinburgh excursion and a rather melancholy inspection of the Highlands his vision centred chiefly upon the barley on the rigs or the barley-bree in the bottle, upon the village lass and the lads that roved and ranted with him, and upon their natural enemies, Holy Willie and the too lairdly laird. Yet, from his parochial Ayrshire, he sang in words which have drifted to the ends of the earth and have lived upon the lips of men scattered from the tropics to the poles. Perhaps the young Scottish emigrants remember him less than did their fathers. I do not know. But surely Ayrshire is worth a visit, with the poems in the pocket, in order to see in what ordinary places this extraordinary thing occurred.

CHAPTER XIII

Glasgow and Clyde

HAVING sniffed the Burnsian zephyrs in his county landscape, we can turn north again. The great city of Glasgow is regarded by many from the South as a murky stepping-stone to better things. Unlike Edinburgh it has no immediate eye-opener for the visitors: it has to be known well before it is properly understood. Those who only tumble out of a train and do some shopping in a downpour and then flit to another terminus and board another train, which is as much inspection as numerous travellers do bestow upon the town, will get an impression as dark as damp. My own stays have often been of this dormitory kind, which I regret, but the Western Highlands are an urgent magnet. Yet at least I have wandered a little, stood on the high places, seen majestic skies with a clear-cut panorama of the water-way and the not so distant hills, basked in the Botanical Gardens on a golden October afternoon, and taken bus to Loch Lomond as a Londoner might take it to Greenwich. Bus to Loch Lomond! Most English people are ignorant that Glasgow has such mountain glory at its gates. Moreover, because so much of its housing was built upward in tenements instead of outward in small-house suburbs, you can escape by road from this city of a million much quicker than you expect, especially if your expectation is based on London's interminable sprawl.

The tenements are gloomy, it is true, and should you chance to come across an eighteenth century poem entitled ' Clyde,' written in the heroic style by John Wilson, who went to school in Lanark and taught later in Lesmahagow and Greenock, you may be surprised at the tribute therein paid to the accommodation of the people.

> *As shines the moon among the lesser fires,*
> *Unrivalled Glasgow lifts her stately spires:*
> *For commerce, glorious with her golden crown,*
> *Has marked fair Glasgow for her favourite town:*
> *She makes her stately edifices thrive,*
> *And merchants rich in princely splendour live;*
> *Extends her spacious streets on every side,*
> *And bids her poor in palaces reside.*

The last line will now strike many Glaswegians as rather more than astonishing. Poor Wilson was compelled to abandon his stately Muse, so respectably embellished with the kindly sentiments of local patriotism. The magistrates and minister of Greenock, when the poet was admitted to a head-mastership there in 1767, would have none of that. These solemn tyrants were horrified by what they called ' the profane and unprofitable art of poem-making ' and made Wilson swear to abjure the vice. He did so because he had a large family to keep and the job was precious. His biographer, John Leyden, M.D., who wrote a prose as copious as Wilson's couplets, described his surrender:

' To avoid the temptation of violating this promise, which he esteemed sacred, he took an early opportunity of committing to the flames the greater part of his unfinished manuscripts. After this, he never ventured to touch his forbidden lyre, though he often regarded it with the mournful solemnity, which the harshness of dependence, and the memory of its departed sounds, could not fail to inspire.'

It did not pay to be a song-bird in the austere groves of Scottish Presbyterian piety. One meets here the kind of world into which Burns was so courageously to break. Yet Wilson had been both kind and prophetic on the subject of Greenock and the River:

> *Where the broad marsh, a shuddering surface, lies,*
> *Fair Greenock's spires in new-born beauty rise;*
> *And many an infant city rises round,*
> *Emerging swiftly from the teeming ground;*
> *So poets tell, that by prolific Nile,*
> *Whole nations issued from the marshy soil;*
> *And if the muse can future fates divine,*
> *They all at last in one vast port shall join;*

Though the vast port, and Greenock itself, speak poorly for man's addition to the natural scene, it is undoubtedly a place with a view. A better outlook on a summer evening than that from the Gourock Yacht Club, a little farther down the Clyde, would be hard to find. Three sea-lochs open up before you and behind them is the mountain-mass at the top of Loch Long, with the jagged Cobbler fretting the sky. But I must not bolt so soon from Glasgow, like one of those who only use it to sleep a night or change a train.

Because of its commercial greatness the city's long nourishment of the mind and recent practice of the arts may be most unjustly over-looked. Nobody is likely to think that I have under-praised Edinburgh, but my addiction to the old capital and its history does not blind

269

me to the fact that Glasgow had been, and is, perhaps increasingly, the Academe of Scotland and has functioned briskly as ' the quick forge and working-house of thought.' In the five hundred years of its University's life it has housed intellectual eminence of every kind: and it has been daring too. Was there ever a bolder and better guess than the election of Gilbert Murray at the age of twenty-three to be Professor of Greek? The Chair of English Literature, with Walter Raleigh and Macneile Dixon as recent occupants, has been a lively fountain of criticism and erudition. Glasgow has now given academic recognition to Scottish Literature, a subject so long and so absurdly regarded as trivial or vulgar by the loftier Scottish minds. What the mandarins of Greenock's intellectual life in 1767 would have thought of Alexander Scott's appointment to be a Reader of Scottish Literature I dare not think, for Scott is himself a skilled practitioner in the ' profane art of poem-making '—and that in the Scottish tongue. Glasgow University has also enriched Balliol and Oxford Senior Common Rooms with its emissaries endowed by the Snell Exhibition and I have owed much to my friends and tutors encountered in that way.

It is a common belief, and doubtless a just one, that no University Magazine ever excelled in wit and pungency that of Glasgow in the years when James Bridie, Walter Elliot, Arthur Wallace, George Fletcher and others were its up-and-coming staff. It was wrong of me, in one way, to include a tribute to Bridie in a chapter on Edinburgh, but I could not mention the latter's Festival of the Arts without him. Here I now salute his shade again, since it was his energy and persistence which chiefly imposed on the people of Glasgow, who should be proud of it, their Citizens' Theatre. There, if the visitor does not mind penetrating across the river to the region known as the

Gorbals (no long journey), he may come across an intelligent play, often both new and Scottish, with a capable Scottish company to play it. For those whose tastes are less courageous, there are always native comedians of abiding popularity to be heard; but they are not easily understood. Glasgow Scottish talk, a half-swallowed perversion of Scottish speech, can be most baffling to a stranger. With at least some ear for Scottish dialects I am myself frequently defeated by the noises commonly made on Clydeside. However, it is worth trying one of the Summer Shows or winter Pantomimes (Glasgow is even more avid of Pantomime than is any town in England) if Harry Gordon, Tommy Morgan, George West, Dave Willis or one of the other notables be in the bill. Duncan Macrae, a Citizens' Theatre discovery and a great comedian with a fine, dry style of absurdity, is also to be looked for by all visitors with a taste for theatre, whether he is still with the Citizens' team or engaged in a commercial enterprise.

The Citizens' Theatre grew on soil once fertilised by John Brandane, James Bridie, and the aspiring amateurs of the Scottish National Players, whose first professional producer was Tyrone Guthrie. That again was working on the legacy of uncommercial theatre left by Alfred Wareing, an irrepressible Englishman who could always turn a deaf ear to defeatists and somehow foisted on the city of his friendly invasion one of the earliest and most gallant of British Repertory Theatres. This was in 1909 and in that year Glasgow was the first city to have a play by Chekhov (then unknown or, if known, unintelligible to most) put on for a run. ' The Seagull ' may not have conquered Clydeside, but at least the quiet beat of its wings beside the Broomielaw made a piece of theatrical history. Chekhov seems now to be everybody's darling; but London was a long way after Glasgow in giving its audiences a chance to be Chekhovians.

The city is, for reasons of population, a principal centre of Scottish newspapers and book-publishing and has had many a distinguished writer at work beside the machinery of print. That Glasgow is almost in the Highlands and draws on them for immigrants is a fact typified by the work of Neil Munro. He was both a romantic novelist of the clans, especially of the Campbells in his beloved Inveraray, and Editor of the Glasgow *Evening News*. He bestowed his rich urban knowledge of Clydeside types as well as his Highland lore and his charming prose upon the daily round of journalism, which takes so much out of a man and may put so much into him too. Neil Munro was both Gael and Glaswegian in outlook and loyalty and his novels, which are still easily purchasable, are ' required reading ' for those who take the steamer up Loch Long to Inveraray or seek an easy and agreeable acquaintance with many facets of Scottish history or of waterside life along the Clyde. His touch in journalism may have gone, but one of the Glasgow editors of to-day, Alistair Dunnett, of the *Daily Record*, has been an adventurer after Neil Munro's heart. His journey with a companion in two canoes from the Clyde to Skye was a remarkable piece of audacious navigation. I recommend his account of their laborious and hazardous sailing and paddling in many and turbulent waters. Those who take safer means of transport from Glasgow to Portree should read ' Quest by Canoe ' to discover what they are missing—to the benefit of their skins, if not of their experience. They will also learn much about the Highlands and Islands by one who has fought the elements to get there in the slowest and hardest way.

One attractive feature of Glasgow journalism has been a liberality of control. The same proprietors own the stately and serious *Glasgow Herald* and the light and lively *Bulletin*: yet these papers have taken a radically different

line about the burning topic of Scottish Home Rule with
no calling to order. As a journalist myself I admire this
editorial freedom.

So, with no disrespect to other Scottish cities, I salute
Glasgow's ability to combine the commercial leadership of
Scotland with abundant and vivacious pursuit of knowledge
and ideas. I raise my hat with cordial veneration when I
enter or pass the University on Gilmore Hill. Its architecture proclaims the mid-Victorian date of its spacious
reconstruction by Sir Gilbert Scott, while its greatness has
no period. From it and across the Kelvin river there is a
view of the red-sandstone City Art Gallery erected in 1902.
It is no beauty by the standards of to-day but it has served
beauty finely, especially under the direction of Dr. Honeyman, whose drive and eagerness to carry ' the best to the
most ' in new and exciting ways has rarely been equalled
in civic administration and official service of the arts.

In visible pleasures Glasgow has benefited greatly by the
treasures of Sir William Burrell's bequest. The traditions
of good architecture and design have long been noticeable
in the older terraces. The thwarted poet Wilson remarked
with accuracy Glasgow's

> *beauty regular and chaste*
> *And elegance correct of Grecian taste,*
> *The comely parts exact proportion show*
> *And to one whole by fit connections grow.*

All did not continue so happily. But around and above the
Kelvin,

> *Here dwell the muses: in their sacred halls*
> *Soft as descending dew their doctrine falls . . .*

Did he foresee Gilbert Murray lecturing on Euripides, and
giving fresh urgency to old saga-stories, making the Greek

dawn yield new, immediate light? Or Dr. Honeyman persuading the young that beauty is not a bore and that we must keep our senses as open as our minds to the new and the unusual thing? While Edinburgh has housed the Scottish National Gallery and the Exhibitions of the Scottish Royal Academy, Glasgow has been a prominent nurse of contemporary painting. It even, through that eminent and successful cateress, Miss Cranston, decided that the equipment of tea-rooms might well prefer the simple and seemly to the trivial and garish long before that idea, revolutionary then, had occurred to others in her useful calling. Her employment of Charles Mackintosh as designer was the sign of her taste and acumen. With all this in view—and I have not even touched on Glasgow's pride of craftsmanship in shipbuilding, which is a service of beauty as well as of transport, and in precision work of all kinds—I suggest that there is also much more to look at and listen to in Glasgow than a hurried survey of its commercial centre would suggest.

It is ridiculous merely to sniff the air of Argyle Street on a drizzly day, loiter round the other shopping-streets, and decide that Glasgow has no particular character because it has not the unique site of Edinburgh and cannot offer the swift and superb impact of Edinburgh's Castle Rock and the Old Town sky-line. You have to work your way into Glasgow's heart. It is not that the people are aloof; far from it. But it is a secretive place that has allowed much of its essence to be obscured. It is a melting-pot of Scots and Irish, Protestant and Catholic, Highland and Lowland, with a fair number of settled Europeans, especially Italians and Poles. Where there is a great river lacing the life of a town there is always the fascination of turning a bend and seeing great ships nosing into the end of the street. Unfortunately docks and building-yards have to be shut off,

274

so that the curious cargoes of the first and the romances of the second are more to be guessed at than to be inspected by the river-side wanderer. Much of Glasgow's character and creation are thus forbidden mysteries. It is a place with a ' round the corner ' quality. You have even to look for its Cathedral, a building which in most cities is dominant. Nor is the Citizens' Theatre where you would expect to find it. That, at least, is the impression it has made on me. This city does not wear its jewellery with a flourish or put its rings outside its gloves. It has given the common-place and even the squalid some of the best positions on its stage; but that does not prevent the presence of comedy and of beauty with strangeness in the programme offered to those visitors who are prepared to wait a little and to get things in proportion.

Glasgow naturally looks to the water for its leisure and at one time its fleet of steamers, partly owned by rival railway-companies, offered a cheap and service to the nooks of the Firth, to the islands of Bute and Arran, and to the Mull of Kintyre. Its water-travel was competitive even to the extent of some friendly racing, a great delight to the young. Who would make Brodick the sooner? But first rationalisation and then nationalisation have destroyed those conveniently combatant speeds and prices; the use of the road, despite the enormous detours compelled by inward-reaching sea-lochs, has steadily increased. When staying at Tarbert, Loch Fyne, I remember thinking, in my old-fashioned way, that the newspapers would only reach us when the boat came in at noon. It surprised me to discover that cars would be speeding through the dawn beside Loch Lomond and Loch Long and crossing the high-flung pass at Rest and Be Thankful in order to serve Inveraray and Tarbert with breakfast-time journals. As far as I am concerned their drivers need not endure their misty mornings.

When observing the seals and sailing-boats, the plunging gannets and the rolling porpoises of the western waters, I can wait to be informed of the crimes and follies of mankind. Of course the services alter from year to year, but in the late nineteen-forties it did strike me as preposterous that I could not get to Campbeltown by sea and had to take a long bus-journey down the Mull of Kintyre. It was a handsome ride, admittedly, with its views over the Atlantic, but to be cramped in a bus is far less agreeable travel than to have the freedom of a deck and the sting of salty air. Since this was first written, public indignation has prevented more of the Clydeside boat-service being abandoned. Glasgow is turning—or being forced to turn its back on its past.

It is a discreditable failure of Scotland not to have done better with its sea-side resorts. Edinburgh's Portobello might have lived up to its beauty-bearing name: instead there is a squalid sea-front (or rather Firth-front) marring the good native quality of some of the houses behind. Glasgow's chief pleasure-towns are Dunoon, Rothesay and Largs. Dunoon, on the north bank of the Firth of Clyde, is cramped under the high Cowal hills which collect and hold a deal of rain. Rothesay, the chief town and harbour of Bute, is shabby at the centre and, though its line of shore-villas is trim enough, it has little attraction for me. Largs, on the south bank of the mainland, is much neater and airier and has magic views of the jagged Arran peaks glinting in the sun, fading in the mist, and reappearing in a sudden shaft of light. Rothesay has a romantic spectre on its unromantic harbour-front; that is the figure of Edmund Kean landing on a boat from Greenock to find his peace on Bute, in his house, Woodend, beside the waters of Loch Fad. He built Woodend about 1822 and made it his refuge when his sins of drunkenness and adultery had made

savagely intolerant the crowds who had previously risen at
the thunder and lightning of his performances: if poem-
making was deemed profane in eighteenth-century Greenock
the play-acting of the ' pomping folk ' was even more
abominable in righteous eyes. And what if the leading
mummer were also a proven limb of Satan, too debauched
even for the endurance of pagan London? Howled down
in Glasgow and proceeding ' only partially sober ' to
Greenock, he was again refused a hearing and the same
night, still in the costume of ' Richard III ' and doubtless
with many a dram taken for consolation, sailed across to
Rothesay. ' Kean's Island Home ' has been very well
described by Alan Dent in his volume of ' Preludes and
Studies.'

> ' By the narrow woodland road near the right-hand
> shore of Loch Fad, proceeding from Rothesay, one soon
> arrives at the lodge-gates of Woodend, to find oneself
> stared at, in this order, by stone effigies of Philip
> Massinger and William Shakespeare, Edmund Kean and
> David Garrick. Shakespeare and Kean are the centre
> pair; Garrick and the creator of Sir Giles Overreach
> have, as it were, to take a back seat. These busts are
> life size, well executed and well preserved, and they
> stand on their pedestals some eight or nine feet high.
> A hundred and twenty snell Scottish winters have
> ravaged them very little. No one knows who cut the
> stone so skilfully, but in my own opinion the sculptor
> has better caught the sad-eyed disillusionment of the
> Shakespeare who wrote " The Winter's Tale " than any
> of the portraitists, and something of Kean's own sardonic
> quality is conveyed.'

Alan Dent, as an Ayrshireman by birth, takes a decent pride
in Ayr's performance when Kean performed there. Received

with an unexpected and most welcome tolerance the English actor in return gave the best of his genius. Perhaps Robert Burns had broken Ayr to the acknowledgment that ' to step aside is human.'

Bute has a prosperous, Lowland look, with a few mild hills in the north and a narrow ribbon of water between it and the loftier mainland at the Kyles. This is one of Clyde's ' beauty-spots ' and passengers in the boats are justly expected to ' alert ' themselves, as we say nowadays, and gaze and admire. Perhaps not all Scots and certainly not all English know the story of the Glasgow man who set out in Fair time to see the Kyles. He settled himself below decks in the well-filled and socially clamorous bar which had developed a fine frowst of friendship, tobacco and beer-fumes. When his wife, more hygienically braving the air on deck, realised that their goal was won and shouted at him, ' Hey, Wullie, the Kyles of Bute! Come up and see the Kyles! ' he roared from the cosy depths, ' Och, to hell with the Kyles! Do you nae ken I'm on holiday? '

From Rothesay you can get buses to various points of the island, unless you prefer, as Wullie would have done had he landed, to settle to a survey of its licensed premises. A good, short journey can be made across the island to Ettrick Bay where the glory of the Firth is well revealed. I remember how, while a member of an undergraduate reading-party at Arrochar on Loch Long, a rain-trap rather than a resort, we grew desperate with the eternal load of cloud upon the Cobbler and its drenching consequence and so took a ship-trip to Rothesay. It poured the whole time and we sampled the town's bars moodily, played billiards among empty beer-bottles with cues that had no tips, looked out occasionally and in vain for better weather, and then in desperation rode off to Ettrick, there to seek shelter

278

in a concert-party's pavilion. (Odd aspect of what I thought was to be a Highland sojourn with strenuous days on the summits!) When we emerged from the dubious relief supplied by comedians and sopranos, the whole sky had lifted. There was an exquisite and universal clarity of air and scene: the maritime and mountain splendours of the Firth lay radiant and unforgettable. Never, I thought, was such a transformation scene. When it does stop raining on the Clyde you have your dividend for a long investment in frustration. That which cloud has so long buried rises from its melancholy grave. It is a glorious resurrection.

Largs, like Rothesay, has its ghosts, but they are dim and distant. One might see a spectral Norseman endeavouring to land from a storm-battered galley and being stone-battered and claymored by the defending Scots, who were batting (or battering) on a good firm wicket. But the battle of Largs was decisive in the long conflict of the landsmen with the alien raiders from the sea. It now seems a singularly serene spot, whose only conflict is in its streets and shops when Glasgow invades it in mass in July. Yes, there is another memory in Largs, that of Jimmy Maxton, M.P., at once so angry and so genial, who made himself one of the most popular Members while holding the most unpopular views. Here, like many another Clyde-sider, rebel or respectable, he liked his vacation and he took his rest.

The inland moors behind Largs and Wemyss Bay do not rise very high, but they can offer some rough, wet tramping with a lavish reward for the eye. Most of south-west Scotland is spread out before you. Plunging through long heather is an exercise for the young and tracks are few, but there is a curious aqueduct leading down from Loch Thom to the reservoir above Wemyss Bay and beside it runs a grassy causeway. That is good walking and good viewing for the seniors; a heron, annoyed by interference with his vigilant angling, flaps sullenly away on great rounded wings; the grouse go scudding off with their own vocal indignation and alarm. The mountains of the islands rise out of the sea like the dreamy cones in a Japanese print. The Clyde area has many such panoramas and, with its shifty weather, they are never the same.

A little to the east, above Paisley, rambled one of Scotland's little remembered poets, Robert Tannahill, a weaver, whose habit was to recover old and neglected airs and find appropriate words for them. This he managed to combine with plying the shuttle. Weaving and melody were old companions, not only in the cottages of the Highlands and Islands, but in the workshops of the growing towns. Shakespeare made Falstaff say: ' I would I were a weaver; I could sing all manner of songs.' Dr. Johnson, commenting on this, said that weavers, having their hands more employed than their minds, amuse themselves frequently with songs at their loom. Tannahill felt himself neglected and was in general an unhappy man; he committed suicide at the age of thirty-six. He was not a mixer and, though he liked his glass, found in taverns what he could not abide and Burns could enjoy, ' the bestial roar of inebriation,' as the former called it.

As a poet he was far behind Burns and does not, as a rule, find a place in the anthologies. Like so many Scots he wrote better in his own tongue than in the English style which he too often attempted. He composed for the ear better than for print and, with the old airs or the new ones devised by his friend Robert Smith of Paisley, he enriched the song-books as he sighed for the braes of Gleniffer or spoke for the maiden all forlorn in ' Oh hey, Johnnie lad, ye're no sae kind's ye should hae been.'

280

I looked by the whinny knowe
I looked by the firs sae green,
I looked o'er the spunkie-howe,
And aye I thought ye would hae been.
There's ne'er a supper cross'd my craig
There's ne'er a sleep has closed my e'en;
Oh hey, Johnnie lad,
Ye're no sae kind's ye should hae been.

(Spunkie-howe is will o' the wisp's dell and craig is throat.) Tannahill's simplicities ripple like a burn which sings its way from the whinny knowe. He is fit reading to carry on a walk above the Clyde, even if he could never bestow upon a jingle the genius of poetry as Burns so often did.

True to his period Tannahill preferred the gentle braes to the soaring bens. But the bens were there for him to see. The summit of Ben Lomond is only twenty-six miles from the centre of Glasgow and the Arran peaks are much closer to Sauchiehall Street than Oxford is to Oxford Street. No great city in our islands—and few outside it—has more adjacent and more excellent wilderness than Glasgow. It is fortunate indeed to have Arran at its doorstep, more fortunate still to have that island in the generous ownership of the Duke of Montrose. When one considers the stubborn tenacity with which many Highland landlords— and not the rich incomers only, though often they were the worst—have repelled the visitor, however innocent of poaching, the availability of Arran, with a huge population just across the narrow water, has been a limitless blessing to the athletic young. Though the north of Arran has deer in plenty, its challenging rocks at the end of its beckoning glens have been open to all campers and climbers.

The island is a geologist's paradise. The vast granite mass is surrounded by a band of slate into which it penetrates, a sign of its once molten condition; the slate marches also with old red sand-stone; in one glen there is quartz with crystals of amethyst. The confusion of minerals gives infinite changes of colour and of form and the prehistoric upheavals have left chasms and knife-edges and pinnacles that cry out to be conquered. The peaks are not enormous and nowhere touch the 3,000 ft. mark, but at a level of 2,600 to nearly 2,900 they dip a little and soar again in a tumult of stone left writhing from its fiery origins. Not as sensational as the Coolins of Skye, the bens of Arran offer the spice of danger, especially with rapid invasions of mist, to youth that will leave nothing unscaled, and must bag the whole cluster in a day of continuous assaults. What a back-garden for a city to possess! The beaches of Brodick are there for the children and the luring defiles of Sannox and Rosa, with the monstrous rockery where these meet at the base of Cir Mhor and Goat Fell, await the strenuous. The last can be gently ascended from one side by those who want no cat-work in their climbing.

Nature has been generously provident in the shaping of Arran, with something for all tastes and aptitudes, while man, in the persons of the owning family, has put no barriers to its enjoyment. The stag is there to be seen, but not to exclude. He has not been turned, as elsewhere, into a jealous monarch of the forbidden Glen. Exploitation by random building has been checked and the accommodation is therefore restricted. But those who get in have ample freedoms and the fishing in most of the streams is at their disposal. Small wonder that so many Glasgow folk have Arran summers printed in red letters in their memories. The trouble is the southerly or south-westerly wind when the clouds are massed and caught by the summits and spill their contents in drizzle or in deluge. It is maddening to have a brief Arran holiday when visibility is almost nil while the mainland may be clear and gay. But peaks are not to be had without paying for. And when the wind veers to the north and the infinite sky breaks open, then does one greet the unseen with a cheer.

The population of Arran actually rose between 1931 and 1951 (from 4,532 to 4,657), an occurrence exceptional among the dismal records of the Western Isles. All of the Hebrides that are counted in with Argyllshire and Inverness-shire showed heavy loss of inhabitants in those twenty years, and that after previous periods of decline. Coll actually lost 113 out of a previous total of 322. I derive from the Census figures, which are not very clear since they include both town and 'landward' folk under the heading of parishes, that Arran's gains were round Brodick with its residential and guest-house appeal, while there were losses on the farms. Still, it is something to find one Scottish island which is not drifting towards the condition of a desert.

There are many forces at work. The higher go the wages in the mainland towns, the less attractive does the crofter's and the fisherman's life become, even with subsidies for some and with higher prices for all their wares. National Service removes many of the young men who, having seen a larger world, may become impatient of their smaller one. One would think that radio would mitigate the dislike of loneliness, but perhaps it rather advertises the pleasures of ' In town to-night.' An extreme and joyless Puritanism, long dominant and even tyrannical in many islands, must certainly add to the appeal of city lights and free, wide choice of leisure occupation. It is significant that Stornoway Parish (in Lewis and counted in with the county of Ross) shows a gain of 680, but Stornoway is quite a town and has ' the pictures.' Various Governments have been reporting on and tinkering with the population problem of the

Hebrides for decades, but the good will which proliferates paper schemes has evidently failed in action. ' The lone shieling ' becomes lonelier.

On more than one occasion my modest sea-faring from Glasgow has taken me by way of Tarbert, Loch Fyne, with the short bus-drive over the land-neck to Tarbert West, and so by sea again to the island of Gigha and on to Craighouses, which is the harbour of Jura. This island, conspicuous afar because of its great mountain-nipples, the Paps, is only sixty miles from Glasgow by air, but it has an immense remoteness of character and atmosphere. Inner Hebrides in fact, it is Outer in quality. It managed to support over 700 people in the eighteenth century; now there are 263. Twenty years ago it had 382. It is thirty miles long, has a single and rough road up the coast, and that peters out into a track as it moves towards the famous whirlpool-straits of Corrievreckan between Jura and Scarba. It is for the most part extremely barren, extremely wet, and over-whelmingly beautiful. On any of its heights you look westward to Colonsay and the Atlantic and eastward over the mainland coast, with its range after range of peaks fading into a white sea of summer cloud. Despite the mist-collecting habit of the Paps, it has its bays and beaches and might have been a paradisal place of holiday for hundreds without any affliction of crowding. But it is ' the island of the deer ' (its name probably signifies that) and where there are deer in Scotland men, except in Arran, are unwanted. So Jura has but one small hotel and a population of less than nine for each mile of its length. It is no easy island to invade and my own knowledge of it and my own feeling for it, love mixed with melancholy, could not have existed without the friendship of Lord Astor and his family who own the middle and perhaps the finest region of the island.

It has had very little history. The Stone Age men tried it and left their marks, though not so conspicuously as in more fertile Arran, and various raiding chieftains found it an unrewarding prey. Islay, to the south, less mountainous and comparatively rich and green, separated by a narrow strait of racing waters, has been worth the seizing, is still rich in distilleries, has golf and a small tourist following, and seems, despite its proximity to Jura, to be in a quite different world from that stern strip of emptiness. Jura once had a distillery: it is no more. And there is no licensed house on the whole island. This is not to say that alcohol never reaches it.

At the north end one gallant and recent landlord has endeavoured to make his estate, Ardlussa, self-maintenant by diligent reclamation and usage of land and by sale of salmon and deer, with as much community life as the tiny village can create under his intelligent stimulation. But the nature of the land is a formidable enemy and motor-boats bring poachers over from the mainland to raid the shores for the free collection of his venison, which now fetches tempting prices. His struggle to restore some island life is a brave experiment. Farther south Lord Astor once tried afforestation, but it was expensive. Only the State can now afford to grow and fence trees in places such as this: the fencing is essential and costly and the Atlantic gales limit planting to a few sheltered spots on the east of the island.

So here, sixty miles from Glasgow, is Caledonia Deserta, no less than in the Dead Vast of the far north. The golden eagle, at least, survives in Jura and does not diminish. I have watched it soar over the lovely, winding inlet of Glen Battrick, a tortuous sea-loch, fit for ' Mary Rose ' romanticism, full of islets which may want to be visited but are not and never will be:

285

Though as he sails and smoothly swings
Round the hillside.
He looks as though from his own wings
He hung down crucified.

Andrew Young, one of my favourite contemporary poets, wrote this and, since he has crossed the Sound and climbed the Jura mountains, clasping rocks ' storm-shattered and sharp-edged ' among the grey ptarmigan and starved moss, it is likely that he saw the same dynasty of eagles as I have seen myself, while he was grappling with the Paps:

And mist like hair hangs over
One barren breast and me
Who climb, a desperate lover,
With hand and knee.

It is a bird-watchers' heaven, and solitudinarians can slake their thirst for the void to the uttermost.

George Orwell lived a Robinson Crusoe life at the northern tip of the island for some years with a rod, a gun, and a piece of land to tame. He collected letters and rations by travelling twice a week for six miles to meet the postman. There he fought a losing battle with tuberculosis and wrote, with moody genius, of the future's menace. He believed that only in such places might life survive after the next war; not that he calculated for his own safety— nobody cared less about that—but he talked to me thus, when he had been removed to hospital in East Kilbride, about his adopted son. In its long, secluded unpopulous life Jura can have had no more gifted resident than this lean, lanky, grim uncommon man, with Eton and Burma behind him, who rebuked the Socialists for not knowing what the common man was like. He conducted his social surveys in the hardest possible way. He made an intimate study of down-and-out life in London, Paris, and English industrial towns; indeed, wherever he went, he determined to find out the worst before he described it and he lived exactly as those whom he was watching. Perhaps it was his pursuit of down-and-outness that attracted him to Jura, where man continually dwindles and the stag stares at you with indignant surprise. For on the bare tumble of the Jura forest you are the curio, not he.

The water laps up against the rocks, making a plaint as sweetly sad as those of Hebridean songs. The call of the pied oyster-catchers adds to the grief; the rains drift over from Colonsay and the clouds scarf the Paps. They pass and the sun glitters on the white sands and on the wild orchids of the sedgy shore. While there are incomers with means to fish and shoot, there will be a few summer occupants, hungry for stags and sea-trout, and a few keepers and stalkers will remain, required for the service of their sport. The Ardlussa experiment will, I hope, succeed. But it is an unlikely bet that the census of 1961 will show a rise in Jura's population, unless Orwell's dark forebodings come true and there is desperate scattering of what's left of the mainland millions. Meanwhile the postman is making his daily drive up the island's single road and the surprise of seeing a human being seems more startling than the hover of an eagle.

It is fine at last and one takes to the hills, plodding first through a lush and boggy glen, with a swarm of flies, midges, and ' clegs ' for company (but not if you are there before July), and so on to the compensation, the exquisite and uninfested air of the tops, with the bare rocks gem-like in the glitter after rain and the lochans a-ripple in kaleido-scopic colour; here, under cloud, is their peaty brown, there, in the sun, a sudden azure. You may walk right on to a sleepy stag, who trots for thirty yards, then turns to glare at your impertinence. Then he is off and his fellows take the hint: the whole hillside starts to quiver with their cavalcade; the stags massed in their own select group go one way: the hinds, in delicate motion, flit to another corrie. Absurdly, if it is early summer, a cuckoo calls. One so much associates this bird with Home County copses and even with Hampstead Heath that its presence among stags and eagles is disconcerting to the ear. But in the Hebrides ' the cuckoo shouts at nothing all day long.' Mountain hares scamper away. Grouse are occasional and rabbits can find no burrowing-ground up here. The stony rocks may have suited Biblical coneys, but Highland ones are more exacting. A trout puts its circling patterns on the still pool of a mountain lochan. You cross the narrow island to the Atlantic shore, where there is nobody and nothing: no, there is a name on the map. It is Corpach, the place of the dead bodies.

Gaelic lingers in Jura and the English, when spoken, has a Highland softness with some intonations which we think of as Irish. Will it endure? The number of persons in Scotland speaking Gaelic only, fell from 6,176 in 1931 to 2,652 in 1951. The bilinguals dropped from 125,419 to 91,630 in the same period. And many of those are in Glasgow and the mainland towns.

The holiday is over. We say good-bye to the grey Astor farm-house, no absurd baronial pile but a Scottish living-place with the reasonable comforts of a softer world. The waves are still beating out their lament on the rocks below. The steamer is coming into the pier at Craighouses, where it calls three times a week. The Sound is soon crossed. The Paps stand sentinel behind us, vainly vigilant, guarding nothing but their own beauty. In a few hours one has changed boats and is passing the Kyles of Bute. (Wullie, art thou drinking there below?) And so to Rothesay where

288

there are more people sitting at a single concert-party show than are living in the whole of Jura. No place so various as the Firth of Clyde. Just opposite Rothesay is dark, forsaken Loch Striven which leads to another limbo, with Glasgow and its millions thirty miles away, some of them with Gaelic on their lips. The Clyde is not a river, but a universe.

CHAPTER XIV

Border and Ballad

THE right road-way into Scotland is the Central route by Carter Bar, with a fine climb, a noble prospect at the summit, and a superb descent. In was, in 1575, the scene of one of the last Border battles in which the men of Jeddart (Jedburgh) defeated the Tynesiders. The coast roads from England are easier, and quicker, and the eastern high-way offers, after Berwick, much agreeable sea-scape; Gretna, in the west, is smirched by some childish forms of showmanship and the journey that way is dull until Lockerbie is past. The true Border country is discovered on the great broad shoulders of the Cheviots and in the sweep downwards from the high pastures of the sheep to the riverside towns of the weavers.

It can be claimed with some reason that the Border makes no sense. The curious slanting line that runs sharply south-west from just north of the Tweed's mouth to the Solway Firth, leaving so much of Scotland almost up to Glasgow south of Berwick, divides country that is alike in its bone-structure and its pastoral economy. The logical division of Britain, based on natural scene and way of living, is roughly a four-fold one. Wales is by geography, language, and tradition a land of its own: in the territory running from John o' Groats and Cape Wrath to Dover and Land's End there are three obviously separate sectors; there are at one end the distinctive Highlands, separated from lower Scotland by a geological fault which runs from the Clyde to the Mearns. There are the south and midlands of England at the other end. Between them, from Derby to the Highland verge, is a great belt of hill-country, whose average height is about 1,500 to 2,000 feet; the 3,000 mark is just missed at Cross Fell, loftiest of the English Pennines, and the largest of the Scottish Lowland summits are not as lofty as that.

On both sides of the formal Border the uplands are not similar to the Dead Vast of the far north. They are serviceable to man. They have more grass than heather and the sheep-flocks are their fortune. Under the lower slopes and level country are coal and iron. The wealth of Yorkshire and of Lancashire has been largely similar to that of Lanark and of Lothian. As far as geology, vegetation, and handicraft go it seems ridiculous that the area should be sharply split between two nations. Why was there such sharp partition of old loyalties? The same sort of men with the same skills and exertions have spoken different tongues in different accents. They have eagerly cut each other's throats and purses. Yet the Pennine shepherd and his fellow in the Lowther, the Moorfoot, or the Lammermuir hills have had the same profession, climate, terrain, and troubles. So have the miners of the Don Valley in Yorkshire and of the Lothian levels around Edinburgh. They are natural partners in man's long endeavours to wrest a living from the hills and to mix his fruitful labour with the meadows and the minerals.

But history is not fashed with logic. The Border in name has remained a border in fact; and it is astonishing that when you have crossed this arbitrary line, parting folk of an identical economy, you know at once that you have entered a new kingdom. The speech differs markedly within a mile or two; there is little distinction in the scene, but a huge one in the social fabric. When racialism rears its head reason flies out of the window and the economic and material interpretations of history seem shallow and null.

Events have made the Border a cock-pit and left its abbeys in ruins. Major battles of the two nations and the minor forays of the raiding clans and families have sown its fields with blood and left forlorn towers of defence and shattered castles where there might have been busy, happy, and tranquil settlements of croft and craft. No view of Scotland better suggests good mutton and good clothing than that from Carter Bar. The sheep on the hills and the cattle in the dales do remain, never more precious than at present, after centuries of plunder and waste, but the Border has missed the riches proper to its natural resources and the inborn gifts of its people. Its water-power became even less valuable in the age of coal and the industrial changes left it endearing to the eye but poor in the pocket. Population was drained away and Jedburgh lost four thousand of its earlier six thousand citizens during the eighteenth century. The symbol of Border history is the broken stronghold such as Neidpath and the lonely, roofless tower.

The towns of the Tweed and Teviot valleys retained their personality, but not their population. They have continued to weave in their own way and well. They are stubborn and small and sometimes, as at Kelso, enchanting. But their culture was overrun time and again by the English, who, like the Romans of old, were apt to make a desert and to call it peace. In 1545 Henry VIII emulated the Edwards in hammering the Scots and the Earl of

Hertford's vandal horde destroyed four abbeys, sixteen castles and towers, five market-towns and two hundred and forty-three villages within a fortnight. The Generals Evers and Leyton pounded the much-assaulted beauty of Melrose Abbey for the last time; there was savage compensation; they were routed and killed at Ancrum Moor on the following day and were charitably buried amid the relics of their rapine. But Melrose and its stately kind had been left in charred and naked calamity; the swarms who now come in by motor-coach to see 'the jewel of the Border' are looking at a rifled treasure.

The Border Scots themselves were no angels of clemency; they gave what they got when they could. But the greater crimes were English and the English tourist of to-day, if his guide-book or his previous reading has given him some awareness of the chronicles, must blush for the English methods of pacification, the sword for the citizens, the fire for the city. At the same time it has to be admitted that Scots were not averse to pillaging Scots and that the Border families were often as awkward and as acquisitive neighbours as were the Highland clans away in the north. The tranquil-seeming hills have a history of horrors.

What a region this might have been had its towns been left to prosper in peace when the masons who raised Melrose were there to practise their superb skill and turn the local stone to the service of man and the glory of a humane religion! But that illogical border-line was there to sunder the men of Tweed from those of Tyne, to make hate endemic, spoliation an industry, and the life that was lived in places appointed by Nature to be sweetly social a mere travesty of what living should be. What Thomas Hobbes wrote of man's natural state was for a long time pitifully apt to the cockpit below the Cheviots. 'No arts; no letters; no society: and which is worst of all, continual fear and danger of sudden death; and the life of man solitary, poor, nasty, brutish, and short.'

One thing, however, the vandal can never kill: that is the word. The Border's fanes might be destroyed and its towns sacked, rebuilt, and sacked again. But the Border ballads and the preoccupation with story in song were not destructible by robbery and murder. The lays and legends might dwindle in local favour and they might cease to be refreshed by new singers, but they were enduring and recoverable things and survived to be renewed and re-fashioned, as Scott and Hogg discovered, and to give themes, both fey and ferocious, to the minstrels of a later day. Many of the subjects were the clarion call to defence and the vengeance cry to attack; the Border, as I said, gave as good (or as ill) as it got. There is a clang of bolted gates in its Muse whose ' flourish and alarum ' provided Sir Walter and other ballad-makers with matter and melody very distant from anything that is called poetry to-day. (This is no argument against the lays.)

> *Lock the door, Lariston, lion of Liddisdale,*
> *Lock the door, Lariston, Lowther comes on,*
> > *The Armstrongs are flying,*
> > *Their widows are crying,*
> *The Castletown's burning, and Oliver's gone;*
> *Lock the door, Lariston—high on the weather gleam*
> *See how the Saxon plumes bob on the sky,*
> > *Yeoman and carbineer,*
> > *Billman and halberdier;*
> *Fierce is the foray, and far is the cry.*

The Muse of the Border, here typified by James Hogg, is often the voice of the recruiting sergeant, the rhetoric of the patriot, the thud of hooves and the clash of steel.

Extremes meet in this minstrelsy. Where there is most severity of temper there is intermittent also, in art as well as in life, the greatest tenderness of sentiment and the queerest veins of whimsy. Gloucestershire's Forest of Dean, another Border country, is I am told by my friends who know it well, a centre of tough living among the miners who regard their own old customs as sovereign over Westminster's laws: yet a belief in goblins and fairies—the kobold or cobalt is the goblin of the mines—strongly abides and a housewife may be seen to take a broom and sweep one of these spooks out of her house. (Puck, at the end of ' A Midsummer Night's Dream,' comes on with a broom ' to sweep the dust behind the door,' but he first mentions the sprites and frolic fairies now at large and his broom links him with the spook-sweeping that is common in all folk-lore and appears to continue still between the Severn and the Wye.) In the same way the Border minstrel who would be roaring ' Lock the door, Lariston ' at one minute would at the next be following Bonnie Kilmeny up the fairy glen to

> *A land where sin had never been;*
> *A land of love, and a land of light,*
> *Withouten sun, or moon, or night;*
> *Where the river swa'd a living stream,*
> *And the light a pure celestial beam;*
> *The land of vision it would seem,*
> *A still, an everlasting dream.*

It is well to have Hogg with you on a Border journey. There is a handy little selection of his poems published by Oliver and Boyd for the Saltire Society which gives in brief all the facets of the astonishing, self-tutored Ettrick Shepherd, who is so richly and so variously expressive of the country of his origin. His was a widely representative voice. He was, like Burns, but with less magic, the singer of the village Lothario and of the herdsman in quest of his quean and his raptures:

> *I lately lived in quiet case*
> *An' never wish'd to marry, O!*
> *But when I saw my Peggy's face,*
> *I felt a sad quandary, O!*
> *Though wild as ony Athol deer,*
> *She has trepann'd me fairly, O!*
> *Her cherry cheeks an' een sae clear*
> *Torment me late and early, O!*
> *O, love, love, love!*
> *Love is like a dizziness;*
> *It winna let a poor body*
> *Gang about his biziness!*

In the intervals of chanting the gay sins of Balmaquhapple, rejoicing in the canty loving on the braes of Birniebouzle, echoing the Jacobite laments for Charlie the Darling, or trumpeting of Border battles long ago, he remembered the ' haunted wild and fairy ring ' and no poem of his is better known, I suppose, than that of the fair Kilmeny and the sights she saw ' so far surpassing nature's law.'

Yet it was this same bard of Balmaquhapple and Birniebouzle, of elfland and St. Mary's Loch, who drove with such penetration into the pyschology of fanaticism in ' The Private Memoirs and Confessions of a Justified Sinner.' That story emerges to-day with a startling freshness and urgency, since the parallel between the extreme Calvinist and the Communist devotee is so exact. All crimes became virtues to the Calvinist if the agent were one of the Lord's

Elect; once marked as a man of God, he knew that his seeming sins were all covered by divine sanction. The Communist, enrolled and taking the Party Discipline, is another of the justified if he does whatever the Party orders; even though it come to murder, he is deemed to be a righteous assassin and to be killing to preserve. It is queer that one should turn to the Scottish Shepherd of the early nineteenth century to discover such light on Russia in the middle of the twentieth.

The enthralling story has its half-lights of magic as well as its bright shafts of psychological illumination. ' This is a book,' wrote André Gide in his introduction to the Cresset Press Edition of 1947, ' so singular and so enlightening, so fitted to arouse passionate interest both in those who are attracted by religious and moral questions and, for quite other reasons, in psychologists and artists and above all in surrealists who are so particularly drawn by the demoniac in every shape—how explain that such a work should have failed to become famous?' To this Dorothy Bussy, Lytton Strachey's sister and Gide's translator, replied that the book was Scottish to its very marrow. The world has been very limited in its acceptance of Scottish literature. It has generously saluted and sometimes it has even overvalued Burns and Sir Walter, and then forgotten the rest. But Scott never wrote anything as arresting or as profound as ' The Confessions,' a book which has been ascribed to another hand than the Shepherd's on the ground that Hogg could never have done it. Shakespeare has been another to suffer from this argument, since his father was a small-town tradesman and he himself a mere player, never at the University. In neither case am I convinced.

The demoniac aspect of this Border book is at once the companion and reverse of the Border concern with the elvish and ethereal. If Satan was abroad and powerful, so was the Queen of Elfland, she who lured Thomas the Rhymer with a kiss and showed him the path of righteousness, the path of wickedness, and the path to fair Elfland and spirited him away to the last:

> He has gotten a coat of the even cloth
> And a pair of shoon of the velvet green,
> And till seven years were gane and past
> True Thomas on earth was never seen.

(A similar fate befell Bonnie Kilmeny. The Border had a marked capacity for effecting mystical disappearances.) But the road to Elfland's ' garden green ' brings one back to the double fascination exercised upon Border folk by the sweet and the terrible and their obsession by actual slaughter as well as by the innocence of never-never-lands. On the way to Elfland:

> It was mirk, mirk night, there was nae starlight.
> They waded through red blude to the knee;
> For a' the blude that's shed on earth
> Rins through the springs of that countrie.

All this is understandable in the curious medley of the Border's history, which is dyed in scarlet, and of its landscape so rainbow radiant in a sunlit valley and so mistily haunting among its hills. The hills are not of a height or form to be terrifying, like the stark, imprisoning peaks that crib up a Highland glen; but those who make the journey by Tweedsmuir from Moffat to Peebles must feel their pressure and their solitude. It may be wondered why men of the English Pennines, which are really the same hills farther south, never spun stories like that of Tam Lin or discovered the inherent magic of simple words in simple rhymes. There was the brutal magic of:

It's narrow, narrow, mak your bed,
And learn to lie your lane;
For I'm gaun owre the sea, Fair Annie,
A braw bride to bring hame.
Wi' her I will get gowd and gear,
Wi' you I ne'er gat nane.

What poem ever opened more savagely? There was the gentler spell of:

Fair Annie served the lang tables
Wi' the white bread and the wine;
But ay she drank the wan water
To keep her colour fine.

I can only surmise that, in the Yorkshire dales, a less eventful history made less responsive men. Those who live, or try in vain to keep alive, in a cockpit may well yearn dreamily for lands of hearts' desire and for elfin country where lily-handed and green-kirtled ladies relieve the heat and stress of war and comfort the weary in green pastures and among the innocence of flowers.

The country itself has, in its softer haughs, a singular witchery and some of the lesser hills, seen in the ground-mist of a September morning, are the fabric of dreams. The Eildons, on such a day, rise up over the lands of Tweed like fantasies. It is the sort of place where legend might grow plentiful and colourful as the broom; the raiding, lawless, homicidal history had long manured the ground with gore to fertilise the sagas on which the songsters drew. When Sir Walter Scott came home to Abbotsford, a dying man, in 1830, Wordsworth joined him and they saw the hills 'purple in an eerie gloaming.' On the Englishman also the Border hills, especially Scott's Eildons, had their

mystical influence and he linked, in a sonnet, their melancholy
with the frailty in decline of the great Scottish writer and
great romantic who so loved them.

> *A trouble, not of clouds, or weeping rain,*
> *Nor of the setting sun's pathetic light*
> *Engendered, hangs o'er Eildon's triple height;*
> *Spirits of power assembled there complain*
> *For kindred power departing from their sight;*
> *While Tweed, best pleased in chanting a blithe strain,*
> *Saddens his voice again, and yet again.*
> *Lift up your hearts, ye mourners! For the might*
> *Of the whole world's good wishes with him goes;*
> *Blessings and prayers in nobler retinue*
> *Than sceptred King or laurelled Conqueror knows*
> *Follow this wondrous potentate . . .*

Wordsworth was long past his best, but the sonnet, so
generous in tribute, is true to the abiding poetic vision
of the Border, spread over many centuries. ' Spirits of
power assembled there.' When Scott's work is added to
that of the ballad-makers, from the anonymous ancients to
the Ettrick Shepherd, it is patent that few rivers have had
such Heliconian springs as Tweed and Teviot, Ettrick and
Yarrow, while few hills have more richly evoked wonder
and pleasure and the words to put them in poignant melody
than have the rolling fells between the Lothian and the
English march.

All the world that makes a Border tour calls at Abbotsford,
the home and now the shrine of Sir Walter. It is handy for
Melrose; it is set by the Tweed, though not, I think, on
the best site that he might have chosen in a region so
abounding in invitations to build with a view. Out of what
had been a farm-cottage with a kailyard and a pond he
created his ' seat.' It must have been quite ordinary, until

he set his plantations around it and raised the extraordinary
mansion of late romantic and Scottish baronial style which
suited the taste of one so versed in and so dedicated to
the Scottish past. Unlikely to be spared by the architectural
criticism of to-day, it might surely have had a kind word
from Ruskin; but even that champion of the Gothic
Revival dismissed it as 'the most incongruous pile that
gentlemanly modernism ever designed.' It was built in
stages over a period of fourteen years; it helped to ruin
the reckless builder, in whom Scottish honour ran so high
while the native qualities of thrift and canniness were
undiscoverable virtues. But he who made it loved it and,
by the wise and humane ordinance of his Trustees when
financial trouble lay heavy upon him, he was allowed to
stay on instead of having it sold over his head; to repay
his creditors and justify the Trustees he made it almost a
factory of fiction, wherein he toiled, as few writers have
ever toiled, to pay for the follies of yesterday with the
relentless industry of to-day. Abbotsford delighted Scott,
burdened Scott, almost to collapse, and in the end was his
sore labour's rest and his consolation as his powers failed.
One cannot avoid deep feeling within these walls. They
enclose the home of a man who had in his maturity won
both the acclaim of the world and the nodding con-
descension of his one-time Edinburgh cronies. These would
mutter 'Poor Walter!' as he passed, lame but unbroken,
on his way to his lodgings in Castle Street.

Parts of it have long been publicly open at a fee and it
is my opinion that those who pay to see a famous house
should be allowed in at the front door and not smuggled
in at the side as though they were a nuisance and disgrace.
But Abbotsford is still a family home, with family precedence
preserved, and so the tourists go round by a sort of tradesman's entrance. What we see is mostly a museum. 'Even

in his sickness,' John Buchan wrote, ' Scott was filling the house with curious mementoes of the past—painted glass representing the Scottish kings copied from a ceiling in Stirling Castle, the old fountain from the Cross of Edinburgh, and plaster models of the Melrose Abbey gargoyles, while buying freely books, armour, pictures, and gabions.' (The last are instruments of fortification.) The library is full of relics and keepsakes, of Rob Roy, Prince Charlie, Flora Macdonald, and Napoleon. The amount of armour and of military hardware of all kinds is overwhelming. In the study, so dark and small, the scene of prodigious energies, you may feel more at home; presumably Scott did not want to be disconcerted by a room with a view: his eyes, when he wrote, were riveted to the desk and its huge surround of chronicles and reference-books.

Sir Walter clapped to it in the early morning, all the year round. Those of the slug-a-bed kind, whose sympathies and practice I share, find it inconceivable that a man can be alert and diligent, and an artist creative, at six in the morning. But Scott had Trollope's way with the clock and with the pen; he wrote three hours before breakfast in this book-lined cell of his, then breakfasted well, and went back to the desk. Afternoons he gave to exercise, according to his age and strength. After dining early, in the manner of the time, he talked or recited his work to the ladies and company—he was a happy and constant host—and then early to bed. So the Waverley Novels flew outward, prodigious in their range of history and vigour of characterisation as well as in their prolixity and in their sometimes burdensome employment of the antiquarian approach. He wrote five of his biggest and best in less than thirty months at a time of severe sickness. Few rooms have seen such application as the study at Abbotsford.

And yet the house, much as he loved it, is not really the

place in which to meet the essence of Sir Walter. That is in the Law Courts of Edinburgh, in the sheriff-court of Selkirk, around his earlier home of Ashsestiel and on the Border Hills or beside the Border waters. He was, despite his lameness, unquestionably active on horse and foot, a follower of field and river sports, a man who liked to feel his body in trim and to relieve his healthy fatigues with good victuals and good wine. That he worked both body and mind too hard, while watching his finance too little, was the easily pardonable error of his life. He was a full man and a fine one, nurtured in the Border country and blood of its blood, a fact too easily overlooked by the thousands who have no more acquaintance with him than school-room yawning over ' Ivanhoe.'

Not even Shakespeare has suffered more than Sir Walter from the educational curriculum. If it indeed be true, as is so often said, that ' nobody reads Scott nowadays ' the fault lies largely in the class-room. Perhaps the actuality of the matter is this. Too few read Scott willingly: too many—and too young—under compulsion. In my school-days, at any rate, the wrong books were chosen and these were wrongly used, that is for reading as lessons and for subsequent examination. My own introduction to Scott was by way of ' Ivanhoe ' and ' The Talisman ' in class; then ' Woodstock ' and ' Quentin Durward ' were imposed as holiday-tasks. Only much later did I recover from this wretched form of conscription and apply myself as a volunteer, with surprising and increasing pleasure, to ' Old Mortality,' ' Rob Roy ' and ' The Heart of Midlothian.' Thence I went steadily on, learning that Sir Walter may, especially in the early reaches of a long book, be quickly thumbed over or even skipped, but that the middle begins to be cogent or even irresistible and that the end is high reward.

But for many young people 'Ivanhoe' and 'The Talisman' have been the first and last of their acquaintance and they laid these down with a will and often, no doubt, with a raven's croak of 'Never more.' That an author should be so victimised by the teacher and examiner was injustice not only to him; our schools have done their pupils wrong, with their dreary examination-papers, their commands and compulsions to compare this and estimate that, and with all their enforced scribblings by the harassed young on hot summer afternoons in quest of the Pass, the Credit, the Certificate. After such preparation we can easily forget the great surge of narrative, as well as the raciness of Scottish character, which leaped up after a too pedestrian start. We were not reminded that Scott was Scottish and that Scottish scenes and humours were his natural theme, wherein he was most likely to be truly himself and truly a story-teller.

But the blame cannot be put solely on the dominies. The visit to Abbotsford is itself an introduction to the worst of Scott, his refusal to look at the present, which was made immensely exciting as much by its social changes at home as by the foreign wars and Napoleon's overthrow. (In 'St. Ronan's Well' he wrote a realistic story of contemporary life in a Border 'spa,' but it is certainly not one of his important books, although it has freshness and that admirable piece of Border character, Meg Dods.) His baronial home, museum as well as mansion, proclaims his excessively antiquarian outlook when at the desk; but in his life he was actively a man of the day. Consequently the wise teacher, if Scott must be brought into the curriculum, would begin by explaining what manner of man the author was, his Border origins and childhood at Sandy Knowe, his fascination by the hills and streams and legends, his zest for sports and exercises, his legal career, his costly misadventures in publishing, and the colossal effort that he made, even when his health was sapped, to struggle out of debt and to see all obligations honourably met. The story of the writing of the Waverley Novels is almost as exciting as any of the novels themselves (and has more 'human interest,' as the magazines say, than 'The 'Talisman') and it should be told as the prelude to the reading of them. Sir Walter was a great man as well as a great master of his craft, but how many, loaded at school with 'Ivanhoe' in childhood, have any inkling of all this?

His devotion to the backward glance and to the events of periods not his own was partly explained by his fear that novel-writing was not quite respectable. It was still, when he began, one of the youngest of British arts and he himself had been greatly influenced in his youth by the new vogue of sensational and fantastic fiction, by 'The Mysteries of Udolpho,' and by the fashions set by Matt Lewis and Mrs. Radcliffe. For a Clerk of Session, sitting under the great lords of Edinburgh's judicature, to be concerned with profitable romancing might, in those days, have seemed to sober citizens to be demeaning his legal office. So Scott, when he began to write, did so as a poet; stories he told, but the rhymed octosyllabics, which he employed with such vitality and variety of touch, invoked the shelter of minstrelsy and the protective title of a Bard. They made him much money, but the epic Muse was his cover from social criticism. Then, when he turned to prose fiction, he could call Clio into court on his behalf. Was he not a historian? Even so, he preferred anonymity, till the secret was public gossip. What books we might have had if only he had turned his observation and his narrative genius unashamedly on to the Edinburgh in which he went to the courts, to the clubs and to the dinners!

So Abbotsford was true to one-half of him, and that not the better half. If it was new, it contained the old. It was a store-chest of romantic lumber as well as of things of grace; it was the seat of an ambitious man and packed full with the rococo notions of an insatiable collector. It was the workshop of a devoted pen, but the raw material which served the racing machine of Scott's invention was outside in the country where he had so long ridden and fished, with an eye and an ear that missed nothing of the picturesque and the vernacular. Abbotsford is true to that part of his great endeavour which lay between tragedy and tushery; for it is tushery in masonry. Beyond it lay the human comedy, and the Eildon and the Cheviot Hills; hence came the books, but not the house, that Scott built. The horror of life's ebb for him was that his own country, so tinted once, had turned drab before his weakening eyes:

The sun upon the Weirdlaw Hill,
In Ettrick's vale, is sinking sweet;
The westland wind is hush and still,
The lake lies sleeping at my feet.
Yet not the landscape to mine eye
Bears those bright hues that once it bore;
Though evening, with her richest dye,
Flames o'er the hills of Ettrick's shore.

With listless look along the plain,
I see Tweed's silver current glide,
And coldly mark the holy fane
Of Melrose rise in ruin'd pride.
The quiet lake, the balmy air,
The hill, the stream, the tower, the tree,—
Are they still such as once they were?
Or is the dreary change in me?

306

He had never taken the way of the defeated or the advice
he put on Lucy Ashton's lips:

> *Stop thine ear against the singer,*
> *From the red gold keep thy finger;*
> *Vacant heart and hand and eye,*
> *Easy live and quiet die.*

He had never lived easily and, only if coma after paralytic
seizure can be called a tranquil end, did he ' quiet die.'

A visit to Abbotsford, if made in June, may coincide
with the ' Common Ridings ' in one of the Border towns,
say Selkirk or Hawick. Andrew Lang said of Selkirk that
' its air is full of ballad notes borne out of long ago,' but
the long ago also becomes brisk, enjoyable present during
these rituals. One June evening each trade or association
brings out its flag and a lady champion to ' buss ' or kiss it:
early on the next day there is a parade of the Town Band
and the Burgh standard is ' bussed ' beside the Flodden
Memorial: all who have or can procure horses and can
manage them without disaster ride after the standard-bearer
and go round the marches of the city, ending up with more
music and the patterned waving of the flags and such airs
as ' Up wi' the Souters (Shoe-makers) of Selkirk ' and ' The
Flowers of the Forest.' Selkirk suffered bitterly in James
IV's folly of Flodden Field. It was small compensation to
bring home an English flag. Hawick's Standard Bearer,
in a similar mid-summer ceremony, is called The Cornet.
After the salute to the past, there comes, in ' The Ridings,'
present revel. Similar rituals are held in other Border
towns; they are genuinely popular and not a fabrication
of the Tourist Industry.

These survivals remind one that the Border is a horseman's country. ' There was racing and chasing on Cannobie
lea ' and young Lochinvar's steed was his boast:

They saddled a hundred milk-white steeds,
They hae bridled a hundred black,
With a chafron of steel on each horse's head,
And a good knight upon his back.

In the Highlands, where the old roads in the glen were at best but stony tracks, a sure-footed pony was of more value than a hunter or a charger; but in the south the battle was to the swift and the well-mounted. The Highlanders charged on foot; the Border reivers went spurring on their quest. Scott himself was a constant horseman and the South of Scotland retains and reveres with the English the habits of hunting and of horse-racing, both on the flat and over fences.

Another oddity of Border sports is the popularity of Rugby Football, which flourishes in strangely separated patches of the British Isles. In the centre of Scotland it is a middle-class exercise, but in the Border Towns it is the people's game. Association Football is the general interest in the industrial belt and even as far north as Inverness. (In a similar odd way in London ' Rugger ' is a ' class ' game, but in the West of England and in Wales it is ' democratic '.) Perhaps the Borderer feels instinctively that a great rush of eight forwards with the ball at their feet —and the Border teams have ever been notable for their mighty scrummagers—is the nearest thing to a cavalry charge. The patterned footwork of ' Soccer ' excites him less than the mass-gallop of eight men of weight and brawn. But Border ' Rugger ' has only a century behind it, whereas the Border Ridings go back into the misty chronicles of boot-and-saddle chivalry and the dominion of the stirrup-jingling ballad.

In English country, despite all the utilitarian conquests of the Petrol Age, the man on a horse remains, without diminution, Somebody. People still turn to look at him and his mount, which does so much less practical service than the engine of a motor-car. So too on the Border a rider is still the observed of the observers, a respectable person in the old and accurate sense of that adjective, and the antique ceremonies of June, held, with backward glance and present pleasuring, in the towns that sent their sons so lethally against the English (and each other) are rightly chivalric. They may not be as old as the hills; they are as old as the horse.

The poetry of the Scottish nation is now made more in the great cities, since poets cannot live by verse alone, than beside the Teviot and the Tweed. But the chief architect of the rebirth of Scottish poetry in Scots, known to letters as Hugh McDiarmid, is by birth a Borderer whose family name is Grieve. He was born and schooled at Langholm in Dumfriesshire: this county is said by the purists to lack Border status, which they limit to the valleys of Tweed and Teviot and their sources. But it is of the southern end and much of it, to the eye and in quality of craft and calling, is of the Border kind. So I shall claim that in Grieve, though as McDiarmid he be no romantic, the Border tradition of poetry endures. Close though his origin may have been to England, he is fiercely Scottish; after some of his pronouncements you might expect him to march on the South, like any callant of the old-time foray.

Dumfriesshire runs into Galloway, which was long famous for its serviceable horses. These nags even trotted into Falstaff's, London. 'Know we not Galloway nags?' cried Ancient Pistol. The district is now perhaps more noted for its cattle. The Galloway 'beltie,' black with a white waist-band, gives a magpie look to the waving pastures of Kirkcudbrightshire. This is an astonishingly inclusive county (Stewartry to be more exact) since it contains not only such essentially Lowland scenery as you encounter on a journey south from Dalry by Loch Ken to Kirkcudbright town, on the estuary of yet another Dee, but the genuine Highlands around Glen Trool. The town itself has a forgotten look, but artists in force have remembered it and made it a home; it has a medieval aroma, to which the castle, Mercat Cross, and Tolbooth contribute. I had a feeling, rather a sleepy feeling since the air is very gentle, that I had wandered into a piece of France. It is best seen at high tide, when the river banks are covered.

Very different are the mountains of the Stewartry, which, if they were farther north and on the main lines of visitation, instead of round the corner and tucked away, would be much more climbed and praised than they are. Colonel Bernard Fergusson, who learned the tough splendours of this country as a boy, has reminded me that behind the great hill of Merrick is ' the highest sheet of water ' in Great Britain, Loch Enoch. I do not know exactly where a ' sheet of water ' ends and a lochan (small loch) begins. But it is a fascinating claim to make for a supposedly Lowland region, especially when accompanied by the kindred assertion that a shepherd's cottage thereabouts, known as Back Hill of the Bush, is the remotest house in Scotland, being nine miles from a neighbour and ten from a road end. There will, of course, be violent counter-claims for supremacy of solitude from the islands and the Dead Vast. But let that pass. The fact remains that those who wish to be alone on mountains as rugged as any of the North (and little walked upon) can have their fill of desolation, and even of danger, between the Merrick and the Carlin's Cairn.

Galloway's population, though it is far more ' landward ' than urban, has actually increased in the last twenty years; the gains are in the small towns, but the countryfolk have declined very little, which is something in Scotland. The district, spared coal and iron, though very close to the South Ayrshire pits, and so escaping the smutch of heavy industry, has put its waters to cleanly service of heat and light. It was a pioneer of Hydro-Electrical development and the result has not been any serious defacement. The loch at Clatteringshaws is no bad contrivance among man's additions to Nature and I have serene memories of a brief holiday at Dalry. Here the river rises and falls according to the electrician's will. But there is no mess. I remember excursions down the smooth valleys and over to Moniaive and the Annie Laurie country; there was also an assault by foot upon the great mountain ridge to the West, but the weather counter-attacked and won a disappointing day.

Yet, given the sun, it is as good a land as any of the Border. It is full of memories—and graves. The tombs of the martyrs (Covenanters) have the Stevensonian whaups (curlews) above them, eternally mourning. Claverhouse and his dragoons destroyed these courageous zealots in plenty and with ferocity. But if you wish to avoid controversy, you must be careful not to say that; I have been violently bombarded for daring to suggest that Claverhouse was not a model of Christian gallantry. For reading here there is Sir Walter's 'Old Mortality' and much of S. R. Crockett, who was born between Loch Ken and Kirkcudbright and went to school at Newton Stewart pleasantly banked upon the River Cree.

Galloway, as Colonel Fergusson points out, has had great concern for schooling; in one parish of the Rhins, the promontory in the far corner of Wigtownshire which runs so far south, towards Ireland, as to be level on the map with England's Durham, the villagers built and furnished their own school in style and payed the dominie with gifts more than a century ago. Another surprise is to come across, in a very unexpected and lonely spot about seven miles from Newton Stewart, a lofty monument. You might think it had been erected by a wealthy town to celebrate a renowned man of arms or proconsul. Instead it honours a shepherd's boy who became a Professor of Greek in Edinburgh. Reverence for scholarship, as well as for the dead Covenanters, was strong indeed in Galloway.

Education (including my own) is linked with Galloway at Sweet Heart Abbey on the Dumfries side of the region. When John Baliol was condemned by the Prince Bishop of Durham to be whipped and to be fined of a sum which would maintain scholars for ever in Oxford, the College of his name was founded. He had taken a highly civilised wife from Scotland, the Lady Dervorguilla of Galloway. She saw to the endowment of a house of learning by the Thames that would carry her husband's name in perpetuity, while she bridged the Nith and founded a monastery in her own Dumfries. After John Baliol's death in 1268 she caused an Abbey to be built with the command that his embalmed heart, which she had kept in a coffer of ivory bound with silver, should be laid on hers when she was buried. That was in the Abbey of her creation. So the name Sweet Heart was given to it and has remained. Like most of the Border fanes it is a ruin; but there is enough to be seen with admiration and to be regarded, by a Balliol man, with gratitude.

Having begun with the Pentland Firth, I end with the Irish Channel. Cape Wrath and the Mull of Galloway are the extremes of a western coast unmatched in splendour and variety of scene. I have never seen the whole of it and I suppose that few have done that. At whichever end you start there is good reason not to hurry: one not only can meander but must meander, since it is a shore of infinite indentations. To see it all would need not one Summer in Scotland, but half a dozen—and some other seasons too.

And then there is the East, from John o' Groat's to Berwick, less majestic but even more diverse, demanding summers yet again. But they would all be spent with reward and I should like to think that some of these many months and journeys may still be mine.

THE END

INDEX

317

INDEX

Tobermory

Loch Ra
Schieh.

Ben Lawers

P E R

Killin

Mull

Loch Linnhe

Firth of Lorne

Oban

ARGYLL

Crianlarich

Lo

The
Trossachs

Loch Melfort

Inveraray

Ben
Lomond

Aberfo

Colonsay

Loch
Lomond

S T

DUNBARTON

Helensburgh

Alexandria

K

Lochgilphead

Ardrishaig

Loch Lyne

Dunoon

Gourock

Dumbarton

Jura

Sound of Jura

Greenock

R E N

Renfrew

Tarbert

Bute

Wemyss
Bay

Largs

Paisley

Islay

Rothesay

F R

W S

H

Goat Fell

Kilbrennan Sound

Ardrossan

Kilmarnock

Brodick

Irvine

Kintyre

Arran

Troon
Prestwick

Mauchli

Yarbolton

Kilmory

Ayr

R. Ayr

Campbeltown

Firth of Clyde

Maybole

Mull of Kintyre

Ailsa
Craig

Girvan

L.
Doon

Merrick
Mt.

Kells
Range

Glen
Troo

New Galloway

R. Dee

KIRKCU

N O R T H

Stranraer

WIGTOWN

Gatehous
of Fleet

Portpatrick

Glenluce

Wigtown

C H A N N E L

Luce
Bay

Whithorn

Mull of Galloway

SOLW